FINDING AND MANAGING
FOREIGN COUNSEL

© Longman Group Ltd 1994

ISBN 085121 1682

Published by
Longman Law, Tax and Finance
Longman Group Ltd
21–27 Lamb's Conduit Street
London WC1N 3NJ

Associated offices
Australia, Hong Kong, Malaysia, Singapore, USA

A CIP catalogue record for this book is available from the British Library.

Printed in Great Britain by Bell and Bain, Glasgow

CONTENTS

CONTENTS

2 DENMARK

CONTENTS

8 JAPAN

9   LUXEMBOURG   193

10   THE NETHERLANDS   205

CONTENTS

12 SPAIN 243

CONTENTS

CONTENTS

INTRODUCTION

Today, most people involved in business can no longer assume that they will never have to deal with a system of law other than that of the jurisdiction in which they are resident. Cross-border commercial transactions, involving more than one (and sometimes several) jurisdictions, have increased dramatically over the past few years, and will continue to do so with the liberalisation of trade that will result from the advent of the European Union and the recent conclusion of the Uruguayan round of GATT.

In addition, the creation of the European Union, the world's largest single market, has not only stimulated trade between its member states, but encouraged enterprises based in it (and thus now enjoying a strong home market) to look outside its borders for fresh markets. Aided by the current GATT agreements they have naturally turned to the US and Japan. Equally, Japanese and US enterprises have, in turn, become aware of the enhanced possibilities for inward trade and investment in the European Union.

Even individuals not primarily concerned with cross-border commercial transactions will find that it is increasingly possible to take advantage of the freedoms of movement and establishment now available throughout the European Union to increase their business or personal activities in other member states, even if it is only for the purchase of a retirement or holiday home in one of the sunnier parts of Europe.

It is a cliché, and not entirely true, to say that the world in the last decade of the 20th century has become a much smaller place but, in spite of the many divisions and differences that still exist, the desire to do business and make a profit constitutes a powerful force for unity.

People involved in business, lawyers and their clients thus have to move with the times and, by becoming more internationally-oriented, play their part in this process of unification. In most cases this does not, and should not, mean becoming aware in detail of the law and legal practice in foreign jurisdictions, although many lawyers continually exposed to international transactions will inevitably gain some familiarity with jurisdictions other than their own. What is required is a general realisation of the legal issues and, in

1

some cases, pitfalls of implementing a transaction in or with the relevant foreign jurisdiction, coupled with a knowledge of when to ask for local legal help, what that help should consist of, and from where it should be obtained.

This book is intended to satisfy those needs. It can be used by the commercially sophisticated individual, whether acting for business or private purposes, and whether on his own account or as an employee of a larger concern, for instance as a commercial manager, to contact relevant foreign counsel direct in order to obtain the advice that is required. Lawyers, however, will find this book equally useful, whether they are in-house counsel instructing foreign counsel on their employer's business, or in private practice acting at the request of a client who has delegated to them the overall legal management of an international transaction, including the instruction of foreign counsel.

The plan of this book is to cover, in 14 chapters, the 12 states currently composing the European Union and its two major trading partners, the USA and Japan. Each chapter follows a standard pattern. The first sections cover the structure of the legal profession in the relevant jurisdiction, with advice on how best to go about identifying, instructing and, in particular, agreeing a suitable fee structure with an appropriate legal adviser in that jurisdiction. These sections are followed by a general analysis of the status and treatment accorded to foreign residents under the applicable laws of that jurisdiction, with particular reference to establishment, litigation in local courts, regulation of inward investment and taxation. Finally, the chapter concludes with a section covering the recognition of foreign judgments in the relevant jurisdiction. The contents of each chapter are broadly current as at the end of 1993.

Finally, it should be emphasised that the aim of this book is not to replace the function of the usual international legal directories which list legal practitioners in various jurisdictions, together with information about them and their areas of specialisation, if any. Indeed it is intended to be used in conjunction with such publications, and is written as a companion volume to *Kime's International Law Directory*, also published by Longman, now in its 102nd year of publication.

—— 1 ——

BELGIUM

——— • ———

CONTENTS

•

BELGIUM

•

 1

BELGIUM

•

STRUCTURE OF THE LEGAL PROFESSION

From a general perspective, there are various legal professions organised in Belgium. A lawyer may work as an attorney (*avocat*), a notary (*notaire*), or a bailiff (*huissier de justice*). The organisation, the conditions of admission, and the professional rules are different for each of these professions.

However, working as a lawyer does not necessarily imply working in one of these organised professions. In Belgium, rendering legal advice is not a regulated activity. Accordingly, virtually all in-house counsel, and many persons or entities giving legal advice, are not members of the bar or of any other regulated profession. It is also within this non-regulated framework that many foreign law firms are established in Belgium.

• ATTORNEYS •

In Belgium, no distinction exists between barristers and solicitors. All attorneys are *avocat* in French, *advocaat* in Dutch and *Rechtsanwalt* in German. The title *avocat* is legally protected.

Other than a few very limited and specific exceptions, Belgian attorneys have a monopoly on representation in court. All Belgian attorneys may represent a client before all Belgian courts, except the Supreme Court (*Cour de Cassation/Hof van Cassatie*). They may also appear and file briefs before the European courts, as well as before the Benelux Court of Justice. Trainees (those in their first three years at the Bar) may not appear before the Council of State (*Conseil d'Etat/Rand van State*), the highest administrative court. Only a very limited number of attorneys, members of the Supreme Court's Bar, may file briefs in front of the Supreme Court.

As well as representation in court, attorneys also provide counsel to their clients and are able to furnish them with a broad array of legal services.

5

Belgian *avocats* are not permitted to work as in-house counsel, or to work directly under the authority of, or in association with, non-lawyers.

Admission to the Bar
Young lawyers can be admitted to the Bar as soon as they have obtained their Belgian law degree (*License en Droit/Licentiaat in de Rechten*). They are sworn in by the Court of Appeals of their district, and their admission takes place shortly thereafter.

During the following three years, young attorneys (trainees) have to meet a number of requirements. This three-year period is referred to as the 'stage'. The requirements of the stage include working under the supervision of a more experienced attorney, handling a number of *pro bono* cases, and passing professional education exams. The only real restriction imposed on the trainees or *stagiaires*, as they are known, is that they may not officially start up their own independent practice.

Organisation
A Belgian attorney is first of all a member of the bar of his or her judicial district. The two main authorities of the judicial district bars are the Dean of the Bar (*bâtonnier*) and the Bar Council (*conseil de l'ordre*). The Bar Council exercises regulatory and disciplinary power on the district's attorneys.

All the judicial district bars are organised within the National Bar Association (*Ordre National*). The National Bar Association plays an important role in setting up national disciplinary rules. It also defends the professional interests of attorneys at the national level.

Disciplinary rules
Disciplinary rules are primarily adopted at the level of the district bars, taking into account the guidelines and the decisions of the National Bar.

• NOTARIES •

Notaries in Belgium play a role which is very different from the role that a notary public may play in a common law country. Notaries are lawyers; they are public officers, appointed by the King, and they certify and pass acts for private parties. Normally, a notary is an independent and neutral agent who acts for the benefit of all the parties, and not for only one client.

Notaries are mostly involved in the incorporation of companies and the transfer of real estate, mortgages, wills, marriage contracts, etc. Notaries can also play the role of conciliator in some specific procedures.

Notaries, like attorneys, are organised professionally at the level of the judicial district. There is a special professional body (*Chambre des Notaires/*

Kamer der Notarissen) in every district, which exercises regulatory and disciplinary powers on the notary. At the national level, the *Fédération Royale des Notaires de Belgique/Koninklijke Federatie van Belgische Notarissen* insures a certain co-ordination between the local bodies. This system is currently under review and a draft bill, which would ensure that regulatory and disciplinary powers would be exercised at the national level, has been presented to Parliament.

• BAILIFFS •

Bailiffs, like notaries, are public officials appointed by the King. Their intervention is required in civil proceedings for the accomplishment of specific tasks, for example, issuing summonses, seizing properties, notifying judgments and supervising public auctions.

• FOREIGN LAWYERS •

Pursuant to the EC Directive of 22 March 1977, non-Belgian EU attorneys may represent their clients in front of Belgian courts. In such a case, these EU attorneys must work closely with an attorney admitted to the local bar, and first be introduced to the Dean of the Bar.

In the bars of the judicial district of Brussels, there also exists a special list (called the B-list) of foreign attorneys established in Brussels. These attorneys are normally not allowed to represent their clients in Belgian courts. They are, however, allowed to establish an office in partnership with Belgian attorneys. Attorneys listed on the B-list are partially subject to local disciplinary rules.

The great majority of foreign lawyers working in Belgium are not listed on the B-list. These lawyers are only permitted to render legal services other than court representation; they may not be associated with Belgian attorneys and they are not submitted to Belgian disciplinary rules.

HOW TO FIND A SUITABLE LAWYER

There is no one single method of locating the right person to handle legal matters.

A basic distinction needs to be made between an in-house counsel and an outside counsel. An in-house counsel is not a member of the Bar in Belgium. He is generally hired, as a company employee, under an employment contract of indefinite duration which can only be terminated upon giving prior notice as defined by case law. He also has employee status, which implies that he enjoys a fair amount of protection both in terms of employment protection and regulations on termination of his employment, and social security coverage.

Hiring an in-house counsel will be carried out, as for any other company executive, through advertising, referrals, personal contacts, executive search firms, etc. When hiring, preference will generally be given to a person who has had experience at the Bar.

Locating a suitable outside counsel is altogether another matter. A basic distinction should first be made between a one-time consultation or litigation, or the setting up of a more permanent and continuous relationship covering a variety of legal problems and services such as consultation, litigation, transactional lawyering, monitoring, etc.

In the first instance, the prevailing factor will be specialisation. For example, if a client wants to engage in trademark litigation he will be able, without too much difficulty, to obtain a list of attorneys specialising in this field.

• LOCAL BAR ASSOCIATIONS •

Most of the bars (in Belgium there are 29 different bars organised in each district – *arrondissement judiciaire/gerechtelijke arrondissement*) keep a list of attorneys as per their respective specialities. In the case of intellectual property, it may also be well-advised to question a patent and trademark agent who will be able to provide the names of one or more attorneys. A foreign client should try to choose from the Bar list the attorneys having the required language capabilities in order to allow for easy communication. The Bar will readily provide this information.

If the client is looking to establish a more permanent relationship with a business, finance and tax firm, the Bar list will not be of great help. Instead, he will be better off relying on embassy, bank or chamber of commerce referrals.

• LEGAL DIRECTORIES •

The prospecting client will also find it useful to consult the various lawyers' directories (*Martindale-Hubbell, Kime's International Law Directory*, etc). Some of the directories list short biographical summaries which can be useful in singling out a few firms.

• CHAMBERS OF COMMERCE AND EMPLOYERS' • CONFEDERATIONS

Chambers of commerce can very often also be of assistance in finding an attorney. The American Chamber of Commerce (50 Avenue des Arts, 1040

Brussels, tel 02/513 67 70) and the British Chamber of Commerce (30 Rue Joseph II, 1040 Brussels, tel 02/219 07 88), for example, are well-organised and have helpful, competent staff. It would be generally less useful to contact an employers' federation although such a federation can be helpful in locating a labour lawyer and in arbitration. In Belgium, this would be the Federation of Belgian Industries (4 Rue Ravenstein, 100 Brussels, tel 02/515 08 11).

• EMBASSIES AND BANKS •

Another source of information for the foreign client seeking an attorney is its local embassy. Banks are also often a reliable source of information. The foreign client can easily contact the local branch or correspondent bank in Belgium of one of the banks with which he is familiar in his home territory.

• LOCAL VISITS AND PERSONAL INTERVIEWS •

The client will then be well-advised to interview a number of firms. The interview is the best method by which to appoint a law firm, as the client will get a better feeling for the existing capabilities and specialities of the firm. For example, he can immediately distinguish and compare the degree of professionalism in the organisation and general set-up: the premises, the reception area, the location of the firm, the atmosphere and the language capabilities of the employees, can all be assessed through the interview.

FACTORS IN CHOOSING A SUITABLE LAWYER

As indicated above, the choice of an attorney will, to a great extent, depend on the type of relationship to be established between the client and the attorney. A different approach is required for a client who needs a one-time consultation or litigation, and a client who needs to establish a permanent relationship with an attorney or law firm.

An important factor in deciding which law firm to employ is the firm's form of organisation. Up until recently, Belgian attorneys worked mainly as sole practitioners, as is the case in other European countries. Even today, the majority of attorneys are sole practitioners even if they present themselves as a law firm working under a firm's name, and share the firm's expenses (rent of the premises, personnel and library expenses, etc). These are not, however, truly integrated partnerships, and do not share profits derived from one profit and loss account.

This consideration may have serious implications in the client/attorney relationship. Lack of availability may be one of the drawbacks. Another difficulty is that the attorney will often act as a general practitioner and the client will not automatically be dealing with the best specialist for any given field of law. Associates in these firms, who are also authorised to handle personal clients in addition to firm clients, will not show the same commitment to the firm client. Alternatively, they might show too much commitment in the hope of 'appropriating' the client.

The firm must also be very well-integrated in the local jurisdiction and therefore well-connected socially and politically. In Belgian society, where all political decisions are built around consensus-building and compromise, and political decision-making is of paramount influence in business life, the attorney must be able to deal with these very complex issues.

• LANGUAGE ABILITY AND SPECIALISATION IN TOPICS •

For a one-time consultation or litigation, preference will be given to specialisation and a good reputation in that area of specialisation, and then to language capabilities. It is probably better to work with the best litigator in a specialised field of law than with a mediocre litigator who speaks the language of the client.

In choosing a law firm – or an attorney – for a more permanent relationship, other factors will play a determining role. It is obvious that if the assignment involves a fair amount of transactional work and lawyering in general, language capabilities will play an essential role.

In a multilingual country such as Belgium, the foreign client must clearly opt for a firm which has not only language capabilities in the three official languages (Dutch, French and German), but which is also seen as serving both of the two larger communities (Flemish and French). In the past, many firms in Brussels were seen as exclusively French-speaking (French is the dominant language in Brussels).

The common law client should also give preference to an attorney who has been exposed to common law. Fortunately, thanks to cultural exchange programmes started immediately after the First World War, many Belgians have had post-graduate experience in American universities.

• TYPE OF TRANSACTION •

In choosing outside counsel in Belgium, the type of work will be a determining factor. EU law, for instance, which constitutes the major legal activity in Brussels, still requires a particular approach in choosing a suitable attorney. Since EU law constitutes a distinct body of law and court procedure, the nationality of the attorney is of no consequence. All attorneys of the Union are admitted to practise before the two European courts.

Tax law will also require a specific approach. Tax law is practised both by attorneys admitted to the Bar and non-lawyers, ie lawyers not admitted to the Bar who work in auditing firms and in separate tax-consulting practices.

COMMERCIAL ARRANGEMENTS WHEN INSTRUCTING COUNSEL

Commercial arrangements with an attorney depend very much on the type of attorney, as well as on the type of the required assistance.

• TIME CONSTRAINTS AND DEADLINES •

In transactional work, time constraints and deadlines are generally treated in the same way as in most common law countries: it is a matter of arrangement between the client and the attorney, and the speed of the assistance essentially depends on the capability of the attorney to meet the client's requirements.

Reasonable delays are therefore the rule, although it is obvious that well-developed law firms, having the staff and expertise as well as the infrastructure, are better placed to tackle complicated or urgent requests.

In the Belgian procedural system the parties, not the judge, conduct the proceedings. Typically, the time periods within which the parties must file their briefs and communicate the documentary evidence are not prescribed under penalty of nullity. If a party fails to file its brief it is up to the other parties to request the court to set a deadline for filing of the pleadings. Also, the time periods to appeal from a judgment start running only on the date of notification of the judgment by the other party. The speed with which proceedings are conducted is therefore to a certain extent in the hands of the parties themselves.

However, even if the parties are diligent and pursue the matter without delay, one can estimate that a judgment in a normal commercial matter, which does not require an expert investigation, will not be rendered within one year after the summons is served upon the defendant.

Another important factor in the progress of proceedings is the excessive workload of many courts which, in some instances, and especially in the courts of appeal, has become a major cause of substantial delays. It may indeed be months or even years before cases can be heard, even though the parties and their attorneys have taken all required procedural steps.

One of the consequences of the abnormal delays in many civil and commercial courts is that more issues are being dealt with by way of summary proceedings.

• FEE STRUCTURE •

The Belgian Judicial Code contains two provisions concerning fees:

- the amount is to be determined moderately;
- the amount cannot be fixed by reference to the outcome of the trial (Art 459).

Contingency fee arrangements are thus prohibited.

According to the Recommendation of the National Bar Association of 24 June 1991, there are basically four methods of determining the fees of an attorney:

- fees per hour;
- fees according to the importance of the case;
- fees per performance;
- annual fee covering any assistance in a given field during that year.

This Recommendation contains various scales for each type of assistance and the calculation of the attorneys' fees.

Although many attorneys do apply one of these methods for calculating their fees, it should be emphasised that the indicated scales are only minimum scales and that the Recommendation has no binding effect whatsoever. Practically, the determination of the attorneys' fees in Belgium is almost completely unregulated.

As far as litigation is concerned, factors such as the importance of the case, the skills and experience of the attorney, the work involved and the financial situation of the client are also taken into account for the determination of the fees.

One should bear in mind in this respect that the fees and expenses of the attorney of the party who has won a suit cannot be recovered from the party who has lost the suit. The award will include only the expenses of the bailiff for the service of the summons, the court fee for the listing of the writ of summons and a small procedural indemnity (*indemnité de procédure/rechtsplegingsvergoeding*) which is meant to compensate the winning party for the expense incurred, including the attorneys' fees. At the current rates, this procedural indemnity is BF 11,400 for proceedings in the first instance and BF 15,200 for proceedings before the courts of appeal. Since in practice the fees of the attorneys by far exceed the amount of the procedural indemnity, the winning party must in fact bear the fees of its attorney.

Finally, it should be noted that the attorneys' fees do not include such expenses as procedural costs, travel expenses, mail, telephone, etc which will generally be billed separately.

• RETAINER •

Many attorneys will request the client to pay a retainer to cover expenses and as an advance on their fees.

• METHOD AND TIMING OF BILLING •

Major law firms working for international corporate clients usually work on an hourly fee rate basis and bill their clients on a bi-monthly or quarterly basis. The hourly fee rate varies depending on the skill and experience of the attorneys involved. The majority of attorneys, however, do not work on an hourly fee rate basis as they are less accustomed to the requirements of corporate clients.

• LEVEL OF EXPERIENCE NEEDED •

Discussing the level of experience needed by attorneys in the firm who will actually be performing the work is only relevant for the major law firms. As indicated previously, the majority of attorneys in Belgium are general practitioners.

However, the major law firms have developed to meet the demands of corporate clients and their emphasis for that reason is on specialisation. Typically, such firms will have different departments dealing with particular fields of law so that the client can at all times be assisted by specialists for any given assignment.

Clients generally have a contact person within the firm, the partner in charge, who co-ordinates the work for that client and delegates the assignments to the competent attorneys in the different departments.

It is obvious that, once a durable relationship is established between the client and the firm, the client often addresses himself directly to the associates with whom he is used to working. The more durable the relationship between the client and his law firm, the more the client may be involved in specifying the level of experience needed by the attorneys who will actually be performing the work.

TREATMENT OF FOREIGN NATIONALS UNDER LOCAL LAW

• RESTRICTIONS, REPORTS AND GOVERNMENTAL APPROVALS • OF FOREIGN INVESTMENT

There is no general restriction in Belgium on foreign nationals doing business and establishing themselves in the country, and no prior authorisation or business permit *per se* is required. However, some administrative formalities must be completed by a foreign company or individual wishing to become established in Belgium.

Individuals

Residence permit and visa requirements

Any foreign national whose stay is to exceed a period of three months must register with the local authority of the place where he is to reside in Belgium within eight days of his arrival. In order to register, a non-EU national must present a visa and, if he is coming to work in Belgium, a work permit or professional card. Spouses and children must also be registered.

Application for the visa is made to the Belgian consulate in the citizen's place of residence abroad on the proper forms and must be accompanied by a medical certificate, five photographs, an employer's certificate and the work permit or professional card. The obtaining of the work permit or professional card is thus a prerequisite for applying for a visa. Applications for members of the family also travelling to Belgium may be made at the same time.

Professional card

Any foreign national, other than an EU national, who wishes to exercise a self-employed activity, ie desires to reside in Belgium to carry on a profit-making independent trade or profession, must first obtain a professional card. Application must be made at a Belgian consulate abroad, or in Belgium through the local municipal authority to the Ministry of the Self-Employed.

The application procedure can be very long (12 months is not exceptional) and involves a full administrative hearing and investigation. The application must be limited to a particular industrial or commercial sector.

A foreign national, other than an EU national, not actually based in Belgium, but who is registered in Belgium as managing director of a Belgian subsidiary or branch manager of a Belgian branch, is normally required to have a work permit or professional card. However, if the Belgian activity is not remunerated and is necessary to another salaried activity exercised abroad (eg with the parent company) it is normally possible to avoid this requirement.

Work permit

Any foreign individual, other than an EU national, who is to be employed by a company or firm established in Belgium must first obtain a work permit.

Applications are, in principle, made before the individual concerned arrives in Belgium. The application is filed by the employer himself or by an appointed representative, with the local branch of the National Employment Office having jurisdiction over the area where the potential employer's firm is located. Application must be made on the prescribed forms and include a medical certificate (in principle issued by a doctor on the approved list of the Belgian consulate nearest to the place where the applicant resides abroad), three passport photographs and a copy of the employment contract. If successful, the work permit is delivered to the employer who should hand it over to the employee.

Companies and individuals

Administrative formalities

In addition to the legal residence requirements mentioned above, a certain number of formalities and registrations must be completed by the foreign national desiring to engage in trade activities and/or by the foreign company wishing to establish a branch or subsidiary in Belgium.

Register of Commerce

Any person or corporate body, Belgian or foreign, proposing to engage in any commercial activity of whatever kind, must first apply to the Clerk of the Commercial Court for enrolment in the Register of Commerce. Craftsmen not involved in commercial activities need to be enrolled in the Craftman's Register. The Registry number assigned must be indicated in all legal documents and on the company's stationery.

VAT administration

Companies (and individuals) planning to engage in activities subject to Value Added Tax are required to register with the VAT administration of the Ministry of Finance.

National Office for Social Security

Any company (or individual) operating in Belgium, and employing one or more people, whether it be incorporated in Belgium or elsewhere, comes under the national social security system. It is therefore required to register with the National Office for Social Security.

Regulated professions

Certain specific activities are regulated and subject to prior authorisation. Among the more important of these activities are banking, insurance, financial leasing, transport and road haulage, stock-broking and commodities transactions, sales of meat and certain other food products, travel agencies, as well as certain professional activities (eg those of lawyers, certain auditors, doctors, architects, etc).

Some activities require recognition of managerial skills and professional abilities sanctioned by a Certificate of Establishment, issued by the Chamber of Handicrafts and Small Businesses of the relevant province.

Contractors of civil works and related activities also require a Certificate of Registration from the Ministry of Finance. Civil works or related activities to be carried out in the public sector require, in addition, a Certificate of Homologation from the Ministry of Public Works.

Licences for specific activities

Dangerous, unhealthy and harmful activities require an exploitation licence from the College of Burgomasters and Aldermen of the commune where the unit is planned. Large distribution units also require the approval of this authority.

Setting up an industrial plant in Belgium involves obtaining permission to carry out the activities concerned. A building licence is needed for the construction of new buildings or the renovation of existing ones. Applications must be filed with the local authorities. Decisions are taken in accordance with the town planning and land zoning legislation.

Investment restrictions on non-residents

A public offer by a non-resident person or corporation to purchase the equity of a Belgian corporation listed on the stock exchange must receive prior approval by the Ministry of Finance. This restriction does not apply to offers made by nationals or registered corporations of one of the EU countries. Government spokesmen have indicated that no intention exists for hindering foreign investment in general.

• EXCHANGE CONTROLS AND OTHER REGULATORY ISSUES •

Belgium and the Grand Duchy of Luxembourg have formed a monetary association called the Belgo-Luxembourg Economic Union (BLEU). Belgium is also member of the European Monetary System (EMS) and the Belgian Franc exchange rate is thus linked to the exchange rates of the other European countries participating in this system.

The foreign exchange control previously used a dual exchange market system whereby commercial transactions took place on the official market, while financing operations were carried out on the free market. The dual exchange market was abolished in March 1990 and all payments and transfers between the BLEU and foreign countries have been freed from obtaining any prior authorisation, and may be executed in Belgian or Luxembourg francs, as well as in other currencies.

The only formality that remains for transfers between residents of the BLEU and non-residents is of a statistical nature and consists of a written declaration of the economic type of any such transaction. The purpose of this is to enable the drawing up of the balance of payments of the BLEU. Where such transactions are executed through a financial institution established in the BLEU, the resident involved has to submit this declaration to the financial institution concerned. For all other transfers, the residents involved have to inform the Exchange Institution directly.

Finally, there are no restrictions on residents holding and operating bank accounts in Belgium. Foreign individuals and companies established in Belgium will be treated as residents for the purpose of the exchange control regulations.

• Tax Treatment •

Foreign nationals, having established their residence in Belgium and being registered with the communal administration of the commune of their residence, are taxed as Belgian residents.

However, in an effort to encourage foreign investment, the Belgian Central Tax Administration has published a tax circular granting a favourable tax treatment to foreign executives temporarily assigned to Belgium by foreign enterprises.

The special tax treatment for qualifying foreign executives provides that the amount paid by an employer as reimbursement for actual and adequate additional expenses resulting from their moving to and working in Belgium are not included in their taxable remuneration, although they are treated as deductible expenses for the employer.

With the exception of educational and moving expenses charged to the employer, other allowances are accepted as tax deductible only to the extent they do not exceed either BF 450,000 for executives of operating companies or BF 1,200,000 for executives of co-ordination and research centres. Moreover, the remuneration corresponding to the foreign executive's professional activity exercised abroad is not taxable in Belgium.

To qualify for the special tax treatment, the foreign executive must show that he has no intention of establishing his permanent residence in Belgium and that his stay due to his secondment is of a temporary nature. In such a case, the personal situation of the foreign executive, as well as the nature of his activity, will be determinant.

To the extent that the requirements relating to the temporary character of the activity are met, no time limit is provided as far as the term of applicability of the special tax treatment is concerned.

A complete file must be submitted by the employer to the Ministry of Finance, in order to have the special tax regime applied.

• ACCESS TO AND TREATMENT BY LOCAL COURTS •

As a general rule, foreign nationals are subject to the same jurisdictional and procedural rules as Belgian nationals for access to local courts or to any Belgian public authority. There are, however, exceptions to this rule.

Security for costs
If a defendant of Belgian nationality so requests, before any other plea or defence and even before entering a plea of lack of jurisdiction, the foreign plaintiff may be required by a judgment to grant a security to cover the judicial expenses in case he loses the suit, as well as the damages he might be liable for. This security will have the amount and the form (bank guarantee, bond, etc) decided by the court.

The obligation to issue a security, however, does not exist if the defendant is a national of one of the states being party to several multilateral and bilateral treaties in which this obligation is waived.

Legal aid
Legal aid is reserved for Belgian nationals and may only be extended to certain defined categories of foreign nationals, as specified by Article 669 of the Judicial Code. A number of treaties also extend such legal aid.

• FOREIGN PARENT LIABILITY •

It is assumed that the act giving rise to the primary liability is that of a Belgian subsidiary, which is a limited liability company (*société anonyme/neamloze vennootschap*).

Definition
Under Belgian law, a subsidiary is a company with respect to which a power of control is exercised (see Royal Decree of 14 October 1991).

Liability of the foreign parent of a Belgian subsidiary
There are no specific legal rules which clearly outline the scope of the parent company's responsibility *vis-à-vis* actions taken by its subsidiary, and only a few reported decisions by Belgian courts deal with this subject.

As a consequence, the usual set of corporate laws apply to parent and subsidiary companies. This means, among other things, that each company has its own legal personality, with the consequences derived from such features (ie limited assets, with liability of the shareholders limited to the stated amount of the registered capital).

However, there has been a tendency in recent years to search for grounds for responsibility of the parent company *vis-à-vis* actions taken by its subsidiary. Also, two specific rules in the case of the subsidiary's bankruptcy may involve the parent company in liability.

Lifting of the corporate veil

If a parent company were to fail to support a Belgian subsidiary, the creditors of the latter could attempt to have the corporate veil of the Belgian subsidiary lifted, which would enable them to exercise their rights *vis-à-vis* the parent company. They could compel the parent company to pay the subsidiary's debts and, if it was unable to do so, to declare the subsidiary bankrupt. Belgian bankruptcy law is silent as regards the extension of the bankruptcy to the parent company, or any contribution by the parent company to the debts of its subsidiary (except for regarding *de facto* directors – see below).

However, extension of the bankruptcy to the *maître de l'affaire* (controller of the business) has been developed by case law, but is only admitted within certain limits. Since the decision of the Supreme Court of 26 May 1978, and 1 June and 26 October 1979, the bankruptcy of a company may be extended to the controller of the business if the following conditions are met:

(1) Circumstances exist which indicate that the controller of the business has not respected the legal personality of the company. Such circumstances are, *inter alia*:
   (a) insufficient company capital;
   (b) non-functioning or irregular functioning of the company organs;
   (c) the exceeding of powers conferred by the charter on the company organs;
   (d) confusion in the accounts of the predominant shareholder and the company;
   (e) absence of regular accountancy;
   (f) use of the company's capital to pay off another company's debt, etc.

   A combination of several of these circumstances is necessary to convince the judge to extend the bankruptcy. (The mere fact that a person holds a significant portion of the shares of the capital of the subsidiary is not sufficient to trigger the extension of bankruptcy); and

(2) The controller of the business qualifies for bankruptcy under Belgian law, ie he is a merchant who has ceased paying his debts and whose credit has been imperiled.

The strictness of these conditions explains why there are no reported cases where this principle has been successfully invoked against a multinational group with a subsidiary in Belgium.

Specific liability in the case of the subsidiary's bankruptcy
The Belgian Co-ordinated Laws of 30 November 1935, as further amended, provide for two instances of specific liability, which could possibly involve the parent company's liability in the event of a bankruptcy of the subsidiary.

Founders' liability
At the time of incorporation, the founding shareholders must provide the officiating notary with a budget forecast (*plan financier/financieel plan*) justifying the amount of the capital. This document is kept by the notary and is not published. The purpose of this is to enable public authorities to assess the liability of the founding shareholders (ie in most instances the principal shareholder) in the event of the company being declared bankrupt within three years of its incorporation. This liability may come into play when, in the court's opinion, the original share capital was, at the time of incorporation, manifestly insufficient to cover the normal development of the proposed activities for a period of at least two years following incorporation (Art 35).

Directors' liability
Article 63 of the amended Co-ordinated Laws imposes a rather strict liability on directors (including *de facto* directors) in the event of bankruptcy of the company and insufficiency of assets.

If it is established that a continuing grave fault on the part of any director or former director, as well as any other person who effectively exercised control over the company (ie a *de facto* director), has contributed to the bankruptcy, these persons may be held personally liable, jointly or otherwise, for all or part of the company's debts to the extent of the insufficiency of the assets.

There are no reported cases where this liability provision has been applied to the parent company of a Belgian entity. However, a court decision was rendered against the Belgian state, which was the majority shareholder of a company that had gone bankrupt and was considered by the court to have been the *de facto* director of this company.

The concept of the *de facto* director was interpreted by the court in a very restrictive way: an actual exercising of power over the company (with regard to contracts, personnel, management policy), as opposed to mere suggestions or even supervision, is required to trigger the qualification of a *de facto* director.

Directors are also, *inter alia*, liable *vis-à-vis* third parties in the case of a violation of the Company Laws and/or the charter of the company, as well as for their tortious acts (Art 62, (2) CLCC and Art 1382, Civil Code). Therefore, it is worthwhile verifying whether the parent company and/or other affiliated companies (or any directors of these companies) have been appointed as directors of the Belgian subsidiary or have the status of a *de facto* director.

• JURISDICTION OF LOCAL COURTS •

International conventions
Bilateral or multilateral conventions provide some rules on jurisdiction. A situation falling within the scope of one of these conventions will be governed by its rules, which prevail over ordinary Belgian law. The most important convention in this respect is the Brussels Convention. (See Appendix for details of the Brussels and Lugano Conventions.)

The Brussels Convention

Scope of application
The Brussels Convention is in force between Belgium, Denmark, France, Germany, Italy, Luxembourg, the Netherlands and the UK. (The Donostia–San Sebastian Convention of 29 May 1989, extending the Brussels Convention to Spain and Portugal, has not yet been ratified by Belgium and is therefore not in force in Belgium.)

The Brussels Convention applies in civil and commercial matters, whatever the nature of the court or tribunal. It does not extend, in particular, to revenue, customs or administrative matters. In addition, a number of matters are expressly excluded by the terms of Art 1 from the scope of the Brussels Convention, ie:

(a) the status or legal capacity of natural persons, property rights arising out of a matrimonial relationship, wills and succession;
(b) bankruptcies, liquidations and other insolvency proceedings;
(c) social security;
(d) arbitrations.

General rule of jurisdiction
The different rules on jurisdiction are not discussed here, because they are, or should be, the same in all contracting states (see Appendix).

The notion of domicile is the key concept in relation to jurisdiction under Belgian law.

Article 2 of the Brussels Convention provides that, except where the Convention otherwise permits or requires, a defendant is required to be sued in the courts of his domicile. The domicile of a defendant is determined according to Art 52 of the Brussels Convention, which states that the court will apply its internal law in that respect.

Under Belgian law a person's domicile is the address where he is officially registered with the local authorities as having his principal residence (Art 36, para 1 of the Judicial Code). Only one such registration can be obtained, which means that a person can only have one domicile. If the party is a company or other legal person or association of natural or legal persons, the 'seat' is treated as its domicile (Art 53, para 1). In order to determine this seat, the court applies the rules of private international law (Art 53, para 1).

Under Belgian law, the seat is the principal establishment of the legal person. The principal establishment usually coincides with the seat mentioned in the charter (registered office). If that is not the case, the real principal establishment is taken into consideration rather than the nominal seat. The principal establishment, however, is to be considered from the viewpoint of the legal rules governing the functioning of the legal person. It is the place where the board of directors or the executives take their decisions and the general meeting of shareholders convenes, not where the business activity takes place.

Belgian law
Where the situation does not fall within the scope of an international convention, Belgian judicial law will determine whether a local court has jurisdiction over foreign nationals or companies. Belgian rules of jurisdiction in this respect may be classified as follows.

Rules if the defendant is a Belgian national
As a rule, the plaintiff can choose to bring the action before any one of the following courts:

(a) the court of the domicile of the defendant or of one of them;
(b) the court of the place where one or all of the obligations subject to the dispute find their origin or where they are, have been or should be performed;
(c) the court of an elected domicile (which is an address chosen by the defendant in a particular act or contract); or
(d) the court of the place where the bailiff has served summons on the defendant in person, if none of the defendants have a domicile either in Belgium or abroad.

There are, however, numerous exceptions to this rule. Particular precaution is therefore recommended as to the verification of the competent Belgian court with respect to the situation at hand.

In connection with the choice of forum of the plaintiff the Civil Code, Art 15, provides that a Belgian national can be sued before a Belgian court for obligations contracted aboard, even if the plaintiff is a foreigner.

Finally, it should be noted that the plaintiff loses his right to choose if the parties have validly agreed upon the forum. As a general rule, the parties can freely choose the forum in all cases and at any time. (However, in matters of bankruptcy, tax law and seizures, the Judicial Code provides for one single competent court, without leaving the parties any possibility of choice whatsoever.) In order to avoid problems of proof, the agreement on the forum should be in writing. It is common practice in Belgium to insert choice-of-forum clauses in contracts, even if these are standard contracts, general conditions of sale, etc. Such clauses are upheld by the court provided that the plaintiff establishes that the defendant has at least implicitly agreed to them. Certain international treaties provide for more stringent requirements for the validity of choice-of-forum clauses.

Rules if the defendant is a foreign national

Applications of the Actio sequitur forum rei *principle*
Article 635 of the Judicial Code lists situations in which a foreign national may be sued before a Belgian court, by a foreign or Belgian national. Under this Article, the jurisdiction of the Belgian court is justified by an objective link with Belgian territory and the foreign defendant cannot contest that court's competence.

The most important of these instances are the following:

(a) the dispute concerns immovable property located in Belgium;
(b) the foreign defendant has a domicile or a place of residence in Belgium, or has elected domicile there;
(c) the obligation on which the action is based originates, is to be performed, or has been performed in Belgium;
(d) the dispute concerns the estate of a deceased person whose last domicile was located in Belgium;
(e) the action concerns the validity or the lifting of attachments or other provisional measures in Belgium;
(f) the action is connected with proceedings already pending before a Belgian court;
(g) the action is aimed at obtaining the authorisation to enforce foreign judicial decisions or authentic deeds;
(h) the dispute concerns a Belgian bankruptcy, a counter-claim or a claim in intervention if the main claim is already pending before a Belgian court;
(i) a claim is brought against several defendants, one of whom has his domicile or residence in Belgium.

Jurisdiction rules based on the domicile of the plaintiff

In all cases not explicitly provided for by Art 635 mentioned above, Art 638 of the Judicial Code provides that the plaintiff can always bring an action against a foreign national before the Belgian court of the place where the plaintiff has his domicile or residence.

Nevertheless, unlike the cases provided for by Art 635, Art 636 grants the foreign defendant the right to contest the jurisdiction of Belgian courts. The exercise of this right is subject to two conditions.

First, the plea of lack of competence should be raised in *limine litis*, ie in the defendant's first pleadings. Second, the defendant who appears and contests the court's jurisdiction has to prove that a Belgian national would have the same right to contest the jurisdiction if sued before a court in the country of which the defendant is a national. The burden of proof of the existence of reciprocity can be met either by referring to a treaty between the two countries or, if no such treaty exists, by submitting a document showing the law of the country of which the defendant is a national.

Finally, Art 4 of the Law of 27 July 1961 on the unilateral termination of exclusive distributorship agreements for an indefinite duration should be mentioned in this context. It provides that the principal to a distributorship agreement for the whole or part of Belgian territory can, in case of termination, always be sued before the Belgian court of the domicile of the distributor.

Once the jurisdiction of a Belgian court over a foreign national or company is verified, Belgian judicial law needs to be consulted in order to determine the particular jurisdiction competent to deal with the case on the basis of its subject matter jurisdiction and its territorial competence.

• FOREIGN LANGUAGE DOCUMENTS AND DOCUMENTS • GOVERNED BY FOREIGN LAW

International conventions

There are a number of bilateral treaties on this issue, notably between Belgium and Austria, France, Germany, Italy and the Netherlands.

Moreover, the Brussels Convention contains two provisions relating to this issue. Articles 50 and 51 of the Brussels Convention provide for the enforceability, in another contracting state, of a document which has been formally drawn up or registered as an authentic instrument in a contracting state.

An order for its enforcement in this other state will be issued provided that:

- the instrument produced satisfies the conditions necessary to establish its authenticity in the state of origin;
- the instrument is enforceable in the state of origin;

- the enforcement of such instrument is not contrary to public policy in the state in which enforcement is sought.

Belgian law

If Belgium has not executed a treaty with the country from which the document originates, Belgian law will determine the conditions under which such a foreign document will be enforceable in Belgium.

Article 586 of the Judicial Code provides that the President of the Court of First Instance, on request, has jurisdiction to confirm or grant a visa:

(a) to arbitration sentences rendered in Belgium or abroad (subject to some exceptions: see the Judicial Code, Art 606, para 1;

(b) to authentic deeds drawn up in a foreign country, pursuant to which mortgages were granted on properties located in Belgium, or deeds of consent of redeemed or reduced mortgages;

(c) to any other authentic deed which is not mentioned above, which was drawn up in a foreign country, insofar as a treaty exists with this country pertaining to the confirmation of said deed.

• RECOGNITION AND ENFORCEMENT OF FOREIGN • JUDGMENTS

International conventions

A number of international conventions on this issue are in force in Belgium, notably with Austria, France, Germany, Italy, the Netherlands, Switzerland and the UK.

The scope of review by the Belgian judge is limited to the matters as set forth in each particular convention and generally gives rise to reduced control.

The most significant convention is the Brussels Convention (see Appendix), which prevails over the above-mentioned conventions when the situation falls within its scope (see the Brussels Convention, Arts 54–57).

The Brussels Convention undertakes to secure the simplification of formalities governing the reciprocal recognition and enforcement of judgments of courts or tribunals from an EU country, in order to promote free movement of judgments within the Union.

The Brussels Convention

Main principles

The Brussels Convention does not, as a rule, allow the court requested to recognise or enforce a foreign judgment to review the jurisdiction of the court of the state in which the judgment was given. There are, however, limited exceptions which pertain mainly to jurisdiction in matters relating to insurance, to jurisdiction over consumer contracts as well as to exclusive jurisdiction (Art 28).

The Brussels Convention extends recognition and/or enforcement to any judgment originating from, and enforceable in, a contracting state even if the defendant in the original suit was not domiciled in a member state and therefore, under Art 4, jurisdiction was determined by the law of that state rather than by the Convention.

Requirements

The Brussels Convention establishes two principles which contribute to promoting the free movement of judgments:

(1) There are no requirements, strictly speaking, for recognition or enforcement. Rather, only grounds for refusal of the application are stated (Art 27).

(2) The conditions for recognition and enforcement are placed on the same level, by setting exactly the same grounds for refusal *vis-à-vis* either of them (Art 34, para 2).

In any event, under the basic rules of Arts 29 and 34, para 3, in no circumstances may the foreign judgment be reviewed in a Belgian court as to the merits.

Procedure for enforcement in Belgium

Since recognition of a judgment originating from, and enforceable in, a contracting state is guaranteed without formal proceedings, only the procedure for enforcement in Belgium will be briefly outlined.

The procedure for enforcement is very simple. The decisions rendered in a contracting state that are enforceable therein may be enforced in another contracting state after a writ of execution has been issued upon request by the interested party.

(1) *Court to which the application for enforcement is made*

Article 32 specifies the court to which the petition has been addressed. In Belgium the petition must be addressed to the Court of First Instance (Art 32, para 1). There are 26 Courts of First Instance in Belgium, each having its own area of jurisdiction.

The chamber of the Court of First Instance which shall decide on the application is composed of a single judge (Judicial Code, Art 91, para 1).

If the party against whom enforcement is sought has his domicile in Belgium, the jurisdiction of the local Court of First Instance is determined by the place of that domicile (Art 32, para 2) (on the notion of domicile, see above).

(2) *The request containing the application for enforcement*

The application for enforcement is to be made by means of *ex parte* proceedings (Art 34, para 1) and is therefore governed by Arts 1025 through 1034 of the Judicial Code, which organise unilateral proceedings.

The applicant has to file a written request, in two originals, with the Office of the Court's Clerk (Judicial Code, Art 1027). A number of points have to be mentioned in the request (see Judicial Code, Art 1026). The request is to be signed and filed at the Office of the Court's Clerk by the applicant's counsel, who must be an attorney-at-law (*avocat/advocaat*). The attorney-at-law has to be licensed to practice in Belgium, which means that he has to be Belgian or a national of one of the member states of the European Union, and the holder of a Belgian law degree (for other conditions, see also Judicial Code, Art 428).

Article 1027, para 3 of the Judicial Code requires the applicant to indicate, on the request, a list of the documents he files together with his request. These are not limited to the documents mentioned in Arts 46 and 47 of the Convention. It is generally advisable (but not required by Belgian law) to also submit translations of these documents in Dutch or French. The language of the procedure before the Belgian court is either Dutch or French, depending on whether the court is located in the Dutch-speaking or French-speaking part of the country. In the German-speaking part of the country, the proceedings may also take place in German. In Brussels, the party making the application for enforcement has the choice between proceedings in Dutch or in French. The proceedings take place in the language in which the request which initiates the proceedings is drafted.

Article 48, para 2 of the Convention provides that if the court requires a translation of the documents to be produced, it shall be certified by a person qualified to do so in one of the contracting states. In Belgium, the profession of translator is not regulated, which means that anyone can be a translator. It is, however, advisable to have the translation made and certified by a sworn translator. This is a translator who has taken an oath in the presence of the President of the Court of First Instance. As a result, his or her translations have the confidence of the court.

(3) *The enforcement proceedings*

Article 1028, para 1 of the Judicial Code provides that the court examine the request. To that effect, the court can summon the applicant to appear in order to provide clarification or to answer questions (Judicial Code, Art 1028, para 2). Generally, however, the court considers itself to be sufficiently informed by the request and the documents submitted.

Once the court has given its decision, the court clerk sends the decision by registered mail to the applicant (and the intervening parties, if any) within three days of it being rendered (Judicial Code, Art 1030, para 1). It is sent to the address given for service of process (Brussels Convention, Art 33, para 2). The applicant's attorney receives an unsigned copy of the decision by ordinary mail (Judicial Code, Art 1030, para 1).

The party against whom enforcement is sought does not receive notice of the decision by the clerk of the court. The applicant can instruct the bailiff to serve the decision on that party. The purpose of this service is twofold. First, it is a prerequisite for the enforcement. Second, it starts the period of one or two months within which the appeal by the party against whom enforcement is sought is to be lodged, in accordance with the Brussels Convention, Art 36.

Belgian law
If Belgium has not executed a treaty with the country from which the judgment originates, Belgian judicial law will determine under what conditions a foreign judgment will be recognised and enforceable in Belgium.

In order to be enforceable in Belgium, a foreign judgment must be declared to be so by a Belgian court. This is done in a special type of adversary proceeding called *exequatur*.

No foreign judgment can be enforced until it has been recognised, but in many cases, a party seeks only recognition. No *exequatur* is required for a foreign judgment to be recognised as a valid instrument of evidence of the facts or acts noted in the judgment. A foreign judgment is furthermore, without *exequatur*, considered as conclusive for *res judicata*, or collateral estoppel purposes, as opposed to enforcement. Finally, a foreign judgment constitutes, even before *exequatur* is granted, a sufficient private title on the basis of which the beneficiary of the judgment can proceed to a third party attachment against the judgment debtor without prior authorisation from the judge of seizures.

Article 570 of the Judicial Code has attributed exclusive jurisdiction to the Court of First Instance to grant *exequatur* to foreign judgments. The beneficiary of the foreign judgment must commence the procedure according to the ordinary rules, ie he summons the person against whom he intends to enforce the foreign judgment in court. The court before which *exequatur* is sought does not have the power to alter the foreign decision; it can only ratify, totally or partially, the foreign decision, but it can neither substitute its own decision for the foreign one nor pronounce a new judgment. When *exequatur* is granted, the enforceable title, ie the instrument on the basis of which one proceeds with an enforcement, is not the foreign judgment but the Belgian judgment granting *exequatur*.

The main difference from the Brussels Convention regarding enforcement is that the Belgian court will review the foreign judgment as to the merits (*révision au fond*), re-examining the whole case which has already been decided by the foreign judge.

The only practical difference between an *exequatur* proceeding and an entirely new proceeding on the original cause of action is the fact that the burden rests on the defendant in the *exequatur* proceedings to show that *exequatur* cannot be granted.

Having reviewed the merits of the case, the Belgian court must further verify whether the foreign decision meets the following prerequisites or conditions in order to grant *exequatur*.

Public policy

The Belgian court examines whether the substance of the foreign judgment is contrary to Belgian public policy or any role of Belgian public law. What constitutes public policy is, of course, difficult to define. It varies from time to time, depending upon the state of the legislation and prevailing political and social tendencies. Therefore, it is important to know that the recognising court must assess the compatibility with the public policy prevailing at the date of the *exequatur* judgment, and not at the date of the foreign judgment. The key issue is to know whether enforcement of the foreign judgment is possible without offending the public policy of the *exequatur* forum. A particular case of incompatibility with public policy is a foreign judgment conflicting with an earlier Belgian judgment, such as when a Belgian court has already decided the dispute between the same parties.

Due process

Belgian law requires that the procedure followed abroad has been regular. This procedural test does not imply that the Belgian judge should investigate whether the foreign proceedings duly complied with all the procedural rules of the country where the judgment was rendered. The Belgian judge must only be satisfied that the defendant was duly served and had a reasonable opportunity to be heard.

Jurisdiction

Most countries agree that in order to be entitled to recognition and enforcement, the foreign judgment must have been rendered by a court having jurisdiction in the international sense. The Belgian court, however, holds the foreign judgment deficient only when the foreign court's jurisdiction was based solely on the plaintiff's nationality.

Finality

In order to be enforceable in Belgium, the foreign judgment must be final. The interpretation of finality varies from country to country. In Belgium, the foreign judgment must be *res judicata* in the country of rendition and all remedies must have been exhausted or the time therefore must have lapsed.

Authentic copy

Finally, the Belgian court verifies whether the copy of the foreign judgment meets all the authenticity requirements set by the law of the country where the judgment is rendered.

Two concluding points should be noted.

First, no *exequatur* procedure is required for the recognition of a judgment in bankruptcy matters. The recognition will be given by any Belgian public authority, upon verification of the five conditions listed above, but without review of the merits of the case.

Second, decisions rendered by an international jurisdiction are considered to be foreign judgments and therefore need *exequatur* to be enforceable in Belgium. The decisions rendered by the European Court of Justice are, however, enforceable in Belgium *ipso iure*, ie without prior *exequatur*. The Ministry of Foreign Affairs verifies the authenticity of the copy of the decision and thereafter the Chief Clerk of the Court of Appeals of Brussels will affix the executory formula, ie the declaration that the decision is enforceable in Belgium.

•

Jean-Pierre de Bandt
De Bandt, Van Hecke & Lagae
Rue Brederode 13
B-1000 Brussels
Belgium

•

—— 2 ——

DENMARK

—— • ——

CONTENTS

•

DENMARK

•

2

DENMARK

●

STRUCTURE OF THE LEGAL PROFESSION

The professional title of a Danish lawyer is *Advokat*. It is a statutory requirement that all practising lawyers in Denmark are members of the Danish Bar
Association (*Advokatsamfundet*). A Danish lawyer may practise as a sole
practitioner, as a member of a partnership or incorporate his business as a
limited company.

Until the mid-1980s many lawyers practised as sole practitioners or as
members of a partnership consisting of two or three lawyers. Since then a
number of mergers has taken place, and the number of lawyers in the larger
firms ranks between 30 and 50. In such law firms a client will usually find the
expertise and knowledge necessary for cross-border transactions, but the
degree of specialisation of such law firms is not as great as is found in UK or US
firms.

Legal advice may be rendered by other professionals, but lawyers have the
sole right of audience before the courts in Denmark. Danish lawyers are not
allowed to participate in so-called multi-disciplinary businesses. Consequently, shares in an incorporated law firm must be owned by lawyers who
are admitted to the Bar.

A lawyer is automatically admitted to the Bar after having been employed as
an articled clerk for three years with a lawyer who has been admitted to the
Bar. After admission the lawyer has the right of audience only before the lower
courts (*Undiarretten*). In order to be admitted to the Courts of Appeal
(*Landsretten*) a lawyer must pass a special test. All lawyers may take this test,
the object of which is to establish that the lawyer is capable of preparing,
handling and arguing cases before the Courts of Appeal. Two actual cases must
be argued before the Courts of Appeal as test cases. The court hearing the
cases decides whether admission shall be granted.

After having been admitted to the Courts of Appeal for five years an
application may be submitted to the Supreme Court (*Hojesteret*) to obtain the

right of audience before it. Such a right is usually granted if the lawyer in question has argued cases before the Courts of Appeal on a regular basis and is of good standing.

Lawyers in Denmark do not have a special right of audience like English barristers.

There is no official institute or agency at which a lawyer may seek certification for having acquired a specialist knowledge within a certain area of the law.

Danish lawyers are not permitted to enter into partnerships or other economic arrangements with foreign lawyers. However, it is quite common for Danish law firms to be members of informal associations of international law firms or to participate in less formal networks.

The major law firms are found in the capital Copenhagen or in Aarhus, which is the largest city in the Jutland peninsula.

HOW TO FIND A SUITABLE LAWYER

When a foreign client considers conducting business in Denmark for the first time, careful consideration must be given to the kind of legal advice which is necessary in connection with the approach to the Danish market. The transaction in question may require advice from a specialist on a specific issue, but the foreign client may also seek to establish a general relationship with a Danish law firm. The first obvious approach is to seek recommendations from the client's own local lawyer, but one may also consider approaching the Danish Bar Association, scanning international listings of lawyers, looking for advertisements, or paying a visit to a number of law firms.

• RECOMMENDATIONS •

If the foreign client's own lawyer has previous and satisfactory experience with a Danish law firm, the recommendation from this lawyer is probably the most important reason for choosing a specific law firm. The lawyer may not have previous experience with Denmark, but may be a member of an international association or participate in a network of lawyers. Other members of such a network may have relevant experience. Recommendations from such sources will therefore play an important role when deciding which Danish law firm to approach.

The major law firms in Denmark cover all areas of the law relevant for business investments, and there is a tendency to establish specialised departments, even though Danish law firms, as mentioned above, are not specialised to the same degree as UK or US law firms. There are also smaller law firms, which possess a special knowledge within a certain area of the law. Recommendations are by far the most useful method for a foreign client to select a Danish law firm.

• LEGAL DIRECTORIES •

Each year the Danish Bar Association publishes a Directory called *Advokatfirmaer i Denmark*. This Directory lists every lawyer in Denmark and each lawyer may choose to list three areas of special interest. However, this must not be considered as an endorsement by the Danish Bar Association that the particular lawyer is a specialist within the three areas indicated. The Danish Bar Association does not, as a matter of principle, give recommendations with regard to law firms.

One may also investigate international directories such as *Martindale-Hubbell* and *Law firms in Europe*, published by Euromoney, or *Kime's International Law Directory*, published by Longman. One should not rely solely on such sources when selecting a Danish lawyer, but these sources may provide useful background information for the selection and confirm the information obtained from other sources.

• ADVERTISING •

Danish lawyers are allowed to advertise, but may not state or indicate that the law firm is a specialist within a certain area of the law. In advertisements or brochures the law firm may mention the areas in which it renders advice and may also state if the firm is a member of an international association of law firms.

Danish lawyers have recently been allowed to approach clients of other law firms without any prior business relationship. Newsletters and other sorts of advertisement material may thus be directly mailed to a target group defined by the individual law firm. Such promotional practices do not seem, however, to be very common.

• LOCAL VISITS AND PERSONAL INTERVIEWS •

Occasionally, a potential foreign client visits a number of law firms in Denmark before deciding which one to instruct for a particular transaction. The object of such visits is to become better acquainted with the structure of Danish law firms, and more often to negotiate fees in major transactions, especially transactions involving land and real property.

FACTORS IN CHOOSING A SUITABLE LAWYER

• PROFESSIONAL QUALIFICATIONS •

A Danish lawyer must obtain a university degree before seeking a position as an articled clerk. After three years of clerkship the lawyer is admitted to the Bar and there are special requirements for admission to the Court of Appeal.

During the clerkship period of three years the Danish Bar Association provides additional education. The Education Department of the Bar Association provides specialist courses within specific subjects to Danish lawyers on an ongoing basis. There is no mandatory requirement for the participation in such post-educational programmes, but most lawyers choose to attend such programmes and/or courses which are arranged by the law firms themselves.

In choosing a law firm the academic qualifications of a lawyer may not be of significance, as one of the most important assets of a lawyer is the experience acquired during years of practice. The prospective client should investigate whether the firm possesses the necessary specialist knowledge, is of a sufficient size to handle the matter in question, and has sufficient experience in international matters. The most reliable source for such information is, as indicated above, the recommendation by other lawyers who have had experience with the Danish firm in question.

• LANGUAGE ABILITY •

A command of foreign languages, especially English, is perhaps the most important factor for a satisfactory interaction between the foreign client and his Danish lawyer. A number of Danish lawyers have taken a Master's Degree at UK or US universities. After having taken the foreign degree many lawyers have worked with UK or US law firms as part of their international education. Such experience usually proves to be an advantage to the lawyer handling international transactions, but generally speaking, lawyers at the major offices all possess reasonably sophisticated linguistic abilities.

However, the need for a translator may arise where the other party to the transaction insists on negotiating and drafting the contract in Danish. If the contract is of a very technical nature, for example, a building contract or a contract relating to the supply of computer hardware and software, it may be unreasonable to expect the lawyer to translate all the technical specifications. The risk of misunderstandings in such circumstances is very high, and the use of a translator under these circumstances may prove to be appropriate.

• Type of Transaction •

A transaction involving the setting up of a business in Denmark will be governed by Danish law, and Danish law will usually play an important role in connection with the acquisition of a Danish company from a Danish vendor. In such matters the need for a Danish lawyer is obvious. The Danish lawyer will play a central role, even though the Danish transaction is only part of a major international deal. The language ability of the lawyer is, in such circumstances, of the essence.

The role of the Danish lawyer may be less important if the transaction is a sale of the shares in a Danish company by and between two foreign companies. Such a contract will usually be governed by foreign law, and the advice necessary from the Danish lawyer will be confined to due diligence aspects and any mandatory provision of relevance to the transaction. Tax issues may also arise from such a transaction.

• Familiarity With Overseas Contract Types •

A typical Danish contract concerning the acquisition of a business used to be less comprehensive than a contract drafted for a similar transaction governed by American state law or English law. The main reason for this approach is to be found in the traditional juridical difference between a common law and a civil law country. Many of the issues dealt with in an Anglo-American contract will usually be regulated by specific legislation in a civil law country. However, as a result of significant increased international experience among Danish law firms, and in order to accommodate the demands and expectations of foreign clients, the drafting of Danish contracts has changed in recent years, and many contracts are now drafted in a typical English style. However, the actual contract is often less voluminous than the English version, but the subjects covered are the same.

• Specialisation in Topics •

As a result of the mergers which have taken place since the mid-1980s, Danish law firms now provide a more specialised service, but one should not expect to find the same degree of specialisation which is typical for the largest UK and US law firms. Danish lawyers, at least in the larger firms, tend to concentrate on two or three specific subjects but are, generally speaking, in a position – sometimes in co-operation with a colleague – to provide advice on most matters which are of interest to a foreign corporate investor.

However, the need for lawyers with in-depth and specialist knowledge of a particular subject becomes more and more apparent, as the complexity of the Danish legal system has increased significantly over the last few years, especially as a result of implementation of EC Directives. The largest firms have established specialist departments in order to cope with this development, but again the Anglo-American degree of specialisation is seldom found.

• ASSOCIATE OFFICES IN BRUSSELS •

Only a few Danish firms have established themselves in Brussels, but most firms have access to a cross-border analysis of EU legislation through membership of informal associations. A potential client should inquire about the availability of such services when instructing a particular law firm, if such expertise is likely to be of importance for a specific transaction.

• CLIENT CONFLICTS •

The Danish Bar Association has issued binding regulations concerning client conflicts. These regulations do not deal in great detail with the issue of conflicts of interest, but state in general terms that a lawyer may not in the same matter advise, represent or provide services to two or more clients if a conflict of interest exists between them. These provisions also apply if there is a significant risk of conflict of interest. Further, a lawyer is not entitled to accept a case if he has previously represented or given advice to the adversary.

A disciplinary action may be brought in the case of a failure to comply with these regulations.

COMMERCIAL ARRANGEMENTS WHEN INSTRUCTING COUNSEL

Legal costs of a transaction play an important role when choosing and instructing a law firm. Before approaching a Danish lawyer the client should have given some consideration to the importance of the matter and consequently the fee he is prepared to pay for the particular case. Certain factors will in this context be of great importance. The complexity of the matter will provide some guidance for the assistance necessary, but also the speed at which the transaction must be carried out will play an important role in calculating the total amount of legal costs the client will incur.

• FEE STRUCTURE •

The main rule concerning the fees a Danish lawyer may charge for legal services rendered is laid down in section 126.2 of the Act on Legal Procedure. This provision states that a lawyer cannot charge a fee for the services rendered in excess of what can be considered as reasonable. The Danish Bar Association has issued tariffs for the fees which may be charged in particular matters. Even though these tariffs are guidelines they are usually followed by Danish lawyers unless otherwise agreed with a commercial client (see below).

The tariffs apply to litigation procedures, matters involving the collection of a creditor's outstanding claim and for acting as trustee in a bankruptcy estate or as an executor under a will. Further, fixed fees are imposed on transactions concerning the transfer of land and property.

The fees which may be charged according to the tariffs are all based on the value of the case and are usually calculated as a fixed percentage of the amount in question.

If no billing arrangement (see below) has been agreed between the lawyer and his client, both the lawyer and the client are entitled to rely on the main principle of reasonable charging laid down in section 126.2 of the Act on Legal Procedure. In order to establish whether a specific fee can be considered as reasonable, a number of factors will have to be taken into consideration.

One of the important items is naturally the number of hours spent by the lawyers involved in the matter. However, the actual figure is not the sole decisive item.

Another parameter is the value of the case. The higher the figures involved, the higher the fees. These factors have to be balanced with the complexity of the matter and the speed at which the client wants the transaction to be carried out. The more complex the matter and the quicker it is to be resolved, the higher the fee which can be justified.

None of the above-mentioned factors is the sole decisive one. When deciding what a reasonable fee is, one has to take all the above-mentioned factors into consideration and then try to establish whether this can be considered a reasonable market price for the services rendered. This may under the circumstances be a very difficult task, but generally speaking, fees charged by Danish lawyers tend to be less than those charged by UK or US lawyers.

If a client feels that the fee charged by the lawyer is excessive, and if no settlement agreement can be reached, then the client may bring the matter before a Complaint Board (*Kredsbestyrelsen*). This Board will then decide the amount of fees which may be considered reasonable under the circumstances.

Commercial matters

In commercial matters Danish lawyers are allowed to enter into special fee arrangements. The Danish Bar Association has in its instructions to Danish lawyers provided examples of the fee arrangements which may be agreed, but the main rule is that individual arrangements may be agreed between the lawyer and his commercial client. One of the examples mentioned is a fixed fee for assistance in a specific transaction. However, such arrangements do not seem to be typical, as both parties at the outset may have some difficulties in estimating the scope of the transaction and the number of hours involved. A very cautious and perhaps a too high estimate will usually be the result of a demand for a fixed fee. This is not, for obvious reasons, in the best interest of the client. However, such fee arrangements are agreed in matters relating to the transfer of land and property. The fee will usually be a certain percentage of the value of the property in question. This fee is then charged without any regard to the complexity of the matter and the number of hours actually logged.

• RETAINER •

If a Danish lawyer is approached by a foreign client with whom he has had no prior business relationship, the lawyer may feel that under the circumstances it is appropriate to ask for a retainer. This will typically be the case if the lawyer is to be involved in a lengthy litigation procedure or negotiations which may last for a number of months. As an alternative to a retainer monthly billing may be agreed based upon the actual number of hours spent.

• METHOD AND TIMING OF BILLING •

The most commonly agreed billing arrangement is hourly billing. The rate charged varies, depending upon the seniority and experience of the lawyer advising on the transaction:

Partners: between DKK 1,500 and DKK 2,000
Associates: between DKK 1,100 and DKK 1,500
Articled clerks: between DKK 700 and DKK 1,100

The above-mentioned rates are only to be considered as the typical range of rates charged, and the hourly rate for a particular matter may differ. Charging at these rates will include overheads and secretarial time.

Hourly billing combined with a success fee may be agreed but is not common practice. In these circumstances the hourly rate may be reduced, and higher rates or a fixed success fee may only be charged if the matter is successfully completed.

Generally, most lawyers tend to bill at the completion of a matter, but the billing frequency varies, and the client may naturally request to be billed monthly or quarterly. In large transactions, which may be expected to last for several months, billing on account is not unusual.

When billing, detailed information about the services provided is usually stated in the invoice and the total number of hours spent may be disclosed, but a computer transcript specifying the number of hours logged in the particular matter is seldom provided unless specifically requested by the client.

TREATMENT OF FOREIGN NATIONALS UNDER LOCAL LAW

• RESTRICTIONS, REPORTS AND GOVERNMENTAL APPROVALS • OF FOREIGN INVESTMENT

The nature and the scope of activities contemplated by the foreign investor is very important when analysing what areas of Danish law will be applicable in the particular case.

Under corporate law a foreign company is required to register a branch if it conducts business in Denmark. The purchase of Danish products through a Danish intermediary is not considered conducting business in Denmark, neither is work of a purely administrative nature. A single agreement concerning the rendering of advice to a particular Danish client is not considered an activity requiring the registration of a branch. However, if the foreign national is represented in Denmark by an individual who has the authority to enter into contracts on behalf of the foreign investor, such an activity would constitute sufficient contact, and registration of a branch would be necessary.

The scope of a foreign investor's tax liability in Denmark depends upon the kind of investment made. Numerous kinds of income received by a foreign investor from Danish sources will be subject to Danish corporate or personal income tax, but a very important exception applies to interest payments from a Danish debtor. No Danish taxation is imposed on interest paid to a foreign grantor of a loan, who otherwise is not subject to Danish taxation.

Value Added Tax (VAT) plays an important role in connection with an investment made by a foreign national. Generally speaking, the scope of liability under the VAT Act may be said to be more far-reaching than the potential liability for corporate or personal income taxes.

• EXCHANGE CONTROLS AND OTHER REGULATORY ISSUES •

Foreign exchange control regulations were in principle abolished as of 1 October 1988. A few reporting requirements apply for statistical reasons and in

41

order to prevent money laundering. However, a number of specific areas of business activities are subject to special regulations, particularly within the financial industry. Activities such as banking, certain investment companies, insurance companies, mortgage associations and consumer financing are subject to special regulations. Most of these regulations are based on EC Directives.

Outside the financial industry, areas such as commercial radio and television stations, the hotel industry and the farming industry are subject to special licence requirements in order to carry out their particular kind of business.

• TAX TREATMENT •

The tax treatment of a foreign investor depends upon the vehicle used for making the investment in Denmark. The foreign investor may decide to invest through a subsidiary of his foreign enterprise. Alternatively, a branch of the foreign company may be established. Several factors may be taken into consideration when deciding whether to establish a subsidiary or a branch. The activities carried out by the foreign company may be of such a nature that the limitation of liability enjoyed by a separate legal entity may be the decisive factor. However, foreign tax considerations may lead to the conclusion that a branch is the most advantageous investment vehicle. This would be the case if a significant tax loss is expected as a result of the start-up expenses, and the business will not generate a profit for a couple of years.

Subsidiary
A Danish subsidiary of a foreign company is subject to taxation on its worldwide income irrespective of the sources from which the income is derived. The corporate tax is 34 per cent and corporate taxes are paid on account bi-annually. If the subsidiary receives income from foreign sources, such income must be included in the Danish taxable income, unless exempt under a particular double tax treaty. Generally, relief under such treaties is granted in the form of a credit for any foreign taxes paid. In the absence of a treaty, domestic legislation provides for such credit for foreign taxes.

The foreign parent company will not be subject to corporate income taxation as a result of having a Danish subsidiary. The establishment of the subsidiary may be made either by an equity investment or a combination of an equity investment and loan financing.

As to the capitalisation of a Danish subsidiary no specific requirements with regard to the debt to equity ratio have to be met. The Danish Corporate Tax Act does not contain a general provision concerning the issue of thin capitalisation. This issue only arises where a Danish parent company is consolidated with its foreign subsidiary for Danish tax purposes, and the capital structure of the foreign subsidiary is highly geared. Under certain circumstances interest deduction on such financing may be disallowed.

As stated above, payment of interest to a foreign parent is deductible for corporate income tax purposes and no withholding tax is imposed. However, it should be noted that all dealings between a foreign parent company and its Danish subsidiary must be at 'arm's length'. If this requirement is not met, any payment in excess of an arm's length payment will be considered as a hidden distribution, and as such not deductible for income tax purposes. The parent company will be subject to Danish taxation of the hidden distribution.

If the repatriation of the foreign investment is made in the form of dividends, the foreign parent company will be subject to Danish corporate taxation on such amounts. The corporate income taxation in this case amounts to 30 per cent of the dividend paid, and is withheld at source.

Relief for the withholding tax on dividends may either be provided in domestic legislation or by a double tax treaty. Under Danish tax law the subsidiary is not required to withhold the 30 per cent tax if the parent company is incorporated in another EU member state and qualifies under Art 2 of the Parent/Subsidiary Directive. A further condition is that the parent company has owned at least 25 per cent of the share capital in its Danish subsidiary, either during the entire financial year in which the dividend is received or through a continuous period of at least two years up till the time the dividend payment is received.

Under most double tax treaties the withholding tax on dividends distributed to foreign companies is reduced to 15 per cent and under certain circumstances to 5 per cent, if the foreign parent owns more than 25 per cent of the dividend paying company. The tax withheld in excess hereof may, upon application, be repaid by the Danish tax authorities.

Any losses sustained by the subsidiary on its trading activities may be carried forward for five years. As long as the subsidiary is owned by its foreign parent company any change in the business activities will not result in a disallowance of the right to carry forward previous tax losses. Certain limitations apply in the case where the subsidiary is sold. If a non-related investor acquires more than 50 per cent of the share capital, and activities in the form of passive investments in shares or bonds are subsequently carried on by the subsidiary, previous tax losses may not be set off gainst such financial income. This does not apply if the subsidiary was engaged in the finance business prior to the sale of the shares.

Branch

A foreign company may, for various reasons, decide to set up its business activities in Denmark through a registered branch. A registered branch is considered a permanent establishment and as such taxed on the income generated by the branch. For corporate income tax purposes only expenses which are connected with the income of the branch may be deducted. The profits of the branch are taxed at the corporate rate of 34 per cent.

The branch in itself is considered a permanent establishment. However, a foreign company is also deemed to have a permanent establishment in Denmark if it participates in a business which has such a permanent establishment. Further, running payments from such a business or the proceeds from the disposal of a business, when such proceeds are not dividend, repayment of the principal of a loan or interest, are subject to Danish corporate income taxation.

The repatriation of profit generated by the branch is not subject to any withholding requirements.

Dealings between the foreign company and its Danish branch must all be at arm's length. The Danish Corporate Tax Act does not specify in great detail under what circumstances dealings are considered to be at arm's length. It is merely stated that terms and conditions for dealings between the foreign company and its Danish branch must be equivalent to such terms and conditions which one may expect will govern the relationship between independent parties.

Value Added Tax

The Danish VAT Act is based on the Sixth EC VAT Directive as subsequently amended. A subsidiary or a branch, which makes taxable supplies or renders taxable services must be registered for VAT purposes. Only if the supply is exempt or the annual turnover of the enterprise does not exceed DKK 10,000 will VAT registration not be necessary. Failing to register for VAT purposes is subject to significant fines. VAT is for the time being imposed at the rate of 25 per cent.

A taxable person may recover any VAT paid on goods purchased or services received as input VAT, and VAT only becomes payable to the extent the output VAT of the subsidiary or foreign branch exceeds the input VAT. Certain limitations may apply where the branch or subsidiary makes partially exempt supplies.

Turnover tax

Sale of Danish shares may, under certain circumstances, be subject to a turnover tax of 1 per cent. This tax is reduced to 0.5 per cent as of 1 January 1995. The tax becomes payable if the vendor of the shares is a resident of Denmark, even though the purchaser is a resident of a foreign country. However, where the vendor is a resident of a foreign country and the purchaser is a resident of Denmark, no tax is payable.

Capital transfer tax

The capital transfer tax of 1 per cent on any amount injected as share capital in a Danish company was abolished as of 19 May 1993.

• ACCESS TO AND TREATMENT BY LOCAL COURTS •

A foreign company or individual may appear in a Danish court as plaintiff without any restrictions. However, a claim for security for costs may be made by the defendant. Such an application must be made on the first day the parties appear before the court. If the application is granted, the security must be made either in the form of a cash deposit or a bank guarantee.

• FOREIGN PARENT LIABILITY •

The concept of lifting the corporate veil is generally not accepted by Danish courts. Under Danish law a company is considered to be distinct from its shareholders. The shareholders are only liable for the amounts injected as share capital. Under the Danish Corporate Act a shareholder may, however, be liable to compensate any loss which he wilfully or through gross negligence has imposed upon the company, other shareholders or a third party by violating the Corporate Act or the by-laws of the company.

• JURISDICTION OF LOCAL COURTS •

Denmark is party to the Brussels and Lugano Conventions (see Appendix). A foreign person or corporate entity may only be sued in Danish courts if the defendant has his domicile in Denmark, or if other grounds for claiming jurisdiction over the defendant set forth by the Conventions are met.

Where the Conventions do not apply, litigation may be initiated in various cases and jurisdictions, as follows:

(a) against a foreign sole trader, in the area where his business is conducted;
(b) in cases concerning rights over land and property, where the property is located;
(c) in cases concerning contracts, where the contract is to be performed; and
(d) in actions in tort, where the accident took place.

Litigation against a company may be initiated in the court having jurisdiction over the area where the company has its registered office.

• FOREIGN LANGUAGE DOCUMENTS AND DOCUMENTS • GOVERNED BY FOREIGN LAW

The language used by Danish courts is Danish and documents in a foreign language need to be translated into Danish by a certified translator.

The parties may agree that a special contract is governed by foreign law but is to be decided by Danish courts. In this case the parties must produce evidence concerning the contents of the foreign law, and the courts will then decide the issue based on such information.

• RECOGNITION AND ENFORCEMENT OF FOREIGN • JUDGMENTS

Under the Brussels Convention (see Appendix) judgments rendered by a court in another EU country may be enforced in Denmark. A request for execution must be submitted to the Bailiff in the municipality where the defendant has his residence. As an exhibit to the request for execution the following documents must follow:

(1) A transcript of the judgment certified by the foreign court.
(2) Evidence that the judgment can be executed in the country where it was made, and that this has been served on the defendant.
(3) In the case of a default proof that a writ of summons and/or a similar document was properly served on the defaulting party.

Denmark has entered into an arrangement similar to the Brussels Convention with the other Nordic countries.

In the absence of a convention a foreign plaintiff will have to initiate legal proceedings in Denmark, where the foreign judgment may be produced as evidence.

•

Hans Severin Hansen
Koch-Nielsen & Gronborg
Applebys Plads 1
Postboks 19
DK 1001 Copenhagen K
Denmark

•

3

FRANCE

———— • ————

CONTENTS

•

•

•

3

FRANCE

•

STRUCTURE OF THE LEGAL PROFESSION

When seeking legal counsel in France one generally turns to the legal services of an *avocat*. The French *avocat* most closely resembles the common law attorney or barrister/solicitor. While many other legal service providers exist, their roles are more specific and their contact with the client is less frequent than that of an *avocat*. Another legal professional with whom a client may come into contact is the *notaire*, who handles the authorisation and mainten-ance of written legal documents primarily in family matters and real estate. Other legal professionals such as process servers (*huissiers de justice*) and judicial administrators (*administrateurs judiciaires*) are public officials and while they may play an important role in resolving various legal problems, their relationship with the client is usually determined by court appointment or procedural requirements.

• **ATTORNEYS** •

In order to reach greater conformity amongst the EU member states, the French government created the 'New Profession of Attorneys', which took effect in 1992 as a merger of two previously independent legal professions – that of *avocat* and that of *conseil juridique*. Prior to this change, a *conseil juridique*, unlike an *avocat*, provided legal advice but was not admitted to the Bar, and thus could not argue a case in court.

A French *avocat* or attorney performs several basic functions. The attorney generally provides legal advice and services to clients in commercial, civil and criminal matters. Furthermore, the attorney oversees litigation, submits briefs and puts forward oral arguments on the client's behalf to all courts except for the *Cour de Cassation* and the *Conseil d'Etat*. The attorney also drafts acts, contracts and other legal documents signed *sous seing privé* on the client's behalf.

The French attorney may practise law in one of three settings:

- in a private practice;
- in the legal department of a company; or
- in an accounting firm.

In private practice, French attorneys may conduct their professional activities as sole practitioners or in group practices. Attorneys may organise group practices in the form of a professional commercial company with shares (*société d'exercice libéral*), a French economic interest group (*groupement d'intérêt économique*), or a joint venture. Law firms (*cabinets d'avocats*) usually consist of partners (*associés*) who have some ownership participation in the firm, associates (*collaborateurs*) and counsel (*conseil consultant*). In their various forms, private practice firms range in size from one or two attorneys to 200, although most firms are much smaller than those in the UK or the US.

A French attorney may also be in-house counsel for a company (*juriste d'entreprise*) located in France. These attorneys are not necessarily members of the Bar since their position generally does not require them to be able to conduct litigation in court.

Certified accountants

In 1994, the accounting profession was reformed, with accountants and accounting interns being merged under one profession of certified accountants (*la profession d'expert comptable*). Alongside these changes, the legal status of certified accountants has been modified. The 1994 law allows certified accountants to be responsible for the administrative and accounting services of their clients, apart from litigation. Moreover, certified accountants may now practise as adjunct legal advisers, thus assuming a quasi-judicial role. Under the 1994 law, accounting firms have five years to adapt their constitutions so as to conform with the present law.

The above-mentioned reforms of both the legal and accounting professions have had tremendous impact on the French legal market by increasing the options available to clients. The accounting firms have expanded their ability to offer legal services from two different directions:

(1) Through the accounting reforms, an auditor may now handle specific administrative legal functions once reserved for legal professionals;
(2) Through the legal reforms and the New Profession of Attorneys, the legal departments that were once staffed with *conseils juridiques* may now perform the full variety of legal services, notably appearances in court which were once reserved for the *avocat*.

Resulting from the creation of a new profession, the former *conseils juridiques* in the firms affiliated to accounting firms may now conduct litigation. This change creates the potential for a 'one-stop' shop for clients, ie clients may be able to have all their accounting and legal needs handled by one firm.

• *NOTAIRES* •

Certain business operations may require a *notaire*. *Notaires*, distinguishable from the US notary, are authorised to receive all acts and contracts required by law or requested by the parties. They also authenticate acts of public authorities and establish the date. Further, they may also manage and retain documents, having custody of original documents and furnishing both common and executory copies. While a written agreement does not require notarial formalities to be valid some transactions, such as real estate transactions and the preparation of antenuptial agreements, do require a notarial act (*acte notarié*) to be valid. Much like attorneys, *notaires* may be members of a professional commercial company with shares or a professional civil company. Also, a *notaire* may be a member of a French economic interest group, a European economic interest group, or a participant in a joint venture.

HOW TO FIND A SUITABLE LAWYER

The best way to find legal counsel in France is through recommendations. However, several other methods may also be useful. With the increasing development of specialisation in particular fields of law, other very good sources for seeking legal counsel have developed including directories and association lists. Often the most effective way for securing counsel is to use a combination of these methods.

• RECOMMENDATIONS •

While recommendations may be obtained from several places, talking to colleagues who have experience dealing with French counsel in the relevant legal field is a good place to start. Asking for a recommendation from domestic legal counsel may also be helpful. Domestic counsel may have representation in France or regularly deal with a particular French firm. Even if domestic counsel does not have such representation or a contact in the country, domestic counsel may be able to recommend counsel based on his or her knowledge of the recommended lawyer's professional reputation. Networking is also a good way to learn about legal counsel in France.

• LEGAL DIRECTORIES •

In searching for an attorney with a particular specialisation, legal directories may be particularly useful. Several directories written in French exist. In France, the 'official' legal directory is the *Guide des Professions Juridiques*. This lists, both alphabetically and by subject matter, all French and foreign legal professionals practising law in France and in the French territories. *Avocats* are listed alphabetically according to the Bar (*barreau*) to which they are admitted. Following the recent legal reform, lists according to specialisation will also be published. Other directories published by private companies are available in French but they may not provide a complete or accurate list of professionals practising law in France, because such directories usually require payment in order to be listed.

French counsel listings are also available in English. *Martindale-Hubbell International Edition* provides a comprehensive list of legal counsel in France. Other directories, such as *Kime's International Law Directory* and the *European 500*, also provide a listing of firms. French legal associations may too provide information. For example, each French bar association has member lists. The *Guide des Professions Juridiques* lists these associations and contacts.

• ADVERTISING •

Advertising by the French legal profession is limited since the Professional Responsibility Code and the individual bar associations severely restrict the substance and format of attorney advertising. For this reason, seeking counsel through advertisements may not be very effective. The Professional Responsibility Code prohibits advertisement by letters, posters, films, radio or television. An attorney may not engage in door-to-door solicitation (*démarchage*) nor offer legal services to secure consultations or legal drafting. A representative of a firm may not be sent to a prospective client's residence or place of business.

However, an attorney or law firm may advertise in certain limited circumstances. Advertising is permitted if the purpose is to present necessary information to the public, but it must be discreet and neutral. Likewise, an attorney may display the firm name and its members on the letterhead, mentioning their studies, specialisations, professional distinctions and diplomas obtained. In this vein, marketing brochures have recently been permitted but are rarely used for promotion. It is customary for law firms to prepare firm resumés describing the firm's activities to potential clients. However, advertising mentioning the identity of the firm's clients is prohibited.

• CHAMBERS OF COMMERCE •

Chambers of commerce may also have information on legal counsel. As with the French Bar Association, they may provide a list either from a legal directory or a membership directory. Many firms who work internationally may be members of chambers of commerce in countries other than France, and therefore a search with a chamber of commerce should not be limited to France or the French Chamber of Commerce.

• BEAUTY PARADES •

'Beauty parades' (*appel d'offres*) are becoming a fashionable way to secure legal counsel. In France, beauty parades do not follow a formal procedure. Usually the prospective client meets the attorney to discuss general legal problems and to ask the attorney specific questions on his qualifications and expertise. The client may repeat this procedure with other firms and makes a decision based on the impression gained at these meetings.

FACTORS IN CHOOSING A SUITABLE LAWYER

Many French firms have taken significant steps toward adapting to the increasingly international and complex needs of clients. They have accomplished this through providing services with international representation and highly-specialised expertise in certain fields of law. Someone seeking counsel in France may want to consider the language capabilities of the firm members as well as their global experience, including the presence of offices in other countries, the work experience of French counsel in foreign countries, and the presence of foreign counsel in the French office.

• PROFESSIONAL QUALIFICATIONS •

In order to join the legal profession one must meet the academic requirements and specific conditions of nationality, morality and competence. An attorney must be a French national, a national of an EU member state, or a national from a state or territory which accords reciprocity by granting the French a right of access to the legal profession. As a result of the *conseil juridique* and *avocat* merging into one profession, the New Profession of Attorneys, all members of the New Profession of Attorneys must be members of the French Bar.

For admission to the legal profession, a French applicant is required to have a *mâtrise* in law (granted after a four-year university programme) or a recognised equivalent, such as a graduate business school degree. The candidate must sit an examination administered by a regional Bar training programme, the EFB (*école de formation du barreau*). Upon successful completion of this examination the candidate registers with the EFB for 12 months' theoretical and professional training. The candidates study the following subjects: professional ethics, pleadings, trial practice, criminal and civil procedure, law firm management and one foreign language. The candidate must also complete a three-month internship (*stage*) in a law firm and a two-month internship with a courthouse, an accountant or the in-house counsel of a corporation. Upon completion of the professional training, the candidate is eligible to take the CAPA (*Certificat d'Aptitude à la Profession d'Avocat*). The candidate may then apply to be registered with the Bar as an attorney in training for two years (*avocat stagiaire*), after which he or she obtains the title of *avocat*.

One issue raised by the formation of the European Union is the ability of foreign nationals to practise law in France. Attorneys who are authorised to litigate in one EU member state file a formal request and take an examination (*Examen d'Aptitude*). Once completed, EU attorneys may conduct litigation before the French courts provided that they comply with all applicable French law governing litigation. Clients may need to consider whether an attorney who does not have a French degree or who may be unfamiliar with French law can still meet their needs.

Attorneys who are qualified to practise law in a non-EU country must comply with more stringent formalities. The non-EU attorney must file a formal request to the CNB for permission to sit for an Equivalency Examination (*Contrôle des Connaissances*). Admission to the French Bar is based on the principle of reciprocity. The concept of reciprocity, however, has not been clearly defined and may depend upon the terms upon which the French Bar Association admits foreign applicants.

• LANGUAGE ABILITY •

With the ever-increasing international aspect of legal services, the client may need an attorney or firm that has the ability to work in multiple languages. When seeking French counsel, the language issue for French clients may only concern legal services required for transactions dealing with another country.

• TYPE OF TRANSACTION •

When seeking legal counsel, a primary consideration is whether the transaction requires French legal advice. Other important considerations are whether a French court will have jurisdiction over the matter. For example, in cases where French law is the choice of law under an international contract, retaining French counsel may be advantageous. These procedural concerns are addressed below. The laws which govern the transaction must also be established. A client may prefer French counsel because of the counsel's familiarity with the French judicial system and law.

Other factors influencing the choice of counsel include the international character of the transaction, the need for highly specialised knowledge, the involvement of complex or new areas of law, and the size or complexity of the transaction.

• FAMILIARITY WITH FOREIGN JURISDICTIONS •

The ever-increasing international aspects of a client's legal needs require that legal counsel have, in addition to regional contacts, contacts all over the world. Growing interest in conducting business in Eastern European countries has made knowledge of these legal systems a valuable asset for French legal firms and their clients. While previously few French firms had offices abroad, many firms have recently established offices in foreign countries, especially in Eastern Europe. French legal representation is developing in other parts of the world where substantial increases in foreign investment and foreign presence have occurred, especially in China and other East Asian countries.

• SPECIALISATION IN TOPICS •

The range of specialisation and expertise in different areas of law is an important consideration for a client seeking French counsel. With the establishment of the New Profession of Attorneys mentioned above, French counsel have the possibility of developing a specialisation. This possibility is especially useful in the fields of tax, employment and corporate law. Legal counsel may now obtain the title of specialist (*spécialiste*) after five years of professional practice in the field of speciality and successful completion of an examination measuring the level of knowledge in the field. Upon request and the fulfilment of these conditions, a certificate is delivered by the regional centre of professional training recognising the attorney's expertise in an area of law. Although carrying the title of *spécialiste* does not require such certification, it may be beneficial for clients seeking counsel with an expertise in an area of law. The Bar recognises the following areas of specialisation:

- administrative law;
- commercial law;
- corporate law;
- criminal law;

- economic law;
- employment law;
- environmental law;
- family law;
- intellectual property law;
- public international law;
- real estate law;
- rural law; and
- tax law.

However, these officially recognised specialisations do not always conform to the attorney's capabilities, or reflect the reality of legal practice. For example, some attorneys specialise in more than one field, while others may further specialise within one of these fields, eg corporate tax law.

• ASSOCIATE OFFICES IN BRUSSELS •

For many law firms, a presence in Brussels is seen as important to enable them to meet the needs of clients conducting international business in Europe, particularly for clients located in Asia and for clients seeking services in international law. A presence in Brussels also provides certain advantages to law firms dealing with European law or various lobbying activities at the European Commission or Council. It may facilitate the ability to litigate in European courts.

• CLIENT CONFLICTS •

The French Code of Conduct calls for attorneys to adhere to principles of honesty, dignity and independence. An attorney cannot simultaneously represent two parties who have conflicting interests. 'Conflicting interests' has a broad significance. The attorney may not be counsel for more than one party in the same matter if a conflict of interests exists or could potentially exist between them. The attorney must also abstain from representing a client if confidential information given by an existing or former client is at risk of being disclosed. He should also not act if he has confidential information from one client, the use of which would give the other client an unfair advantage.

The relationship between the *avocat* and the client is confidential. If there has been interference with the attorney/client relationship the client may always dispense with the services of the attorney. The client may also file a complaint against the attorney if there is any breach of this confidentiality.

• Rights of Audience in Local Courts •

One important facet of the attorney's role is to present oral arguments and to perform functions in conducting litigation. In France, bars are organised by court district. One factor, therefore, which the client must consider is to which bar the attorney has been admitted. For certain courts, an attorney may only represent his client in procedural matters before those courts included in the bar to which he is admitted. However, for substantive matters, an attorney may plead before any French court without territorial limitation. Instances may thus arise where a second attorney must be taken on to the case to perform certain procedural acts before courts located outside the jurisdiction of the bar to which the principal attorney is admitted.

COMMERCIAL ARRANGEMENTS WHEN INSTRUCTING COUNSEL

• Fee Structure •

An attorney fixes fees according to agreement with the client, the guidelines in the Essential Principles of the Professional Responsibility Code and the principle of *délicatesse* (tact or consideration). In the absence of an agreement between the attorney and client, the fee is fixed according to customary practices established by jurisprudence. The setting of fees may depend upon several factors, including the nature of the legal problem and the particular attorney and client involved. Conditions affecting the setting of fees therefore include:

- the nature and importance of the interests involved;
- the difficulty of the litigation;
- the outcome of the litigation;
- the urgency of the case;
- the private or commercial nature of the litigation;
- the diligence and reputation of the attorney;
- the services rendered;
- the degree of specialisation required and the general expenses of the law firm;
- the amount of time devoted to the client's affairs;
- the financial status of the client; and
- the permanent or temporary status of the client.

All of the above factors must be considered when setting a fair and reasonable fee.

These criteria explain the variation in billing rates and why, for example, fees for securities law issues may be higher than fees in other matters. Furthermore, firms of different sizes will have fees reflecting structural expenses such as attorney teams, computer teams, secretarial staff, night secretaries and other resources provided. Matters which involve extensive technical research will also be reflected in the attorney's fees.

An attorney may develop a reputation through exposure in the media or through the limited personal advertisement allowed. Although a recognised factor, it is often difficult to put a price on an attorney's reputation. The diligence of the attorney is measured in relation to the scale of the procedures and the complexity of the case, so that the attorney's fees may be increased if more time is spent preparing the case.

It should be noted that the *Ordres des Avocats* in Paris set up the Institute on Fees (*Institut de l'Honoraire*) whose role is to collect information on the actual practices involved in fee setting. The Institute also recommends methods for calculating fees, the current trend being towards greater transparency in the interests of the client.

• RETAINER •

Upon accepting a case, the attorney customarily requests a retainer from the client, which must be agreed to in writing. The retainer is most commonly requested in the area of company law but also in other sectors such as divorce and trusts and estates. The retainer is negotiated between the attorney and the client based on an estimate of how much the litigation will cost.

• METHOD AND TIMING OF BILLING •

To avoid disputes regarding fees, the establishment of attorney fees by prior agreement is highly recommended. The agreement must provide for an allocation of fees that is fair and reasonable. In France, several methods are used for setting an attorney's fees. Fees may be calculated at an hourly rate according to the services rendered by a partner or associate assigned to the case. Contingency fees (*quota litis*), which set the attorney's remuneration according to the outcome of the litigation, are prohibited. Nevertheless, in 1991 a limited form of contingency payment was authorised where a fee agreed upon between the attorney and client may be based on the outcome of the litigation although it is only a complementary fee added to the fee charged for services rendered.

A flat rate, which corresponds to the total sum that the client must spend, may also be charged. Once a flat fee is stipulated, the attorney may not solicit or obtain any additional fee. However, depending on the particular case, a complementary fee (*honoraire de résultats*) may be charged in certain cases.

• FEE DISPUTES •

If a client feels that the attorney's fees are excessive, disciplinary action may be instituted against the attorney by the intervention of the *Conseil de l'Ordre*. Generally, contesting attorneys' fees first requires a decision by the President of the Bar with the right to appeal to the presiding judge of the *Cour d'Appel*.

TREATMENT OF FOREIGN NATIONALS UNDER LOCAL LAW

This section is intended to provide an overview of some of the legal aspects that might affect a foreign investor who anticipates investing in France. This brief summary in no way gives a full picture of the issues and legal provisions to be taken into account by a foreign investor. How such a foreign national is affected by laws governing business transactions varies with the circumstances. For example, most investors who establish a presence in France are considered to be resident for foreign direct investment and tax purposes.

• RESTRICTIONS, REPORTS AND GOVERNMENT APPROVALS • OF FOREIGN INVESTMENT: EXCHANGE CONTROLS

Generally, the French government favours foreign direct investments and even facilitates these investments in certain circumstances. Recently exchange controls have been eased to this end. However, some government intervention in foreign direct investment and exchange control remains. Potential foreign investors should be aware of these measures since they often require disclosures or cause delays. French regulations governing direct investments and exchange controls apply to France and all of its Overseas Departments and Territories as well as certain countries whose central banks have a privileged relationship with the French Treasury Department including Congo, Gabon and the Ivory Coast.

Under these regulations there are two categories of foreign investors, residents and non-residents. A resident is an individual, legal entity or branch of a legal entity whose interests are principally centred in France. Legal entities do not have to be incorporated in France to be considered residents. Any legal entities established in France are considered residents for exchange control purposes. Individuals who are foreign nationals are considered residents upon proof of residence in France.

Non-residents are all French and foreign nationals whose interests are principally centred abroad, including foreign civil servants stationed in

France. For exchange control purposes, all establishments of French and foreign legal entities created abroad are deemed to be non-residents. Special procedures exist for non-residents who are EU nationals.

A number of organisations are involved in the regulation of direct investment and exchange controls. The Treasury Department (*Direction du Trésor*), a subdivision of the Ministry of Economy, is in charge of all international financial relations and prepares publications on the application of exchange control regulations. It is also responsible for reviewing the declarations of direct investments made by foreign investors.

The General Customs Department (*Direction Générale des Douanes et Droits Indirects*) enforces the exchange control regulations. For these purposes, it has the authority to monitor international transfers of funds and transfers of funds relating to import-export transactions. Customs also monitors international transfers of financial instruments and supervises payment methods used by importers to France.

The Bank of France (*Banque de France*) is the Central Bank. It oversees technical procedures for exchange control regulations and also manages the exchange control stabilisation fund (*le fonds de stabilisations des changes*) through which all purchases and sales of foreign currency are made on the foreign exchange market on behalf of the Treasury Department.

The Central Fund for Economic Co-operation handles exchange control matters relating to the overseas departments and territories.

Direct investment
Under French law, a direct investment consists of the purchase, creation or extension of a company, partnership, a going concern, branch or sole proprietorship. A direct investment may also include any operations or series of operations which allow the investor to take or to increase control of any legal entity which engages in an industrial, agricultural, commercial, financial or real estate activity. A foreign direct investment transaction is a transaction made by:

- a non-resident;
- a company which is directly or indirectly under foreign control;
- a French establishment of a foreign company; or
- a transfer of an interest in a resident company from one non-resident to another.

This means that if a French company which is owned by a foreign legal entity invests in another French company, this transaction is considered a foreign direct investment.

All investments made by a non-resident, other than a national of the EU, require prior authorisation from the Treasury Department. Non-resident investments subject to prior authorisation include the control of a resident company, an interest in a resident company under the control of non-residents, and an interest in an unlisted resident company which when combined with interests already acquired by other non-residents, constitutes foreign control of that company. Foreign control of a company which is listed on the stock exchange exists where more than 20 per cent of capital or voting rights is held directly or through foreign companies controlled by residents. For companies not listed on the stock exchange, the foreign control exists when more than 33.33 per cent is held directly or through a foreign company controlled by residents.

However, some investments by non-residents do not require prior authorisation. Among these investments exempted from prior authorisation are:

(a) the creation of a branch office or newly-formed enterprise;
(b) increases in the holding of a French company under foreign control where that investor already holds 66.66 per cent of the capital or voting rights in the company;
(c) a subscription for an increase in shares of a French company under the control of a foreign investor, when that investor does not increase its percentage of participation in the company's capital;
(d) merger transactions or other sales of assets, when made between French companies under foreign control where the companies belong to the same group.

These exceptions and other exemptions from prior authorisation still require that the transaction be reported to the Treasury Department within 20 days of being made.

Direct investment by nationals of the European Union not residing in France are subject to slightly different regulations. An EU national does not need to have authorisation, it must simply make a declaration, and it benefits from all the exceptions extended to those foreign investors who need an authorisation. In order to facilitate investment transactions, by eliminating the requirement of receiving prior authorisation other than those mentioned above, an EU investor may be granted permanent recognition by the Ministry of the Economy. The Ministry may grant permanent recognition if the investor qualifies as an EU investor, if the investor had a turnover during the previous fiscal year exceeding FF 1 billion and if the investor has carried on a true economic activity for at least three consecutive fiscal years.

The Ministry of the Economy recognises an investor as an EU national if that investor is either an individual who resides in one of the member states of the European Union, or a legal entity which is directly or indirectly controlled by an EU resident, regional or local authorities located in one of the member states or an EU member state. Generally, a legal entity is considered an EU investor if the EU shareholders or partners hold over 50 per cent of share capital and a majority of the voting rights.

However, a legal entity will not be considered an EU national if non-EU shareholders:

(a) may appoint or dismiss the majority of the board of directors;
(b) may determine the outcome of shareholders' decisions as a result of the voting rights held;
(c) hold an unconditional option on part of the shares which allows for the acquisition of a majority holding; or
(d) hold a *de facto* dominant influence in the company.

Conversely, if an EU national meets the conditions above for a legal entity which is majority-owned by a non-EU national, then that legal entity may be considered to be an EU investor.

Although most transactions by an EU investor do not require prior approval, such approval may be required in certain limited circumstances. EU investors must still obtain prior authorisation for investments which relate to the exercise of a government activity, public health or safety and the defence industry. Also, investments designed to avoid the application of French law must receive prior authorisation.

Once the Ministry of the Economy grants recognition, it can only be withdrawn if the investor's control is significantly modified such that it may no longer qualify as an EU investor. Because of this possibility, the EU investor must inform the Ministry of the Economy within 30 days of any changes in shareholding or effective control which could disqualify its recognition status. EU investors are still required to file subsequent declarations within 20 days of each investment.

Sanctions

Non-compliance with the regulations governing direct investment or exchange controls may result in penalties being imposed. Those liable to such penalties include investors who do not make a required declaration or those who do not obtain required prior approval before proceeding with a restricted transaction. Sanctions include imprisonment for from one to five years, confiscation of the particular transporting vehicle used to violate the law, confiscation of the amount of money used and a fine of up to double that amount. Furthermore, the underlying contracts relating to the contravening transactions may be declared null and void.

• TAX TREATMENT •

The tax treatment of foreign individuals and legal entities may be subject to bilateral tax treaties as well as EU Directives. France has entered into treaties with approximately 80 countries to limit double taxation. A foreign national will have to pay French taxes if that national either carries on an activity in

France or invests or operates a business through a subsidiary in France. The French taxes on foreign nationals with a presence in France may be divided into two categories:

- direct taxes imposed on income; and
- taxes, such as Value Added Tax (VAT) imposed on specific transactions.

The tax treatment of foreign individuals depends on the category into which the individual falls, pursuant to French and EU tax law. Foreign individuals domiciled in France are subject to taxation on their total revenue whether it has its source in France or abroad. Foreign individuals domiciled outside France are subject to taxation if they have French source income. Foreign individuals domiciled outside France who maintain one or more residences in France are subject to French taxation on either their French source revenue or their property holding. If an individual has little or no revenue the revenue is taxed on a flat sum equal to three times the value of the property. The above does not apply if the revenue from France is greater than three times the value of the property.

French-sourced income is divided into two types, revenues from assets, rights or activities in France and revenues received from a debtor situated in France. Revenue from assets include:

- revenues from real property located in France;
- French securities;
- operations in France;
- professional activities whether salaried or not, exercised in France;
- capital gains and profits from operations related to a business operating in France as well as buildings located in France;
- capital gains on transfers of holdings of less than 25 per cent of a company with a registered office in France.

It should be noted that taxpayers domiciled outside France are not taxed on capital gains from the transfer of unlisted securities representing a holding of less than 25 per cent, on the transfer of shares of a partnership, or on the transfer of movable property.

Foreign taxpayers are subject to a progressive tax rate as well as family status and dependency exemptions. The minimum tax rate is 25 per cent, although, this is not applicable if the taxpayer can show that the minimum rate that will result from the imposition in France of tax on the total of his revenue of worldwide income will be less than the minimum rate. Nevertheless, if the taxpayer is domiciled in a country which has a double tax treaty with France, the minimum tax rate of 25 per cent applies to revenues effectively connected with France.

Under certain circumstances, there is a withholding tax which the debtor pays directly to the French Treasury. This applies to certain non-salaried revenues and royalties. The debtor's activities must be in France and paid to a foreign individual with no permanent establishment in France.

In summary, income from real property, investments in securities and salaries is subject to French tax. Royalty payments for intellectual property rights made by a French resident to a foreign national are also subject to a withholding tax. Pension payments made in France are taxable, regardless of the country in which the services giving rise to the payment were rendered. Foreign nationals are taxed at the same rate as French nationals.

Corporate income tax
French corporate income tax is a standard rate of 33.33 per cent and is imposed on the net taxable income from those operations conducted in France by all corporations and other limited liability companies doing business in France. A foreign corporation with operations in France, ie a permanent establishment, is subject to French corporate income tax on all income received from operations carried out in France and assets related to such a permanent establishment and to a qualified agent, real property in France and passive foreign sources such as royalties, dividends and interest. Income earned from real property in France is also subject to French corporate income tax. In the absence of any taxable income, all corporate taxpayers are subject to a minimum annual corporate income tax.

Transfer-pricing
French tax authorities have the power to verify that transactions between French companies and foreign companies are at arm's length. Use of transfer-pricing schemes solely for tax avoidance purposes may be deemed to be constructive income. The French tax administration may review direct or indirect transfers of income between a French company and a foreign enterprise if there is an element of control between the entities. The transaction is judged in the light of similar transactions conducted at arm's length. In addition, income improperly transferred to a foreign entity may be treated as an undisclosed distribution of profits if the foreign enterprise is a shareholder of the foreign operations company and subject to a French withholding tax.

Value Added Tax
Value Added Tax (VAT) is a non-cumulative tax imposed on each of the taxable transactions necessary for the production, distribution or delivery of goods and services and importation into France. Each taxpayer must invoice his customers and pay VAT to the tax authorities on the value of the taxable goods and services. Each taxpayer pays VAT only on the value that is added to the goods subsequently sold or services rendered.

• ACCESS TO AND TREATMENT BY LOCAL COURTS •

French law essentially provides full access to French courts for anyone who wishes to bring a claim. Although previously distinctions were made between the treatment of French and foreign nationals in French courts, these distinctions have been eliminated. For example, previously non-French nationals were required to lodge security before bringing a claim (*judicatum solis*) where French claimants had no such requirement. Under current French law, this requirement has been abolished.

French statutes of limitations limit the time in which a claimant may file suit. These statutes fix periods which vary from three months (for libel or slander cases) to 30 years (for other civil claims). The limitation period starts to run from the first day on which legal action could begin for the claim in question. Parties may by agreement shorten the applicable time period, but they may not extend the time period nor may they renounce their rights arising from a statute of limitations before those rights mature.

Once a claim has been filed in a French court, the judge may not rule on a case without giving the parties an opportunity to be heard. The parties must promptly give their evidence and factual and legal claims to each other. The judge cannot base a decision on any evidence which has not been subject to formal open debate. Once a judgment is given, the parties have a right to appeal.

• FOREIGN PARENT LIABILITY •

As a result of the various limited liability structures existing in French company law, the circumstances in which the parent company of a French-based company would be liable for any claim brought against its French subsidiary is limited. However, a plaintiff may 'lift the corporate veil' of a parent company for claims brought against a subsidiary. Generally, the parent company can be held liable if it has not complied with the corporate formalities, with the result that its subsidiary has not acquired a separate corporate identity. The potential for liability may also depend on the nature of the legal problem. A creditor of a French subsidiary may obtain compensation from the parent corporation in a bankruptcy proceeding more easily than, for example, in the case of mismanagement or interference with the subsidiary's business or fraudulent bankruptcy.

• JURISDICTION OF LOCAL COURTS •

The French courts generally have jurisdiction over a claim to which a French national is a party. However, there are certain rules limiting the competence of the court at the domestic level. For example, the *Tribunal de Commerce* hears cases dealing with commercial matters. Certain procedural rules must also be followed. The chosen forum (the specific court where a case is heard) is often the jurisdiction within which the defendant resides. Disputes concerning real property are among the few exceptions to this rule and, in these cases, the forum is the jurisdiction where the real property is located. Contractual matters may be brought either in the jurisdiction where the defendant resides or where the contract was or should have been performed.

• FOREIGN LANGUAGE DOCUMENTS AND DOCUMENTS • GOVERNED BY FOREIGN LAW

All documents for any French court proceeding must be in French. If any documents in a foreign language are required for evidence, they must be translated into French. If a submitted document is not in French, the judge has the authority to reject its admittance into evidence. In certain circumstances, parties may request that the documents be translated by a sworn translator who is appointed by the court from a list.

French courts may apply foreign law pursuant to the French rules of Conflict of Laws. Whether a foreign law is applied depends on a number of variables including the subject matter, the place where the events leading to the cause of action occurred, the parties involved, and the facts of the case. On a more general level, the courts may also take into account national and international interests.

If a judge applies foreign law, it does not have the same authority as French law. In the lower courts, foreign law is treated as a fact rather than as a rule of law. Therefore, it is the parties' responsibility to present the law into evidence, with proof of its validity as a rule of law. It is not presumed, as is the case with French rules of law, that the judge knows the foreign rules of law. However, once the lower court judge reviews the evidence on the foreign law, he reserves the right to review the law and interpret it accordingly. Since foreign law is treated as a question of fact, if a case involving foreign law is appealed, the court of appeal may not review the lower court's interpretation.

• RECOGNITION AND ENFORCEMENT OF FOREIGN • JUDGMENTS

Generally, a party seeking enforcement of a foreign judgment in France must petition the appropriate *Tribunal de Grande Instance* for recognition and enforcement (*exequatur*). The party seeking enforcement must file a petition accompanied by an original or a court-certified copy of the foreign judgment.

The French court verifies that the court which rendered the decision had jurisdiction and that the judgment did not violate fundamental principles of law, including the rights of defence. However, the French court may not review the merits of the substantive issues of the case. Once recognition is granted, the foreign judgment has the same legal force as a French judgment. In certain limited cases, formal recognition by the courts may not be required. A foreign decision may be considered a fact and is clothed with a certain authority, regardless of any prior approval of a French court.

In addition to the French rules governing the enforcement of foreign judgments, France is a party to bilateral and multilateral agreements that have been established to facilitate the application of judgments from the other signatories' jurisdictions. France is a party to two multilateral treaties among the European countries concerning the enforcement of foreign jurisdiction, the Brussels Convention and the Lugano Convention (see Appendix).

In addition, France has entered into signed several bilateral treaties:

(1) In Western Europe, with Austria, Monaco, Spain, Switzerland and the UK. (France has also signed bilateral treaties with Belgium and Italy, but these treaties have been pre-empted by the Brussels Convention on the applicable subject matter.)
(2) With former socialist countries Poland, Romania and Yugoslavia.
(3) With many countries which were formerly French territories including Congo, Gabon, Morocco, and Vietnam.

France has not entered into any agreement for the enforcement of judicial decisions with any North or South American countries.

•

Dominique Borde
Moquet Borde & Associés
Société d'Avocats
30 avenue de Messine
75008 Paris
France

•

4

GERMANY

•

CONTENTS

•

4

GERMANY

•

STRUCTURE OF THE LEGAL PROFESSION

In order to be admitted to the German Bar, the prospective lawyer has to undergo an average of eight years of legal education, with extensive training in all major fields of the law. The first part of this education is received at a university and the second part, referred to as the *Referendar* period, is acquired through practical training in courts, law firms and various bodies of public administration. Thus, the German lawyer traditionally tends to view himself as being an all-round lawyer, litigating and counselling on every aspect of the law rather than inclining himself to a heavily-specialised practice.

The structure of the German legal profession has been characterised by lawyers practising as sole practitioners or, if at all, in very small partnerships. Moreover, the rules and regulations on legal practice tended to be tight, limiting the practice of each lawyer to small judicial districts and prohibiting the formation of partnerships with lawyers admitted in other districts within Germany. In interaction with the heavily-decentralised structure of political and business activities in Germany, these rules formed a rather infertile ground for the emergence of large law firms. Only a few firms, by and large concentrated in the few German cities that can be regarded as business centres, grew to a considerable size.

Beginning in the late 1980s, the grip of professional rules eased and mergers between law firms located in different cities became possible. Many of the larger law firms specialising in business practice took the opportunity to gain additional expertise by combining their resources. Others decided to grow internally and started to open offices in cities other than their domiciles.

Shortly thereafter, the German legal profession was hit by German unification. This dramatically increased the demand for legal advice, thereby providing German law firms with unmatched opportunities for growth. As a consequence, most of the law firms specialising in business practice opened up offices in Berlin and/or other cities within the old East Germany.

Today, the market for legal advice in Germany is still growing and German law firms are expanding at a considerable pace. Nevertheless, only a few German law firms employ more than 100 lawyers. It has to be borne in mind, however, that many potential issues of concern to a lawyer practising in a common law system have been taken care of by statutory provisions of the German Civil Law system, thus reducing considerably the manpower needed, eg for drafting legal documents.

For the last couple of years, German lawyers have been permitted to bear the title of *Fachanwalt* (specialised attorney) for a limited range of fields, such as tax law (*Steuerrecht*), administrative law (*Verwaltungsrecht*), labour law (*Arbeitsrecht*) and social insurance and welfare law (*Sozialrecht*). The usefulness of these titles is rather controversial, and many lawyers with excellent expertise in these subjects have not cared to undergo the official filing process for obtaining such titles.

In some of the German Federal States, such as the State of Hessen (Frankfurt/Main), lawyers with long experience as practising attorneys may also serve as public notaries. As a notarisation or notarial certification is required for many transactions under German law, eg real estate, transfer of shares in limited liability companies, applications to the Commercial Register, this additional qualification facilitates the process of executing a transaction.

The needs of foreign clients seeking German legal counsel will be met by numerous German law firms providing full-scale service for complex commercial transactions. In addition, a couple of large foreign law firms – mainly from the UK and the US – have begun opening up offices in Germany during the last few years, adding competition to a growing market.

HOW TO FIND A SUITABLE LAWYER

• RECOMMENDATIONS •

One of the best approaches to finding a suitable lawyer in Germany will be to follow recommendations from persons having experience in dealing with German lawyers. Ideally, the person giving the recommendation should have been involved in the same kind of transaction as the person who is seeking the legal advice. If, however, a disparity exists between those two transactions, then it is still worthwhile to contact the lawyer recommended and to inquire whether he or his firm has the expertise to handle the matter. As a general rule, the size of a law firm can serve as an indicator of its competence in handling complex commercial transactions and of having expertise in all segments of business or law. Notwithstanding this general rule, there have also been mergers of law firms which are largely dedicated to local practice – usually having only a few lawyers in numerous locations. Significantly, there are also small firms ('boutiques') with excellent expertise in their field of specialisation.

• LOCAL LAW SOCIETY OR BAR ASSOCIATION •

Every lawyer admitted to practise in Germany has to join the local bar association (*Anwaltskammer*). Many will also be members of the local and national law society (*Deutscher Anwaltsverein*) and/or member of international associations like the German-American Lawyers' Association, German-British Jurists' Association, etc. Although these associations normally maintain a strict neutrality and will be reluctant to give a specific recommendation, they will be able to hand out the addresses of lawyers and law firms in a specific city. The same purpose may be served by contacting the local chamber of commerce (*Industrie-und Handelskammer*).

• LEGAL DIRECTORIES •

In the absence of, or in addition to, a personal recommendation, an international law directory may help in selecting a German lawyer. Most directories list the fields of specialisation, thus giving an idea of whether a specific law firm will be in a position to assist in a particular transaction. It has to be borne in mind, however, that the listings are often based on self-evaluations by the respective firms, leaving its reliability to the truthfulness of the listed firms. The listing of the educational background of the lawyers may be of special interest. A considerable number of lawyers in German business law firms have spent at least one year of their professional education at a foreign law school or with a foreign law firm, and some are admitted to practise law in more than one jurisdiction. This international element of their education will not only help to overcome language problems but also helps the lawyer to understand better the needs and demands of foreign clients.

• ADVERTISING •

As a general rule, German lawyers are prohibited from actively seeking clients. Although the very restrictive professional rules seemed to have been relaxed somewhat in recent years, it is still considered unethical for a German lawyer to place advertisements. German lawyers therefore attract clients mainly via recommendations of existing clients, by publishing articles in law reviews and by giving lectures at specific seminars.

FACTORS IN CHOOSING A SUITABLE LAWYER

• LANGUAGE ABILITY •

For a client not fluent in German, one of the most crucial qualifications a German lawyer must have is his ability to communicate in a language with which the client is familiar. Generally, this will be the English language. Most German lawyers specialising in business law will be able to communicate in English, although the quality of language skills will vary. As an untroubled and detailed communication between the lawyer and the client is fundamental when dealing with legal problems, one should not compromise on this issue.

As stated above, a considerable number of German lawyers have degrees from foreign universities or have spent some time with foreign law firms, mostly in the UK or US, so that communication in English will not be a problem. Ordinarily, one can expect that lawyers in large firms dedicated to business practice will be fluent in English.

The second language most often spoken by German lawyers is French. This number is more limited than that of those familiar with English, however. If one is not comfortable communicating in either English or French, the search for a suitable lawyer will be more difficult. Finding a Spanish or Italian-speaking lawyer, however, should not be too difficult as there are still a fair number of German lawyers who are familiar with these languages.

The international law directories will provide useful information when looking for a lawyer able to communicate in your language. As the listings are based on the self-evaluation of the respective lawyers, one will be on the safer side if the listed language skills are backed by the indication of time spent in a country matching the listed language skills.

• TYPE OF TRANSACTION •

After resolving the language question, the next problem is choosing a suitable lawyer to fit the particular transaction. If the transaction has German law elements but is governed by non-German law, a law firm outside Germany will typically be involved in the first stage. The German law firm will then be needed to spot and to handle the specific German law issues. For example, a merger, a joint venture or a distribution agreement might have effects on the German market (even if the companies do not have subsidiaries in Germany) such as to invoke the applicability of German cartel law with its strict provisions. Improper filing with the German Cartel Authorities can have the effect of voiding the transaction and can result in the imposition of considerable fines.

If the transaction involves the transfer of shares in a German GmbH (limited liability company) or of real estate, the transaction needs to be notarised in order to be valid. Only very few public notaries outside Germany are regarded as qualified to perform a proper notarisation under German law. Where a German notarisation or notarial certification is required (eg real estate transactions, transfer of shares in limited liability companies, applications to the Commercial Register), one might find it helpful to contact a German law firm having lawyers who are licensed public notaries as well. Due to the German Federal system such lawyers are only found in some of the German states. In transactions governed by non-German law, a foreign law firm will generally be able to recommend German law firms. It should also be noted that where a law firm is involved through its notaries, it must remain neutral thereafter and can no longer represent one of the parties in any litigation regarding such matter.

• SPECIALISATION IN TOPICS •

Typically, the domicile of an office may give some indication of specific fields of specialisation depending on the needs of the local clients. Therefore, some cities are regarded as strongholds for specific issues, for example:

- Düsseldorf (law of large stock corporations, cartel law);
- Frankfurt (banking law, international transactions, import/export);
- Munich (media law, intellectual property);
- Hamburg (law of international transportation); and
- Berlin (investment in the new German states).

• ASSOCIATE OFFICES IN BRUSSELS •

Because of the increasing relevance of EU law and its supra-national implications, many German law firms have opened offices in Brussels. This is designed to further the assistance offered to internationally-active clients.

• CLIENT CONFLICTS •

In cases of conflict, the German code of ethics provides that a lawyer may not represent a second party if he has already advised another party in the same matter with conflicting interests. This rule imposes only a limited restriction in that it refers only to the 'same legal matter'. Thus, there is the much wider question of economic conflicts of interest, where a law firm is advising two clients on different matters, but there are matters of highly confidential information due to competitive pressure between clients from the same industry. In such a case the attorney should, for reasons of fair conduct of matters, represent one party only. In the case of such sensitive matters, the client should also ask the attorney to act on a specific issue for him alone and mention this in initial contacts.

• RIGHTS OF AUDIENCE IN LOCAL COURTS •

Germany has a rather homogeneous legal system. The civil and criminal law is uniform in all German states and only in the field of administrative law do minor variations exist. The domicile of a law firm therefore does not affect its ability to counsel on transactions in any part of Germany. It is certainly more convenient and cost-efficient, however, to choose a law firm having an office in the proximity of the city in which the negotiations will take place.

As the rights of audience in local courts are still restricted to lawyers domiciled in the respective judicial district, the domicile becomes a more important issue for litigation work. As every state is divided into many judicial districts, it will quite often be difficult to find a law firm with international experience which is domiciled in the district of the locally competent court. However, one should not hesitate to contact a law firm matching one's needs even if this firm is not domiciled in the relevant district. Due to the tight restrictions on the rights of audience, German lawyers are used to co-operating with lawyers domiciled in other districts for litigation work. It is standard practice that a law firm not domiciled in the relevant district will nevertheless do the bulk of the work, including the communication with the client, research and drafting of court actions, whereas the assisting lawyer in the relevant district will restrict himself to the courtroom work. Frequently, a lawyer not domiciled in the respective district will appear before the court and argue the case; this is permissible when he is accompanied by an attorney domiciled in the district.

COMMERCIAL ARRANGEMENTS WHEN INSTRUCTING COUNSEL

• TIME CONSTRAINTS AND DEADLINES •

When instructing German counsel, or indeed in an ongoing lawyer/client relationship, time constraints generally fall within one of two categories, namely time constraints caused by third parties, such as the court during litigation, or business partners during commercial transactions. Alternatively, time constraints may be caused by the client himself, ie self-imposed deadlines or coercive business reasons.

Deadlines are of particular relevance in litigation because the failure to meet deadlines imposed by statute or by the competent court may lead to the party in default losing certain rights. The court might have to disregard certain information or material introduced in the case by the defaulting party, or might refuse to hear witnesses, and obviously this might lead to the defaulting party losing its case.

By contrast to the Anglo-American legal systems, there is no pre-trial discovery of any sort under the German system of civil procedure. Furthermore, civil proceedings are not concentrated in one long oral hearing on many consecutive days or even weeks so it is not necessary to have one's case prepared to the slightest detail. Instead, German litigation is in effect mainly conducted in writing. The plaintiff presents its case in a detailed statement of claim, to which the defendant replies in equal detail within a certain deadline set by the court (generally between two and four weeks). The exchange of the statement of claim and the defence between the two parties will be followed by a preliminary oral hearing which on average lasts less than 15 minutes. The function of this short preliminary hearing is to give the court an opportunity to tell the parties its first understanding of the case in question and to inform them if they ought to present further evidence or explore and explain certain facts in more detail.

Generally therefore, after such a preliminary hearing further written pleadings are exchanged between the parties. This again will be followed by another short oral hearing. This may lead to yet further written pleadings and eventually the examination of witnesses. The technique of cross-examination is not really provided for in German law and is therefore much less refined in Germany than in the Anglo-American legal systems.

As German civil proceedings are document-based and as the plaintiff has the opportunity to introduce additional facts and evidence at a later stage, it is possible to start legal proceedings relatively quickly. It must be borne in mind, however, that civil proceedings are regulated by strict formal rules and their time-frame follows from a mixture of deadlines set by statute and deadlines set by the court. The missing of any of these deadlines may have very deleterious consequences. However, upon a well-founded application to the court the court is generally prepared to postpone its own deadlines, eg as regards the time-frame within which the defendant has to respond to the initial claim or as regards the handing in of pleadings, or indeed the date of the oral hearing.

Reasons for the postponement of such deadlines would, for instance, be that the defendant is not reasonably able to produce a proper defence within that time because of communication difficulties in cases with an international element. It should be borne in mind, however, that the parties' ability to influence the timing of a court case is limited.

Any party to civil proceedings in Germany, and in particular a foreign party, should take the various deadlines in such proceedings very seriously and follow the general guidance of its counsel and particularly the request by its counsel for further information diligently and promptly. It should be taken into account that in proceedings involving an international element documents to be handed in as evidence may have to be translated (which takes additional time). Some major district commercial courts do, however, accept documents in the English language without a translation.

Obviously, German lawyers will make an effort to meet deadlines set, or time constraints imposed upon their clients by their clients' business partners during a commercial transaction. Clients should, however, inform their lawyers as soon as possible about such deadlines. It may, of course, be that due to the limited time available in a particular transaction the respective lawyer will only be able to give his advice subject to the proviso that perhaps some aspects of the transactions would normally require further legal research.

Time constraints caused by the client should be openly discussed with the German legal adviser. As lawyers provide a service to their clients they will try to meet the needs of their clients as far as possible.

Timing of a commercial transaction

The timing of a commercial transaction is often of great importance to the success of the transaction. Therefore, lawyers should be informed as soon as possible about the intended timing in order to avoid unnecessary time constraints or the wasting of time. For example, many merger and acquisition transactions have to be approved by the Federal Cartel Office and are subject to pre-merger notification requirements. Until and unless such approval is actually or constructively given, the respective transaction is void. There are certain time-frames within which the Federal Cartel Office must review an application for approval, and if the Office does not act within that time the approval is deemed to have been granted. However, the parties to a transaction might put themselves in jeopardy if, for example, they have agreed in a letter of intent to a short-term exclusivity clause, ie a duty of the prospective seller not to negotiate the sale of his business with a third party during a certain period of time.

However, there may be regulatory requirements in other legal systems which are not applicable in Germany, so that in other aspects a transaction might move quicker in Germany. Therefore, instructing lawyers at an early stage of a transaction actually serves cost-effectiveness.

Unreasonable deadlines should be avoided because they serve no useful purpose and do not enhance the lawyer/client relationship. Practical difficulties might arise where a major transaction has gone to sleep for some time and is resurrected after some weeks. In such a situation it is generally the intention of the parties to close almost immediately whereas it takes some time for the respective lawyers to again get on top of the transaction, and it may force them to rearrange their own working schedule and to postpone work to be done for other clients. If such additional pressure leads to excessive working hours (nights and weekends), this might be reflected in the billing of the transaction.

• FEE STRUCTURE •

Lawyers
By law, German attorneys are required to charge for their services pursuant to the provisions of the *Bundesrechtsanwaltsgebührenordnung* (BRAGO, the Federal Code on Attorneys' Fees). The BRAGO contains detailed regulations how different types of work are to be charged for. In particular, it contains a sliding scale of legal fee units, the amount of which is determined by the amount in dispute or the economic value of the matter at hand. The higher the amount in dispute the higher the basic fee unit.

Depending on the particular nature of the work performed, lawyers in some instances have a discretion to charge only a certain percentage of a fee unit. In most instances, however, they are required to charge a certain fee unit or indeed a multiple thereof. For instance, in a court case involving the examination of witnesses, three multiples of the relevant fee unit would be charged. For most international business transactions which require the negotiation of agreements, two multiples of the respective fee unit would be chargeable. For example, one fee unit in respect of the value of a transaction of DM 100,000 is DM 1,889. The corresponding amounts for DM 1,000,000 and DM 10,000,000 are DM 5,789 and DM 32,789 respectively.

In a contested case the losing party has to bear by law its own costs, the legal costs of the winning party, and the court costs. The court costs amount to approximately 50 per cent of the legal costs of one party.

Although the BRAGO is applied by the average lawyer on almost all of his work the picture is different for international legal work. The BRAGO allows lawyers to agree to a fee arrangement with their clients, and this has become customary in particular in international legal work. It is open to doubt, however, to what extent the professional legal rules for German lawyers allow them to enter into fee arrangements below the rates prescribed by the BRAGO. However, as in some legal matters, eg in particular banking work, capital markets and some merger and acquisition transactions, the application of the BRAGO would lead to very high fees, it would appear that a fee arrangement resulting in lower fees than those prescribed by the BRAGO should not be seen as conflicting with the professional rules, as the aim of the lawyer in those particular cases is not to attract business by under-cutting adequate fees but simply to reduce extreme fees to adequate fees.

When coming to a fee arrangement, an internationally working German lawyer will, apart from looking at the commercial value of the matter at hand (which he is obliged to do under his professional rules), take equally into account the time spent on the respective matter, which in many cases will be the basis for charging the client. He will look also at other factors, such as the type of work performed, the difficulty of the questions involved, the skill and special know-how required to perform the service properly, his firm's resources which are required, the fee customarily charged for similar services by firms similarly situated, and also special factors such as time limitations imposed by the client or other special circumstances of the individual case.

Out-of-pocket disbursements (such as telephone, fax, travel costs, etc) are usually itemised and charged in addition.

In accounting for time spent, generally only the time of fully-trained professionals should be considered. The work of legal assistants, such as trainees and other support staff, should be included in the lawyer's work.

Notaries

Notaries charge for their work according to the *Kostenordnung* (Federal Cost Code). The principles of the *Kostenordnung* are similar to that of the BRAGO. However, the fee units chargeable under the *Kostenordnung* are lower. For some notarial matters there are statutorily prescribed caps. Finally, the rate of increase in the fee units slows as the economic value in question rises (eg for a contract which needs to be notarised and is worth DM 100,000,000 the notarial fee is DM 103,020 and for a contract worth DM 200,000,000 the fee is DM 109,020, ie only an increase of approximately 6 per cent in fees for an increase of 100 per cent in value).

Transactions requiring notarisation include, in particular, the sale and transfer of shares in a limited liability company and the pledge of such shares, the entering into and amendment of articles of association of a limited liability company or a stock corporation, capital increases in such companies and the sale and transfer of land. Notaries' fees are prescribed by law, non-negotiable and quite independent of attorneys' fees.

• RETAINER •

If a client has a constant and continuing need for legal advice in certain areas, it may make sense to agree on a retainer with a German law firm. Under such an arrangement, the client would pay a fixed monthly sum which would cover all advice given. However, court cases are generally exempt from this arrangement and there is also in most cases an understanding between the client and the lawyer that if the client asks for help in an extraordinary transaction, that transaction would not be covered by the retainer arrangement. Obviously, the amount payable as a retainer would depend on the type and amount of work expected to be performed by the law firm and will be agreed upon after a thorough discussion of these matters. Additionally, the law firm will undoubtedly monitor the amount of work done in order to ensure that the retainer represents an adequate fee. If one of the parties reaches the conclusion that the retainer arrangement is substantially disadvantageous for one or other of them, it will probably be re-negotiated.

Whether or not a retainer arrangement is sensible depends on the needs of the particular client. The advantages are that there is no continuing fee discussion, the client can budget its legal costs and can be sure of obtaining legal advice at any time. The difficulty of a retainer arrangement is to ensure that it is always fair to both parties.

• METHOD AND TIMING OF BILLING •

The method and timing of billing does not follow a fixed pattern, although the following general remarks can be made: if a matter is billed according to the provisions set out in the BRAGO the client is likely to be billed at the end of the matter, ie the finalisation of the litigation or the closing of a commercial transaction. However, by law German lawyers are allowed to ask, and sometimes do ask, for payments on account. A bill drawn up according to the BRAGO will state the economic value of the matter, the sections of the BRAGO specifying the multiples of the fee unit to be charged for the particular matter and give a figure for costs and expenses. The work done is not itemised. This applies *mutatis mutandis* to a notary's bill too.

In cases where the German lawyer does not bill pursuant to the BRAGO, generally for international legal work, and if there is no retainer arrangement, the method of billing varies and in practice to a large extent depends on the type of work. If there is a continuing client/lawyer relationship and if bills are sent at certain periodical intervals, the bills will generally specify and itemise the work done. However, where a bill relates to one particular transaction only, it is quite usual for the bill to refer only to this particular transaction and not to itemise and break down the work performed in connection with that transaction. The names of the individual lawyers involved in a particular matter and the respective time spent by those lawyers is not disclosed in the bill.

There appears to be no general practice as regards the timing of billing for general and ongoing advisory work. Some clients prefer to be billed at certain regular periodic intervals, and their lawyers will certainly oblige.

• LEVEL OF EXPERIENCE NEEDED •

On average, German law firms are much smaller than UK or US firms. A firm with 100 lawyers would be regarded as very substantial in Germany. At present there are indeed very few firms of that size. Due to the German legal system, which is codified to a greater extent than the Anglo-American legal systems and where certain general principles in respect of the construction of the language of a document are applied by operation of law, eg in particular that agreements are to be interpreted *bona fide*, German legal documentation in general is much shorter than Anglo-American documentation. In litigation, there is no pre-trial discovery.

Additionally, there is the principle that the court knows the law so that in theory the lawyers should only present facts to the court. Legal business transactions and litigation, therefore, need much less legal manpower.

Moreover, professional training is very long and German lawyers in general specialise much less than their UK and US counterparts. It is, for instance, not uncommon that one lawyer handles one side of a merger and acquisition transaction by himself without any assistants. Teams of lawyers are only put together by the major German law firms for very large transactions or transactions requiring special know-how in different areas. However, it is not customary to specify in detail the level of experience needed by lawyers in the firm who will actually be involved in such a transaction, although of course, the respective firms will try to satisfy requests from their clients in that respect.

TREATMENT OF FOREIGN NATIONALS UNDER LOCAL LAW

Foreign investments have always been highly welcomed in Germany and, therefore, there are few discriminatory regulations regarding business with foreign nationals. Such restrictions are limited to reporting requirements, approvals for the exchange of goods in the fields of national security, foreign policy and currency protection.

The same non-discriminatory policy applies to the access of foreign nationals to German courts which generally honour foreign legal documents as long as they comply with the German Constitution and public order, and reciprocity is guaranteed.

• RESTRICTIONS, REPORTS AND GOVERNMENTAL APPROVALS • OF FOREIGN INVESTMENT

There are only a few restrictions on foreign investments in Germany. They are concerned with the protection of the German currency, reasons of national security and foreign policy.

As far as tangible goods are concerned, import and export to or from Germany as well as contracts between Germans and foreign nationals are generally not subject to any restrictions. However, some transactions regarding specific goods require governmental approval according to a regulation under the *Außenwirtschaftsgesetz* (AWG, the German Law on Foreign Trade).

Exports
Governmental approval is required for the export of tangible goods and know-how of military/strategic significance such as weapons, ammunition, war goods, nuclear energy goods, other goods and technologies of strategic significance, chemical plans and chemicals and plants for the production of biological substances. The same restriction applies to goods in the field of agriculture, nutrition, and hardware trade for the purpose of commodity coverage, quality insurance and according to regulations of the European Union. As a consequence of an agreement between the EU and the US the export of specific hardware products requires governmental approval in order to avoid US import restrictions.

Further restrictions on the export of goods and technology arise from the implementation of international non-proliferation arrangements (covering nuclear, biological and chemical weapons) such as the UN embargo against Iraq. The embargo on military/strategic goods also applies to all goods serving military purposes such as arms' production and maintenance of arms or nuclear plants in specific countries.

In addition to the requirement of a governmental approval, exports that are not in accordance with the German Foreign Trade Law may lead to severe fines or imprisonment. As a consequence of questionable or illegal exports to Libya and Iraq, governmental practice has become increasingly rigorous in recent years.

Imports
The importing of goods by German nationals from the US, Japan and the EU countries is generally not subject to any restriction as long as such goods originate or have mainly been produced in those countries. This applies specifically to the free exchange of goods within the EU. Restrictions can mainly be found with respect to the textile and clothing industry. Except for these goods, reporting obligations or the requirement of governmental approval exist only for few specific goods such as sheep, grape products, coal and fuel, etc.

Foreign nationals
According to German legislation on aliens, every foreign national has to apply for an alien's residence permit in order to enter and reside in the Federal Republic of Germany. Different regulations apply depending on the nationality of such alien.

EU countries
Foreign nationals from EU countries may enter Germany without a visa and will receive a residence permit upon application if employed and residing in Germany for more than three months. Foreign nationals from EU countries are not required to apply for a work permit.

Non-EU countries

Foreign nationals from countries outside the EU generally need a residence permit in order to enter the Federal Republic of Germany. Such a permit is issued by German embassies in the form of a visa. Regarding Austria, Finland, Sweden, Switzerland and the US, the residence permit may also be applied for after entry into Germany. Entry without a required visa may be a reason for refusal of a residence permit.

Foreign nationals from other than EU countries planning to work as employees for more than three months in Germany may only obtain a residence permit under specific circumstances. One of these circumstances is the issue or prospective issue of a work permit. Regarding foreign nationals from Austria, Finland, Sweden, Switzerland and the US, obtaining a residence permit should generally be no problem.

For foreign nationals from other than EU countries who continue to have their usual place of abode in a foreign country and want to work in Germany, work permits are normally only granted if the duration of the employment does not exceed three months. If their usual place of abode, however, is transferred to Germany, work permits are also granted for longer terms. In deciding whether to grant a work permit the labour office will take into consideration whether any unemployed person registered with the labour office would be available for the job position the foreign national is meant to assume in Germany. It is therefore advisable to provide a job description tailored to the specific knowledge and abilities of the foreign national.

• EXCHANGE CONTROLS AND OTHER REGULATORY ISSUES •

As far as the German currency is concerned, transactions between residents of Germany may generally only be effected in Deutsche Mark, but no such restrictions exist for transactions between residents and non-residents.

German banks and German nationals are required to report on investments, receivables and payments, such as:

- reports of residents on the purchase and sale of participations in foreign companies and branches, including an annual status report;
- reports of non-residents on the purchase and sale of participations in domestic companies and branches, including an annual status report;
- monthly reports by residents on claims against and liabilities to non-residents;
- individual, monthly or semi-annual reports on payments by residents to non-residents and vice versa.

Generally, reports on investments in excess of DM 50,000 are required. These reports to the state branch of the German Federal Bank are for statistical purposes only.

However, the most important restriction is contained in the Bretton Woods Agreement of 1944 to which Germany has been a party since August 1952. According to Art XIII, s 2(b), p 1, exchange contracts which involve the currency of any member and which are contrary to the exchange control regulations of that member maintained or imposed consistently with the Agreement are unenforceable in the territories of any member. As a consequence of the Agreement not only the German exchange control regulations but also those of foreign nationals entering into exchange contracts are applicable. Foreign investors should, therefore, be aware of the exchange control regulations of their own country and of any country the currency of which may be influenced by the exchange contract. If such exchange contract is not in accordance with the Bretton Woods Agreement the obligations of the respective parties are not enforceable and therefore in practice invalid.

• Tax Treatment •

Individuals having their residence or permanent abode in Germany are subject to taxation in Germany on their worldwide income, unless otherwise provided by a double tax treaty which might mainly concern foreign source income. Corporations are taxed in Germany on their worldwide income if they have their statutory seat or place of management in Germany. Again, foreign income may be tax exempt in Germany if so provided in a double tax treaty.

Non-residents are subject to taxation on German source income only if certain criteria are met.

(1) Income from a trade is taxed in Germany only if there is a permanent establishment or permanent representative in Germany. Tax rates for non-resident individuals vary between 25 per cent and 53 per cent. Foreign corporations are subject to corporation tax of 42 per cent.

(2) Income from self-employment is subject to taxation in Germany if there is a fixed place of business in Germany. Such income is subject to the same tax rates as those described above. It is generally not subject to withholding taxes. Income from a position on a supervisory board, artistic, sporting and some other activities in Germany are subject to 30 per cent withholding tax in the case of a seat on a supervisory board and to 25 per cent in other cases. These withholding taxes may be reduced under applicable double tax treaties.

(3) Income from employment in Germany is subject to wage withholding if the employer has a permanent establishment in Germany. Even without such permanent establishment of the employer it is subject to income tax if the services are performed or used in Germany. Most

double tax treaties provide for an exemption from taxation in Germany if:

- the employee does not spend more than 183 days in Germany;
- his salary is paid by or on behalf of an employer not residing in Germany; and
- such income is not charged to the permanent establishment of such employer in Germany.

The tax rates are the same as provided under (1) above.

(4) Income from capital investments (dividends, interest, etc) are subject to 25 per cent withholding tax on dividends and generally no withholding tax on interest paid to foreigners. The withholding tax on dividends may be reduced to as little as 5 per cent within the EU, depending on applicable double tax treaties.

(5) Income from letting and leasing is subject to income tax if the real estate or the asset leased is located or registered in Germany. In the case of income from leasing movable assets or intangibles the income is subject to 25 per cent withholding tax. Again, this is often reduced under applicable double tax treaties.

• ACCESS TO AND TREATMENT BY LOCAL COURTS •

Individuals as well as juridical persons have access to German courts if these courts have jurisdiction over their actions irrespective of the claimant's nationality.

In litigation before the *Amtsgericht* (lower district court) each party may conduct its own case personally. Regarding claims where an amount of more than DM 10,000 is involved, or the defence against such claims, the *Landgericht* (higher district court) is competent and the parties may only conduct their case by means of an attorney admitted to the district's Bar.

Tax advisers and auditors may represent a party in any tax procedure including the tax court. The same applies to union representatives and the representatives of employers' associations with respect to labour cases.

• FOREIGN PARENT LIABILITY •

Operations which are only branch offices of a foreign parent are part of the parent corporation. Thus, actions of the local branch are actions of the foreign parent, who have full liability for those actions.

If there is a subsidiary which is a legal entity independent of the foreign parent with only limited liability, the parent's liability may, however, result from specific regulations of German law. For example, a foreign parent may be treated as quasi-producer for the purposes of the German *Produkthaftungsgesetz* (Law on Product Liability). A quasi-producer is any person pretending to be a producer by attaching its name, its trade mark or any other distinguishing mark to the product.

According to German jurisprudence, the main kind of quasi-producers are persons or business entities marketing products as a producer or under their own name or trade mark without indication of the real producer, although such products have actually been produced by other persons or business entities (eg a sports car producer marketing sunglasses or watches; mail order houses marketing products of other persons or business entities under the house's name). Distinguishing marks attached to a product or its package by a quasi-producer are names, firms, registered or non-registered trade marks as well as characteristic features such as colours, etc regardless of who attached the distinguishing mark.

One of the most important quasi-producers is the grantor of a licence under which a licensee produces and trades goods to which the trade mark or any other mark of the grantor of the licence is attached, thus giving the impression that the grantor of the licence is also the producer. In this case, the licensee and the grantor of the licence may both be liable. A parent corporation treated as a quasi-producer is liable for damages caused by defective products or insufficient or misleading product information.

The German *Aktiengesetz* (Corporation Law) is based on the principle of the legal independence of juridical persons and, therefore, generally does not hold liable a shareholder or person otherwise controlling a corporation for such corporation's obligations. In general, creditors of a corporation may only seek payment from the corporation's capital and may not demand payment from the shareholder. The same principle applies to companies with limited liability under the German *GmbH-Gesetz* (Limited Liability Company Law). However, there are exceptions to this rule, one of the most important being abuse or misuse of a subsidiary's legal independence. In this case the separation between the legal entity and its shareholders is set aside and the subsidiary and its shareholders are regarded as one entity, thus causing the shareholders to be liable for the subsidiary's obligations. However, the legal existence and independence of a company or corporation may only be ignored if otherwise results contravening the principles of good faith will occur.

There is no general rule as to when the legal existence of a subsidiary may be ignored. However, the shareholder's liability has been established in German jurisprudence where:

- a single shareholder confuses its own private assets with a company's or corporation's assets;

- a single shareholder uses the subsidiary as a means to receive or keep personal advantages;
- a single shareholder voluntarily creates the impression of personal liability; or
- a company or corporation is incorporated by trustees in order to create a false impression of financial circumstances (dummy company/corporation).

A second important exception to the above-mentioned principle is provided by German law in cases of agreements between enterprises entitling or enabling the parent to dominate a subsidiary or to take over the subsidiary's profits. In cases of such a control agreement or agreement to transfer profits, the parent is obliged to compensate the subsidiary for losses caused by the agreement or by specific actions under the agreement. Generally, this obligation exists only *vis-à-vis* the subsidiary and does not give any rights to the subsidiary's creditors. However, upon termination of the agreement between parent and subsidiary, the subsidiary's creditors are entitled to demand security from the parent in order to ensure the satisfaction of the subsidiary's claim for compensation.

In several recent judgments the *Bundesgerichtshof* (German Federal Court) has held a German parent company liable for the debts of its Germany subsidiary in circumstances in which the parent had conducted the business affairs of its subsidiary in a continuous and comprehensive manner. As a consequence, the creditors of a subsidiary that had filed for bankruptcy were able to bring claims directly against the parent. The *Bundesgerichtshof* appears to favour a broad interpretation of comprehensive conduct.

The court has indicated that it considers that comprehensive conduct exists if a parent company has centralised the decision-making power regarding its subsidiary's financial matters on a group management level. The same result may arise if there has been centralisation of the operative functions of a subsidiary that are crucial for its existence (ie product distribution or research and development). The exercise of influence over the subsidiary's management via interlocking directorates could also be considered as an indication of the existence of comprehensive conduct, at least if a majority of the managing directors of the subsidiary are also executives or directors of the parent.

A parent company's possible defence against the imposition of liability for the debts of its subsidiary appear to be limited under existing law. The *Bundesgerichtshof* has recognised the possibility of a defence based upon the argument that the losses suffered by a subsidiary are a result of circumstances having nothing to do with the influence exercised by the parent. The plaintiff has to prove the parent's exercised influence, the damage and the fact that such damage was due to the influence. To the extent that the plaintiff is not in a position to prove all this it can request some assistance from the corporation, if the corporation can provide the information and the request is reasonable.

• JURISDICTION OF LOCAL COURTS •

In the absence of specific bilateral or international regulations German courts have jurisdiction over foreign persons only in a number of restricted circumstances.

Generally, the court of a district in which a debtor is domiciled has jurisdiction for any action brought against the debtor. There are, however, some important exceptions to this rule. If the debtor is not domiciled in Germany the competent court is located in the district where such debtor holds assets. As far as claims regarding real property are concerned, jurisdiction is where such property is situated. For any action resulting from a property management or trusteeship the court of the district where the management or trusteeship is performed is competent for such action. In cases of tort, German courts are competent if the unlawful action was committed in Germany. In some specific cases of environmental liability, German courts are competent if the environmental damage as well as the defective plant are in Germany.

The most important exception to the general rule that German courts have jurisdiction over residents only, applies to the place of performance. Actions based on a contract can be brought before German courts if the obligation in issue has to be performed in Germany. The importance of this exception results from the parties' ability to agree on the place of performance in the contract, provided that both parties are acting in the course of a business or juridical persons. Such agreement on the place of performance may also be contained in standard terms and conditions of trade or business if the respective provision regarding the place of jurisdiction is clearly pointed out to or separately signed by the parties.

The parties may, in addition, agree upon the place of jurisdiction itself, provided that both parties are acting in the course of a business or juridical persons. Such agreement on the place of jurisdiction has to be made in writing, or at least to be confirmed in writing. The restrictions for agreements on the place of performance apply as well to agreements on the place of jurisdiction contained in standard terms and conditions of trade or business. The agreement must refer to a specific legal relationship. If at least one of the parties of the contract is not domiciled in Germany no further restrictions apply to the agreement on the jurisdiction. If both parties are domiciled in Germany the parties may only agree on the place of jurisdiction:

- after a claim has arisen, or
- in a case where the defendant's domicile is unknown at the time of the filing of an action, or

• if the defendant's domicile is moved out of Germany.

However, even if German courts are not competent they may have jurisdiction if the defendant disputes the substance of the claim without challenging the court's competence.

• FOREIGN LANGUAGE DOCUMENTS AND DOCUMENTS • GOVERNED BY FOREIGN LAW

Such documents can only be used to prove a claim before a German court and cannot be directly enforced. However, court judgments or orders, court and so-called attorneys' settlements and documents notarised by a German notary public are generally enforceable. In all other cases the party demanding performance of an obligation resulting from such a document has to file an action and to obtain a court decision in order to enforce the respective claim. The court will then apply foreign law if the particular obligation is governed by foreign law but a German court has jurisdiction. However, the document containing the obligation has to be translated into German.

• RECOGNITION AND ENFORCEMENT OF FOREIGN • JUDGMENTS

Foreign court decisions may be recognised and enforceable under German or EU law. Recognition and enforceability of judgments rendered in one of the EU member states is governed by the Hague Convention of 1968. Under the Hague Convention court decisions rendered in one of the EU member states are generally recognised in Germany. The claimant has to file for a court decision declaring the judgment enforceable, with the President of the *Landgericht* (higher district court) where the defendant is domiciled. If the defendant is not a German resident the *Landgericht* of the district where the enforcement will take place is competent to decide on the enforceability.

The same regulations apply to official documents and court settlements which are enforceable in their state of origin. Judgments, official documents or court settlements are not enforceable:

• if they do not comply with the German public order;
• if the defendant was not correctly summoned by the foreign court;
• if the above-mentioned decision does not comply with a second decision given in Germany with respect to the same parties and the same matter;
• in cases of specific violations of German international private law; and

- if the decision is contrary to a previous decision given after litigation between the same parties in a non-EU member state, as far as the previous decision is recognised and enforceable in Germany.

Judgments given in states which are not party to the Hague Convention, such as the US and Japan, may be enforceable according to the German Procedure Law. Enforceability requires a foreign court decision – official documents, authorised documents or court settlements are not sufficient – and an application filed with the competent court. The foreign court decision is not recognisable and/or enforceable if:

- the foreign court has no jurisdiction according to German law;
- the documents with which the claimant has filed an action have not been properly served on the defendant;
- the decision does not comply with a German or a recognisable foreign court decision given previously or the procedure leading to the decision is contrary to previous litigation in Germany;
- the recognition of the decision would lead to a result contrary to the basic principles of German law especially the German constitution; or
- no reciprocity is guaranteed.

As concerns non-recognition of a decision because of a violation of basic principles of German law, a ruling of the *Bundesgerichtshof* regarding recognition of a US court decision on past medical damages, future medical expenses, cost of placement, anxiety, pain, suffering and general damages of that nature, and exemplary and punitive damages ('John Doe') has to be mentioned because of its significance as to what does or does not comply with the basic principles of German law. According to the *Bundesgerichtshof* neither a pre-trial discovery nor the American rules of costs prevent a US court decision from being recognised in Germany. The same applied to the US court decision as far as it entitled the claimant to demand past and future medical damages, the cost of placement and damages for anxiety, pain and suffering. As far as exemplary and punitive damages are concerned, the *Bundesgerichtshof* held that the US court decision did not comply with the basic principles of German law and, therefore, could not be recognised in Germany.

Although punitive damages are regarded as a specific kind of compensation between private persons, such compensation complies with German law only as far as the claimant has actually incurred a damage or loss. However, punitive damages are granted under US law also for the purpose of punishing the defendant. German law does not know of such punishment between private persons but reserves the right to punish the defendant to state officials or authorities as a state monopoly. To the extent that the US court decision did not distinguish between compensation and punishment with respect to the punitive damages, such a decision was not recognisable or enforceable in Germany. However, enforceability of punitive damages would not prevent the court decision from being recognisable and enforceable with respect to other damages or claims.

The second most important restriction applying to the recognition of foreign court decision is the guarantee of reciprocity. As far as Japanese court decisions are concerned, such reciprocity is mainly accepted in German legal practice although not yet confirmed by German courts. As far as US court decisions are concerned, reciprocity is accepted in some cases but varies according to which state of the US is concerned.

•

Konstantin Mettenheimer
Bruckhaus Westrick Stegemann
Taunusanlage II
D-6000 Frankfurt/Main 1
Germany

•

—— 5 ——

GREECE

———— • ————

CONTENTS

•

•

5

GREECE

•

STRUCTURE OF THE LEGAL PROFESSION

• GENERAL •

The legislation that governs the legal profession comprises mainly the Legislative Decree 3026 dated 6–8 October 1954, On the Code of Lawyers, as subsequently amended and supplemented. There are also other enactments on lawyers:

(1) Penal Code, Art 175, para 2, on usurpation of lawyers' duties, Art 233 on intentional harm of client's interests and Art 371 on violation of professional obligation of secrecy;
(2) Code of Penal Procedure, Arts 111–112 on competency of courts for crimes committed by lawyers, etc;
(3) Civil Code, Art 250 on time-bar of lawyers' claims;
(4) Code of Civil Procedure, Arts 15–16 on powers of courts over lawyers, Art 400 on lawyers as witnesses, etc.

• DEFINITION •

According to the Code of Lawyers, Art 1, 'the lawyer (*dikigoros*) is a honorary public official, appointed by a ministerial decision and subject to disciplinary authority exercised in accordance with the provisions of this Code', and further, according to Art 38 of the same Code, 'the lawyer is a honorary public official entitled to respect and honour by the courts and any authority'. In this definition, as it has been interpreted by the courts (*S Plenary of the Council of the State*, judgment No 2244/1970), the reference to 'public official' is only for the purposes of underlining the public character of the lawyer's duties, and it does not imply that the lawyer is connected with the government in any way whatsoever.

The legal profession is therefore a completely independent liberal profession.

• BECOMING A LAWYER •

The duties of a lawyer can be exercised only upon registration in any one of the bar associations of Greece. The right to exercise the duties of a lawyer ceases upon disbarment, resignation or retirement.

Greek citizenship or the citizenship of any of the member states of the European Union is a requirement for becoming a lawyer. The other requirements are:

(1) A degree from a law department of any law school of a Greek or a recognised foreign university, according to the provisions of Presidential Decree 52/1993, which implemented the provisions of EC Directive 89/48 into Greek law;

(2) Practical training as a trainee-lawyer for a period of 18 months after obtaining the above degree;

(3) An age of not more than 35;

(4) Passes in examinations taken in the Appeal Court of the area where the trainee-lawyer is registered. Such examinations are organised twice a year, in March and September, by the bar associations of the areas of the courts of appeal throughout Greece.

If the above requirements are met, any eligible candidate has the right to apply to be appointed as a lawyer in any first instance court of Greece, provided that a number of certificates are produced, together with a certificate evidencing that the applicant has no record of serious criminal convictions, as provided for in Art 26 of the Code of Lawyers.

Within three months from the date of the appointment by a decision of the Minister of Justice, the candidate must take a prescribed oath, otherwise he is considered not to have accepted the appointment.

• OBLIGATIONS OF A LAWYER TOWARDS HIS BAR • ASSOCIATION

Every lawyer is obliged to file with his bar association an annual statement countersigned by another two lawyers, stating that he actually practises law and that there exist no legal impediments to his exercising the duties of a lawyer.

The above annual statement must say whether any retainer on a monthly remuneration basis exists, as every lawyer is entitled to have only one such retainer.

An annual contribution to the bar association, presently amounting to Drs 7,000 to 15,000, depending on the seniority of the lawyer, must be paid by all lawyers. A card of identification is then given to the lawyer bearing his photograph, name and surname, the number of his registration and the court to which he has been appointed.

A lawyer who has citizenship of any of the member states of the European Union has the right to be established and practise in Greece, according to the provisions of Presidential Decree 258/1987, which implemented the provisions of EC Directive 77/249 of 22 March 1977 and to Presidential Decree 29/1992, issued in compliance with Arts 48, 52 and 59 of the Treaty of Rome.

• PROMOTION •

As mentioned above, lawyers are appointed in any first instance court of Greece. The lawyer so appointed has the right to appear before the First Instance Court and the Court of Peace of that area.

Any lawyer, after four years of practice before the First Instance Court, may be promoted to lawyer before the Appeal Court and after four further years he may be promoted to lawyer before the Supreme Court (*Arios Pagos*), provided that he proves he has adequate experience (eg by producing writs and pleadings that he has drafted) and that certain contributions are paid.

• RIGHTS AND OBLIGATIONS •

The duty of the lawyer is to represent and defend his client in court or before any authority or committee of special jurisdiction and to provide legal advice and opinions. The rendering of such services by non-lawyers is strictly prohibited and constitutes a crime. Lawyers also have exclusive authority to represent litigant parties in any kind of court, in registrations of trademarks and patents, in making inquiries in public land registries, and also to be present, as is necessary, in notarial contracts of any kind, eg sale, purchase, mortgage, donation, transfer of real rights on immovable property and ships, company statutes and articles of incorporation, provided that the value of the contracts is more than Drs 5,000,000 for the areas of Athens and Piraeus and Drs 750,000 in all other areas.

Litigant parties are permitted to appear in court without a lawyer only in the following cases:

(1) In penal cases, except:
    (a) before the Supreme Court, and
    (b) for cases of serious intentional crimes;
(2) Before the Court of Peace;
(3) For the avoidance of an imminent danger, especially for filing appeals and for interrupting a time-bar;
(4) In procedural acts abroad (eg before Greek consular authorities);
(5) In ecclesiastical courts and generally in any other case provided for specifically by the law.

Any lawyer has the right to practise in the area of the bar association of which he is a member, except in penal cases, in which lawyers have the right to appear in all courts throughout Greece. Lawyers are obliged to have their office and practice in the area of the bar association of which they are members. The lawyers appointed to every First Instance Court of the state constitute a bar association of which they are all obliged to be members and which bears the name of the city in which it functions.

Any bar association is a legal entity governed by public law. Its organs are:

- the General Assembly, comprising all the member-lawyers; and
- the Board of Directors, including the members and the President.

There is a Co-ordinating Committee of all the bar associations of the state, the president of which is the President of the Athens Bar.

Lawyers also have the right to form companies for rendering professional services, according to the provisions of Presidential Decree 518/1989.

The Code of Lawyers lays down rules of professional conduct, and the Athens bar association has drafted a complete Code of Professional Ethics. Any violations of the above rules constitute a breach of discipline, adjudicated on by disciplinary boards of the lawyer's bar association. Punishment may be a reprimand, fine, temporary suspension of the lawyer's status for up to six months, or even permanent disbarment.

If a lawyer becomes an employee, salaried by any agency of the state or of any municipality or other public entity, he loses the status and capacity of a lawyer, with the exception of lawyers retained for providing exclusively legal services, members of Parliament, ministers and under-secretaries, general secretaries of ministries and municipalities, mayors, university professors, reporters and a few other categories.

In addition, a lawyer loses his capacity as a lawyer in cases where he becomes professionally engaged in commercial activities, scientific activities or any other employment incompatible with the dignity and independence of a lawyer, eg becoming the managing director or the manager of a corporation or other commercial entity, or an employee of any natural person or legal entity for rendering non-legal services.

• OTHER BRANCHES OF THE LEGAL PROFESSION •

The legal profession also includes, apart from judges and public prosecutors, notaries, who must have a full legal education. Notaries draft all contracts, deeds and acts concerning real rights on immovable property and other important transactions (public wills, articles of incorporations, etc) and also hold public auctions.

Finally, there are court-bailiffs, who serve writs and other judicial and extra-judicial documents and receive instructions from lawyers for enforcement proceedings. Court-bailiffs are not required to have a legal education but they must take training courses and examinations on the basic principles of the law.

HOW TO FIND A SUITABLE LAWYER

• RECOMMENDATIONS •

There are no statutory or other rules regarding recommendations. A lawyer or a firm may be recommended by an existing or previous client or by another lawyer or law firm.

• LOCAL LAW SOCIETY OR BAR ASSOCIATION •

There are several law societies in Greece, for example:

- the Society of Greek Penal Lawyers;
- the Society of Greek Commercial Law Lawyers;
- the Society of Greek Constitutional Law Lawyers;
- the Society of Greek Procedural Law Lawyers;
- the Society of Women Lawyers;
- the Society of Maritime Law;
- the Society for the Protection of Intellectual Property;
- the Greek Society of Arbitration;
- the Society for the Protection of Human Rights;
- the Society of Tax Law; and
- the Greek Society of Employment and Social Security Law.

There exists also the Greek Institute of International and Foreign Law, which is an official state-run body providing exclusively to lawyers information and opinions on any legal matter of foreign law. The opinions of the above Institute are used in Greek courts to prove the contents of a foreign law, in cases where such law is applicable to a dispute which is to be solved by a Greek court.

• ADVERTISING •

Advertising by lawyers is expressly prohibited by the Code of Professional Ethics of the Athens Bar. Lawyers are also forbidden to try to obtain clients by methods incompatible with the dignity pertaining to the legal profession, to visit persons in detention rooms and prisons without their prior invitation, to make announcements in the press or to send letters of solicitation.

• CHAMBERS OF COMMERCE AND EMPLOYERS' • CONFEDERATIONS

In the shipping area, the most important organisations are the Union of Greek Shipowners, the Greek Shipping Co-operation Committee, and the Maritime Chamber of Greece.

In the area of industry, the most important employers' confederation is the Association or Federation of Greek Industries. There also exist local associations of industries, such as the Association of Industries of Attica and Piraeus, of Northern Greece, of Thessalia and Central Greece and also the Association of Greek Food Industries, etc.

In the area of commerce there exist local commercial societies or associations, such as the Commercial Association of Athens, of Piraeus, of Thessaloniki, etc. Also there are the Association of Retail Enterprises, the Association of Supermarkets, the General Federation of Tradesmen and Craftsmen, the Co-ordination Committee of Commercial Associations, etc.

There are several chambers of commerce and crafts, the most important of which is the Athens Chamber of Commerce and Crafts. A union of all the chambers of commerce and crafts also functions.

Finally, there exist international chambers of commerce for the promotion of bilateral commercial relations between Greece and certain foreign countries, including Arabia, France, Germany, Italy, Japan, the UK, the US and Yugoslavia.

• LOCAL VISITS AND PERSONAL INTERVIEWS •

There are no rules on local visits and personal interviews, and these depend on the arrangements made between the lawyer and the client.

FACTORS IN CHOOSING A SUITABLE LAWYER

• PROFESSIONAL QUALIFICATIONS •

In order to qualify as a lawyer in Greece there are two prerequisites: a law degree from a Greek university or from a recognised foreign university, and the passing of a special examination before the local bar, after a minimum period of training of 18 months. The degree need not be a postgraduate one; a first degree in law is sufficient.

Every Greek lawyer can practise in all fields of law. Specialties are developed as a matter of practise and do not require a formal qualification.

• LANGUAGE ABILITY •

Greek is spoken by very few people on earth, and foreigners consider it a difficult language to learn. Moreover, a foreign national who is interested in doing business in Greece but does not intend to establish himself permanently in the country, may find it a waste of time to learn Greek. However, anyone doing business in Greece cannot avoid frequent contacts with public officials and apart from the top echelons, Greek civil servants are not renowned for their foreign language skills. It is therefore of paramount importance for a foreign client to choose his Greek advisers, and especially his lawyers, on the basis of their language ability.

By this we do not just mean a capacity to communicate in day to day matters which, thanks to tourism, almost every Greek citizen can do. It is also necessary to be able to communicate on more sophisticated matters such as legal issues, tax and accounting problems, banking and financial transactions and other topics of interest to the client. In recent years there is a growing number of Greek professionals, especially lawyers, who have acquired a good command of foreign languages, usually due to studies in universities outside Greece.

It is undeniable that the most common foreign language spoken by Greek lawyers is English, although many lawyers also speak French and to a lesser extent German and Italian. Consequently, although the language barrier may at first appear insurmountable to a foreign client, it can easily be overcome by the choice of a lawyer who speaks fluent English, or even the client's own language.

In order to locate a lawyer with the required language ability it is often easier to search in the various international directories listing law firms, which usually mention the languages spoken by the members of the firm. However, these are by no means the only lawyers speaking foreign languages and the best way to find out is still personal contact (interview, or at least written and oral communications).

• Type of Transaction •

Many international transactions relating to Greece are governed by foreign law, usually the law of the country of origin of the foreign client or company, and such choice of law is generally valid under Greek law (provided the chosen law has some connection to the parties or to the contract). There is always, however, an element of Greek law involved in each transaction concerning Greece, even if it is only on the procedural level. Moveover, there are certain types of transaction where the application of substantial Greek law is compulsory, such as rights of ownership and similar rights on assets located in Greece, incorporation of Greek companies, tax law, investment law, banking and foreign exchange regulations and other matters of public interest.

As a result it is necessary to obtain legal advice or assistance from a Greek lawyer and it is advisable to do so before embarking on any project. As mentioned above, there is now a growing number of lawyers in Greece who are familiar with international transactions and who are able to advise on these issues.

Examples of transactions where foreign law is usually chosen are international loan agreements, joint venture agreements, distributorship and agency agreements, licensing agreements, sale and purchase of ships and other similar transactions, where one party at least is a foreign entity. However, even in transactions which are very loosely connected with Greece (eg a loan agreement in foreign currency, where only the borrower is established in Greece) the involvement of Greek law cannot totally be avoided. For example, if the borrower is in default and the lender wants to enforce on assets located in Greece, the relevant procedure (by auction or otherwise) will be regulated by Greek law. In addition, if the proceeds of enforcement are in Greek currency, the lender will have to follow Greek foreign exchange regulations in order to try to repatriate his funds.

• Familiarity With Overseas Contract Types •

As international transactions increase, and since the English language is often used irrespective of the nationality of the parties, the familiarity of Greek lawyers with UK/US contract types has also increased. In addition, Greece has one of the largest shipping industries in the world, and it is well-known that the international language of shipping is English and that English law governs the majority of shipping contracts. As a result the use of, and therefore the familiarity with, UK/US contract types has grown considerably in recent years. Very often Greek lawyers are now able not only to comment on and apply such contract types, but also to draft them from the beginning, subject to obtaining a legal opinion by a qualified foreign lawyer whenever necessary.

• SPECIALISATION IN TOPICS •

Traditionally, Greek lawyers were willing to undertake almost any kind of legal work, and the main distinction was between civil and criminal lawyers. Nowadays specialisation is rapidly increasing, together with the need to co-operate in larger firms. Although the Greek legal profession is still quite far from the high degree of specialisation of certain other jurisdictions, it is now possible to identify lawyers dealing mainly with commercial, corporate, banking, shipping, investment or tax matters and who are able to provide services of an international standard, in addition to the more traditional civil or criminal law practitioners.

Increasing specialisation has led to the creation of larger law firms of more than one or two lawyers, although the number and size of these law firms is still very limited compared to the Anglo-Saxon type. It is estimated that in Athens there are no more than a dozen relatively large law firms (ie with more than ten lawyers) which comprise sufficient specialists to be able to cover all the main needs of an international corporate client.

• ASSOCIATE OFFICES IN BRUSSELS •

Very few Greek law firms have associate offices in Brussels in the strict sense. There are, however, many links between Greek and foreign law firms, usually on an informal basis, and therefore most large law firms in Greece have correspondent firms in Brussels.

• CLIENT CONFLICTS •

The Greek Code of Lawyers contains some general provisions on matters of client conflicts. In addition, violation of the Code of Ethics, which was adopted by the Athens Bar Association a few years ago, constitutes a disciplinary offence.

The general principle is that a lawyer should never use a client's confidential information for the benefit of another client, even if the former is no longer a client, and that a lawyer should not represent clients whose interests conflict, at least not without their full knowledge and consent.

• RIGHTS OF AUDIENCE IN LOCAL COURTS •

Every Greek lawyer belongs to the bar association of a particular city, and except in criminal cases cannot represent a client in the courts of another city without the assistance of a lawyer from the bar association of that city.

Moreover, every Greek lawyer, when starting his profession, can only appear before the courts of first instance. A minimum of four years' practice is required for a lawyer to request promotion from his local bar and be able to appear in courts of appeal, and a further four years' practice are required for appearance before the supreme courts.

COMMERCIAL ARRANGEMENTS WHEN INSTRUCTING COUNSEL

• TIME CONSTRAINTS AND DEADLINES •

One of the most important issues in instructing foreign counsel is to find out his time constraints and make sure that he will comply with deadlines, if any. In the initial instructions the deadlines should be very clearly stipulated followed by the relevant question to the foreign counsel on whether he feels he will be able to comply with them or not. However, problems may arise either because the foreign counsel in his eagerness to take on the work over-estimates his capabilities, or because he unintentionally miscalculates the time needed for the provision of the requested services. A possible way to overcome these problems is to request a very specific analysis of the hours needed to be devoted to the case and of the lawyers who will be involved, in order to induce a more careful calculation and to receive information which may lead to more accurate conclusions. If you see, for example, that in order to comply with the agreed deadlines a lawyer will have to work on this case for more than five hours per day, you have to wonder what will happen to his other cases or, if he does not have any other cases, whether you have made the right choice. Obviously all the above comments apply mainly when you instruct sole practitioners or very small law firms, since bigger law firms usually can involve more than one lawyer in a case and can comply with deadlines more easily.

• FEE STRUCTURE •

Most of the large law firms in Greece and the sole practitioners who are accustomed to work with foreign clients have adopted a billing method of charging for the time spent on working on the specific case. The currency mostly in use in international transactions is United States dollars, and depending on the seniority of the lawyer involved in the case you can find rates varying from $60 to $300 per hour. Naturally, when instructing a lawyer or a firm in Greece you will request information about his fee structure. If the system is to charge for the time devoted to the case you will also request the rates applicable in your particular case.

A very important aspect of the fee structure system is whether or not the foreign counsel is keeping a detailed and accurate time-sheet. Obviously you cannot ask such a question and expect to receive a negative reply, so you can only deduce what the situation is by asking some indirect questions. If, for example, you warn beforehand that you will request a detailed analysis of the time spent and the reason for such request, and as a guide you request a copy of a time-sheet used by this law firm or lawyer, the reply you get will assist you in reaching some useful conclusions.

• RETAINER •

In some cases, especially those expected to be very lengthy and time-consuming, it is possible to negotiate a monthly retainer. However, it is our view that in most cases the retainer is an unfair system either for the client or for the lawyer and it makes sense only when one or both parties aim to create a strong bond between them.

• METHOD AND TIMING OF BILLING •

The billing method most commonly used for foreign clients is charging for the time spent working on the specific case. Other billing methods sometimes used are lump-sum fees or contingency fees.

Usually, bills are submitted when work is completed and the lawyers' file for the case is closed, but if the case is lengthy billing is normally effected at agreed intervals, usually quarterly. Further, if the anticipated expenses are high, an advance payment on account is requested so that funds are available in order to avoid any delays in the handling of the file.

A note of caution: make sure that your agreement regarding the method and timing of billing is on record (fax, telex or letter), because if there are any disputes the fees of Greek lawyers provided by the Code of Lawyers in some cases are very high. For example, the minimum fee for drafting and filing a lawsuit is 2 per cent of the amount of the claim, and a further 1 per cent is due for drafting and filing pleadings at the first hearing. Thus, theoretically the minimum fees for reaching the first hearing is 3 per cent of the claim, although in practice when large sums are involved a special agreement is made.

• LEVEL OF EXPERIENCE NEEDED •

If you instruct a large law firm, make sure that you will not be charged the time of a senior lawyer for simple work that can be successfully carried out by a junior member of the firm. In order to accomplish this, if you do not want to leave the decision to the instructed firm, you will have to request a detailed analysis of the work which is needed to be done and by whom, in order to understand what will really happen, and see whether the proposals made to you are justified or not.

In conclusion, if you are lucky enough to instruct a firm or a sole practitioner who has experience in dealing with foreign companies, usually you will not have any problems provided that a clear agreement is made at the beginning of the relationship. If you have been unlucky in your selection, you may wonder why deadlines have not been met as promised and why the bills you receive seem to be higher than you expected.

TREATMENT OF FOREIGN NATIONALS UNDER LOCAL LAW

• RESTRICTIONS, REPORTS AND GOVERNMENTAL APPROVALS • OF FOREIGN INVESTMENT

Generally speaking, there are no investment restrictions on foreign non-resident investors. A foreign investor may choose to do business with a permanent presence in Greece either by setting up or joining in a type of business provided for under Greek legislation or by establishing a branch of a company constituted under the legislation of a foreign jurisdiction. Depending on which option is chosen, there are specific requirements as regards foreign nationals.

Subsidiary
Under Greek law there are various types of companies, of which the ones most used in business are: the corporation (*Société Anonyme* – SA), the limited liability company (EPE), the general partnership (OE) and the limited partnership (EE):

- The *Société Anonyme* (SA) requires a minimum capital of Drs 10,000,000 and at least two founders, individuals or legal entities;
- In SAs the board of directors must have at least three members. There is no obligation for the directors to be Greek citizens or to be resident in Greece, with the exception of the managing director who must reside in Greece and have residence and work permits;
- The limited liability company (EPE) requires a minimum capital of Drs 3,000,000 and two founders, individuals or legal entities. In EPEs the administrator (one or more) must be resident in Greece, and must have residence and work permits.

The procedure for the issue of the above permits is made more simple to EU nationals.

Branch

A foreign limited liability company may open a branch in Greece upon authorisation by the Ministry of Commerce, provided:

(a) it has been formed in accordance with the laws of the country of its registered office;

(b) it has duly appointed a representative in Greece and reports to the competent Greek authorities the address of its registered office and the names of its directors; and

(c) reciprocity exists between Greece and the respective above country.

A foreign corporation may also establish a branch office in Greece if prerequisites (a) and (b) are met. For this type of company there exists an obligation to file a balance sheet annually with the Ministry of Commerce, together with information on the branch's activities in Greece. Furthermore, notification of any changes in the board of directors must always be lodged with the above Ministry.

The Minister of Commerce may not approve the establishment of the branch of any type of foreign company in Greece, where such company's objects are wholly or even partly prohibited in Greece.

Non-trading branches: Law 89/1967

A foreign company (shipping, commercial or industrial) may establish an office in Greece in accordance with Law 89/1967, following an approval by the Ministry of National Economy, or the Ministry of Merchant Marine in the case of shipping companies. The prerequisite for the approval and operation of this offshore type of company is that it must necessarily carry out its activities outside Greece. These companies have an obligation to import foreign currency (yearly minimum $50,000) to meet their local expenses.

Restrictions on border areas

By virtue of legislation dating from before the Second World War, certain areas of Greece were designated as 'border areas', where it was in general forbidden, for reasons of national defence, for foreign nationals to purchase property or acquire any property rights. The relevant legislation was radically amended in 1990. It is now possible for EU nationals, individuals or legal entities to purchase property anywhere in Greece, although there are still restrictions in some areas (which, however, apply to Greeks as well).

The restrictions cover not only direct sale and purchase, but also indirect acquisition of property through the purchase of shares or parts of a company which owns property in the so-called border areas. The above restrictions may be lifted by the administrative authorities upon request, after examination of the purpose of the purchase and of the nationality of the prospective purchaser. Where the purchaser is a legal entity, the nationality of its shareholders and/or persons who control it and the origin of the capital invested are also examined prior to approval, which in case of non-EU nationals is entirely discretionary.

• EXCHANGE CONTROLS AND OTHER REGULATORY ISSUES •

Greece is a country with strict foreign exchange regulations. The importation of foreign capital, either equity or loan capital, is free. However, a prerequisite for repatriation of capital and remittance of profits or interest is that the investment must have been first approved according to the provisions of either Law Decree 2687/1953, or of Presidential Decree 207/1987 or Bank of Greece Governor's Decision No 825/1986.

In the case of loans the regulations of the Bank of Greece must be followed (Decision 1976/1991).

Law Decree 2687/1953 provides, irrespective of the investor's nationality, for the granting of certain privileges to foreign capital investments, such as the repatriation of capital, cumulative remittance of profits or interest, etc. Approval for the importation of foreign capital under Law Decree 2687/1953 is needed from the Ministry of National Economy. Most of the major investments in Greece prior to 1986 were made in accordance with this Decree in order to benefit from its privileges, which, for EU investors and in view of Presidential Decree 207/1987, have now lost most of their significance.

Although the foreign exchange environment is closely regulated by the Bank of Greece and the Ministry of National Economy, the situation has recently been relaxed and the new regulations are designed to lift the main existing restrictions, considerably more so with regard to EU member states, on exportation of royalties, fees, dividends, capital, interest, etc.

EU countries
Presidential Decree 207/1987, regarding the free movement of capital between Greece and the other EU member states, radically relaxed capital transfers in favour of EU-based individuals or legal entities. In accordance with this Decree approval is required for capital, interest and profits expatriation rights. This approval is granted following an application by the investor to the Ministry of National Economy, where the genuineness and origin of the investment are examined. Furthermore, EC Council Directive 92/122 of 21 December 1992, which will be implemented in Greece by a Presidential Decree to be published very shortly, will supersede Presidential Decree 207/1987.

This EC Directive provides that Greece is authorised to defer liberalisation of certain short-term capital movements and may still apply temporary restrictions to the following capital movements only:

(a) operations in current deposit accounts with financial institutions;
(b) operations of a duration of less than one year carried out by residents with foreign financial institutions;
(c) financial loans and credits of a duration of less than one year;
(d) personal capital movements;
(e) loans of a duration of less than one year;
(f) physical importation and exportation of financial assets;
(g) means of payments.

Apart from the above categories, all other categories of capital movement within the EU are fully liberalised.

Royalties, know-how, fees, etc to EU countries are not covered by the above restrictions, and prior to such payments the commercial banks, which handle such matters, examine only the legality of the relevant agreement and the EU status of the beneficiary.

Non-EU countries

By virtue of Bank of Greece Decision 825/1986 the regulations concerning direct investments from non-EU countries have become very similar to those of Presidential Decree 207/1987 described above. The main difference is that prior approval is essential and that such approvals are granted by the Bank of Greece. Direct investment covers the establishment or extension of a branch office, new companies, participation in new or existing businesses for the purpose of establishing long term links, etc. Important changes are also expected very soon in this field.

As regards payment of royalties, know-how, fees, etc to non-EU countries, a considerably more detailed examination is carried out by the Ministry of National Economy, where royalty rates are subject to decision by an administrative committee.

• TAX TREATMENT •

Foreign and Greek individuals domiciled (resident) in Greece and Greek legal entities are subject to income tax for their worldwide annual income, whether remitted to Greece or not. The determination of domicile depends on the individual's physical presence in a specific place and his intention to base his overall activity there. In cases where tax has been paid on non-Greek source income outside Greece, it is deductible up to the amount of tax payable in Greece on the same income. Individuals domiciled out of Greece as well as those temporarily resident in Greece are taxed only on their income derived from a source within Greece.

Foreign legal entities are taxed on their income in Greece provided they have a permanent establishment in Greece. Permanent establishment is a concept determined according to national tax law. Foreign legal entities acquire permanent establishment because:

(a) they maintain an office or a branch or other place of operation (plant, warehouse, laboratory or other processing facility in Greece;

(b) they are engaged in manufacturing activities in Greece;

(c) they conclude transactions or render services through a representative in Greece;

(d) they render services of a technical or scientific nature in Greece even without a representative;

(e) they keep inventories of merchandise for their own account from which they fill orders; or

(f) they participate in various forms of business organisations (EPE, OE, EE).

Greece has concluded treaties for the avoidance of double taxation with the following countries: Austria, Belgium, Cyprus, Czechoslovakia, Denmark, Finland, France, Germany, Hungary, India, Italy, the Netherlands, Norway, Poland, Sweden, Switzerland, the UK and the US. These treaties, according to Art 28, para 1 of the Greek Constitution, prevail over national tax law. The key terms 'permanent establishment' and 'domicile' are defined in each treaty in a different way than in national law, and this may result in a different, and sometimes preferential, taxation of individuals and/or legal entities covered thereby, as compared with Greek national tax law. The tax treaties cover, *inter alia*, the withholding tax treatment on payments of profits, interest and royalties from Greece to residents of the treaty parties and vice versa.

Non-trading branches: Law 89/1967
Companies operating under this law (see above) are not, despite their 'permanent establishment', subject to income tax in Greece. These companies are exempt from turnover taxes, import duties and all other charges on imported equipment for the operation of the branch.

• ACCESS TO AND TREATMENT BY LOCAL COURTS •

In Greece any natural or legal person may, subject to jurisdictional rules, bring an action in the Greek courts, regardless of nationality. In fact, according to Art 4 of the Greek Civil Code, a foreign national enjoys in Greece the same civil rights as a Greek national. The principle of equal jurisdictional treatment of litigants regardless of nationality is emphasised by Art 3, para 1 of the Code of Civil Procedure. In particular, a foreign national, natural or legal person, may be involved in an action in Greece as a plaintiff or as a defendant, may be added as a party to the proceedings at the request of one of the existing parties or may intervene in existing litigation to pursue its own claims or to support one of the existing parties.

A foreign national, whether a natural or legal person, does not need to have any kind of establishment in Greece in order to be involved in an action as a plaintiff. Of course, the appointment of a lawyer is obligatory (except in the cases mentioned above). This lawyer may be appointed not only as a legal representative but also as the appropriate person on whom service of documents concerning the case will be effected (agent for process of service).

However, a foreign national, natural or legal person, can not be subject to an action in Greece as a defendant unless such person is domiciled in Greece (for natural persons) or has within Greece its real (actual) seat (for legal persons), ie the place where the board of directors actually meets and the administration of the company is effected or, at least, has its registered office.

• FOREIGN PARENT LIABILITY •

The term 'subsidiary' usually applies to Greek companies owned or controlled by a foreign parent company. Such companies are distinct legal entities, and except for partnerships, where at least one partner has unlimited liability, in all other Greek company forms the liability of the shareholder or partner is limited to the amount of capital invested in the company.

If, however, the term subsidiary is used for a branch of a foreign company this is not a separate legal entity, and the parent company is fully liable for all the actions of the branch.

• JURISDICTION OF LOCAL COURTS •

If the defendant has no domicile in Greece, a Greek court may nonetheless have jurisdiction under one of the provisions of the Brussels Convention (see Appendix). This Convention was ratified in Greece by Law 1814/1988 and became applicable in Greece as of 1 April 1989. If the Convention does not apply, Greek courts may have jurisdiction under the jurisdictional rules on the specific grounds of jurisdiction set out in Art 27 *et seq* of the Code of Civil Procedure.

For instance, proceedings related to a company and its members or related to the members may be brought in the appropriate court for the seat of the company (Art 27). Proceedings relating to real property must be brought in the appropriate court for the place where the property is situated (Art 29). In matters of tort the proceedings may be brought in the appropriate court for the place where the wrongful act was committed (Art 35). In disputes arising out of contracts the plaintiff has the choice of suing the defendant in the local court of the defendant's domicile, or of the place where the contract was concluded or is to be executed (Art 33).

For admiralty matters, the Code of Private Maritime Law contains certain specific jurisdictional provisions. Disputes relating to co-ownership of Greek flag vessels are to be brought before the court of the port where the vessel is registered. Greek courts have jurisdiction over claims arising from collision on the condition that:

(a) the defendant has its domicile or residence in Greece;
(b) the ship carries the Greek flag;
(c) the collision took place in Greek territorial waters; or
(d) the ship was arrested in Greece.

Greek courts have jurisdiction over a case if the parties have so decided. However, this is possible for pecuniary claims only. Regarding future disputes, the relevant agreement must be made in writing in advance and must refer to a specific legal relationship. Failure by the parties to object to the jurisdiction of a court at the first hearing also confers jurisdiction on that court.

A foreign national may be involved in criminal proceedings in Greece as a defendant if he has committed a criminal offence in Greece or, as the civil claimant, if he has been the victim of such an offence in Greece. In any case, jurisdiction to try a criminal offence lies with the appropriate court of the place where the offence was committed or where the residence of the defendant is situated.

• FOREIGN LANGUAGE DOCUMENTS AND DOCUMENTS • GOVERNED BY FOREIGN LAW

Foreign language documents drawn privately are taken into account by the court as documentary evidence, on the condition that the original (or a certified copy) is presented to the court or to the authorities in general, together with an official translation into Greek by a lawyer or another person having such authority.

Moreover, a document drawn by a foreign civil servant or other person exercising a public function, which is considered a public document in its place of issue, has the same force in evidence as a Greek public document (Art 438 of the Greek Code of Civil Procedure). In this case also an official translation is needed if the document is produced to a court or other authority.

• RECOGNITION AND ENFORCEMENT OF FOREIGN • JUDGMENTS

Recognition of foreign judgments in Greece is governed by the relevant provisions of the Brussels Convention (see Appendix) or, if the Convention does not apply, by Art 323 of the Greek Code of Civil Procedure, which lays down a rule very similar to that of the Convention.

According to this rule, a foreign judgment is recognised in Greece without any special procedure being required, if evidence is tendered that such judgment is enforceable in its state of origin. It must further be proved that:

(a) the foreign court had jurisdiction over the subject-matter according to Greek law;

(b) the party against whom recognition is sought was not deprived of its rights of defence and in general from its right of participation in the proceedings (unless the law of its state of origin applies the same restriction to its citizens);

(c) the judgment is not irreconcilable with an earlier judgment given by a Greek court involving the same cause of action and enforceable between the same parties; and

(d) it is not contrary to morality or public policy.

Recognition of foreign judgments of the so-called 'voluntary' jurisdiction (ie *ex parte* or non-contentious affairs including, for instance, declaring a lost negotiable instrument as void, authorising the alienation of a pledged thing, pronouncing the interdiction and guardianship or judicial supervision of a person, etc) is even simpler. Such a judgment is recognised in Greece without any special procedure (subject to the provisions of international treaties) if it is shown that the foreign court had jurisdiction under the applicable substantive law, that the law applied was that which would have applied under Greek choice of law rules and that the decision is not contrary to good morals or public policy.

While recognition takes place automatically and without the need for any proceedings, in practice difficulties may be encountered in persuading particular authorities that the judgment satisfies the criteria of the law. To remove this uncertainty, proceedings are often instituted seeking confirmation of the recognition. While recognition is often sufficient for some foreign judgments, when the judgment orders the payment of money or the performance of an act, then it must be rendered enforceable. In the absence of any applicable bilateral or multilateral convention on the recognition and enforcement of judgments, a foreign judgment can only be enforced if an order for its enforcement is obtained from the competent Greek court. The appropriate court is that of the judgment debtor's domicile or, if he has no domicile, the court of Athens.

The procedure is commenced by an application. If the conditions enumerated above concerning the recognition of foreign judgments are satisfied, there is no examination of the factual or legal merits of the case. When the enforcement order is granted, the foreign judgment is enforceable by whatever method is appropriate as if it were a Greek judgment. This applies both to money judgments and to non-money judgments.

A foreign arbitration award (ie an award made abroad or under foreign law) is enforceable in Greece if:

(a) the arbitration agreement was valid under the applicable law;

(b) the subject matter could be subject to arbitration under Greek law;

(c) the award is not subject to appeal (although it need not be enforceable) in the country of origin;

(d) the person against whom enforcement is sought was not deprived of the right of defence;

(e) the award is not contrary to morality or public policy.

•

Loukas Roufos
Vgenopoulos & Partners
96–98 Filonos Street
Piraeus 18536
Greece

•

---- 6 ----

REPUBLIC OF IRELAND

———— • ————

CONTENTS

•

REPUBLIC OF IRELAND

•

6

REPUBLIC OF IRELAND

•

STRUCTURE OF THE LEGAL PROFESSION

The legal system in Ireland is a common law system similar, though by no means identical, to that of England and Wales. The structure of the legal profession in Ireland is also very close to that in England and Wales. There are two different types of legal practitioner in Ireland, namely solicitors and barristers.

• SOLICITORS •

The professional title for a solicitor is 'Solicitor of the Courts of Justice'. Solicitors provide advice and services to clients in all areas of the law, including representation in court and acting in transactions on a client's behalf. At present there are 5,200 solicitors on the Roll of Solicitors in Ireland, servicing a total population of some 3.5 million. There has been an enormous growth in the size of the profession in the last 15 years and it is estimated that two-thirds of all solicitors currently practising have been admitted to the rolls since 1980. The 'sole practitioner', traditional form of practice remains strong with 57 per cent of all practices being of this type. Indeed 80 per cent of all practices have either one or two proprietors. The vast bulk of major transactions and international work is carried on by four or five firms based in the capital, Dublin. There are five firms in Dublin with more than 50 lawyers and two of these firms engage around 100 lawyers.

While, in practice, both solicitors and barristers specialise in many areas such as commercial law, banking, property, probate, taxation, arbitration and intellectual property, there is no form of recognition for such specialisation. Moreover, regulations governing advertising prohibit solicitors from claiming specialist knowledge of any particular area of law or practice.

Solicitors may also become Commissioners for Oaths. The function of a Commissioner for Oaths is the swearing of persons who come before him as to the truth of written statements in such documents as affidavits and declarations. However, it is expected that currently pending legislation in the form of a Solicitors Bill will provide for all solicitors to be Commissioners for Oaths.

• BARRISTERS •

Barristers have a particular expertise in the area of advocacy and may not be engaged directly by a member of the public. They are retained through solicitors for the purposes of issuing expert opinions on complex legal matters and acting as advocates for clients, particularly in the higher courts. At present there are approximately 860 barristers practising in Ireland, most of whom are based in the Law Library in the Four Courts in Dublin.

Barristers are referred to as senior or junior counsel. The different titles denote levels of expertise and seniority. The process of transition from junior counsel to senior counsel is known as 'taking silk', a traditional expression which refers to the silk gown which a senior counsel wears. In order to become a senior counsel, junior counsel must apply to and obtain the approval of the Chief Justice.

HOW TO FIND A SUITABLE LAWYER

Selecting a lawyer in a foreign jurisdiction requires forethought and investigation. It is obviously important when selecting a law firm to represent you on the establishment of a software development centre in Ireland to ensure that the 'best lawyer in Ireland' recommended to you from a newspaper clipping does not turn out to be the best matrimonial lawyer in Ireland.

• RECOMMENDATIONS •

Recommendations from other enterprises that you know have used Irish lawyers in the past are often of assistance. If you are referred to a major Dublin law firm with respect to the legal issue that faces you in Ireland, it should not matter at all where the 'action' is to occur. However, if, for instance, you are referred to an excellent firm based in Donegal who provided superb service to your German affiliate, establishing a branch in Donegal, that law firm may have certain limitations which would make it very difficult to provide a similar level of service to your company setting up business in Waterford.

Recommendations from other companies that have engaged Irish lawyers are often helpful, as are recommendations from lawyers in your own jurisdiction who have referred work to Irish law firms. It is not unusual for foreign law firms to recommend Irish lawyers to their clients and the fact that there are very few Irish law firms who are members of international legal associations means that one can be reasonably assured of an 'impartial recommendation'. In taking a recommendation from a foreign law firm, one must try to ascertain the capacity of the Irish law firm to perform the transaction and assess what foreign law firm involvement (if any) will be required.

• LEGAL DIRECTORIES •

Legal directories give information on the size and, often, specialties covered by law firms. All of the major commercial law firms in Ireland are listed in the top international legal directories.

• ADVERTISING •

Advertising by solicitors is regulated by the Solicitors (Advertising) Regulations 1988. Under the Regulations, solicitors are not entitled to carry on practice in such a manner as to attract business unfairly or engage in 'touting', but otherwise may advertise their services in such way as they think fit. Advertising must be in good taste and must not contain any inaccurate, false or misleading information. The Regulations prohibit advertisements which claim superiority for the quality of a solicitor's practice or services over those offered by other solicitors, or which contain a criticism of other solicitors. Moreover, advertisements must not make reference to any specific fee for services or contain a comparison of the solicitor's fees with those of other solicitors.

Block advertisements may be a source of information although very few firms advertise in the press and reliance on such advertising is very questionable. What may be of much more value is to obtain the corporate and specialist literature issued by the law firm or firms that have been short-listed since they may give you a substantial amount of additional information.

• LOCAL VISITS AND PERSONAL INTERVIEWS •

For the more significant transaction on which you require Irish legal advice, it may be important to select lawyers on the basis of an interview at the law firm's Irish address or alternatively have a representative from the Irish law firm visit you locally. The larger law firms in Dublin are well used to 'beauty parades', particularly in the area of corporate and commercial work, though outside of the four or five top law firms the concept of a beauty parade may be novel.

An interview in Ireland or at head office is an ideal way to get a feel not only for the competence of the firm and for such matters as fees and conflicts, but also for whether the attitude of the firm being interviewed fits in with your own way of doing business. For example, is the firm more likely to give just straight legal responses to a set of circumstances rather than working with you to achieve your commercial goals?

FACTORS IN CHOOSING A SUITABLE LAWYER

• PROFESSIONAL QUALIFICATIONS •

The first step in becoming either a solicitor or a barrister is to spend either three or four years obtaining a primary degree from an Irish university. This degree will usually, although by no means always, be in law. There is an increasing trend of obtaining, prior to the commencement of professional training, post graduate degrees in law from universities or other educational institutions either in Ireland or abroad.

On completion of the academic stage the student must choose to train either to become a solicitor, by entering into indentures of apprenticeship with a solicitor of more than five years standing and then enrolling with the Incorporated Law Society of Ireland, or else to become a barrister by enrolling with the Honourable Society of the Kings Inns.

The three-year professional training course with the Incorporated Law Society comprises an apprenticeship of 18 months spent in a solicitor's office sandwiched between intensive training courses which operate on a 'learning by doing' basis and are provided by the Incorporated Law Society. The three-year course of the Kings Inns is lecture based and qualification is followed by a compulsory one-year 'devilling' with an established barrister.

Though there is at present no compulsory form of continuing legal education in Ireland, this is likely to change when the anticipated Solicitors Bill is enacted. At present, however, the Law Society provides programmes which are attended on a voluntary basis and some universities have also commenced the provision of courses in recent years. A few law firms provide continuing legal education courses internally.

• LANGUAGE ABILITY •

English is spoken by everyone in Ireland and is the language in which business is transacted. The Irish language is spoken on a very limited scale in several of the less populated areas of the country.

• TYPE OF TRANSACTION •

The type of transaction in which one might propose to engage a solicitor is a very important factor in deciding whom one might engage. A large Dublin-based law firm may be appropriate for giving comprehensive advice on the establishment of a major manufacturing plant in Ireland but may not be the most suitable choice for collecting a debt of £150 in the provinces.

• FAMILIARITY WITH OVERSEAS CONTRACT TYPES •

Irish law is based on the common law system and therefore there is great similarity with UK and US legal structures. Most international contract law is handled by the top four or five firms in Dublin, most of which have a depth of specialist experience in all areas of contract law between Irish and overseas contracting parties.

• SPECIALISATION IN TOPICS •

Over the past ten years or so lawyers, particularly those practising in international work, have had to become more and more specialised. Whereas ten years ago one might have specialised as a corporate or commercial solicitor, one now finds that lawyers in the larger firms specialise in specific areas within a corporate/commercial department. Examples of such 'sub-specialty' include inward or overseas investments, mergers and acquisitions, computer and software contracts, telecommunications law, media and entertainment, pharmaceuticals, health care and chemicals groupings, EC and competition, aviation, shipping, asset financing, securitisation and so on. Litigation is another area on which foreign clients frequently instruct Irish law firms and there again choosing the lawyers with the requisite specialisation is critical. Some of the larger firms have groupings devoted to professional liability, building contracts, intellectual property, etc.

Though much expertise is centred in the top firms in Dublin, some areas are well catered for in the provinces. For example, one of the foremost lawyers in the area of EU milk quotas is a sole practitioner. Likewise, one of the acknowledged experts in labour law in Ireland practises on her own.

• CLIENT CONFLICTS •

The Incorporated Law Society of Ireland has laid down general guidelines on the code of conduct that should be pursued in the event of a conflict of interest arising. The guidelines state that where a solicitor acts for two clients and a conflict arises between their interests, he should cease to act for both clients.

In non-contentious business there may be circumstances where a solicitor may, with propriety, choose the client he will continue to represent, but only if the other client (who has to instruct another solicitor) does not object. Where a solicitor acts for two or more clients in non-contentious business, that solicitor has a duty to ensure that each client will be independently advised in the event of any contentious matters arising between those clients. The guidelines go on to set out specific rules in relation to conflicts of interest in property transactions.

It is probably correct to say that solicitors in Ireland are not as 'conflict conscious' as lawyers in some other jurisdictions. This is due to the relatively small size of the economy and the very limited number of law firms who handle large-scale commercial work. In reality the larger commercial law firms frequently have as clients a number of companies which are competitors. Where the interests of these competitor companies come directly into conflict on a particular matter the above guidelines of the Incorporated Law Society may be applied. However, the experience over many years is that clients fully accept the situation, 'Chinese-walls' are erected where necessary and problems very rarely arise.

• RIGHTS OF AUDIENCE IN LOCAL COURTS •

In contrast with the UK, solicitors have full rights of audience in all courts. Although these rights of audience have existed since 1971, they are very rarely exercised by solicitors in the High Court or Supreme Court where almost all cases are pleaded by barristers. In the Circuit Court solicitors exercise their rights of audience increasingly frequently and in the District Court advocacy by solicitors, rather than barristers, is the norm.

COMMERCIAL ARRANGEMENTS WHEN INSTRUCTING COUNSEL

It is very unusual when engaging lawyers in Ireland to have an engagement or retainer letter. It is more normal to have an oral understanding which is not subject to trade or customary terms. It is, therefore, most important to reach a clear understanding with the firm that you have selected as to the precise terms of the engagement. In particular:

- the ambit of responsibility of the local lawyer;
- from whom the local lawyer receives instructions and to whom he provides advice;
- which lawyers will be involved in the project and, if time pressure dictates, their home addresses and telephone numbers;

- a time-table for the provision of services by the local lawyer;
- the basis on which these will be charged and an estimate of likely fees and outlays which the lawyer might properly expend; and
- the timing of billing.

• FEE STRUCTURE •

Whereas there is a good deal of freedom in negotiating a basis of charging fees with a solicitor in Ireland, solicitors usually charge for non-contentious work that is not related to property transaction on a statutory basis. This is so that the solicitor is paid such 'sum as may be fair and reasonable' having regard to all the circumstances of the case and with particular reference to certain specific issues. General commercial work is regulated by Sched II of the Solicitors General Remuneration Order 1986. A number of factors make up what is considered to be an appropriate charge but the instruction fee is by far the most important. The 1986 Order provides that the instruction fee shall be:

such fee as may be fair and reasonable having regard to all the circumstances of the case including:
- (a) the complexity, importance, difficulty, rarity or urgency of the questions raised;
- (b) where money or property is involved, its amount or value;
- (c) the importance of the matter to the client;
- (d) the skill, labour, and the responsibility involved therein and any specialised knowledge given or implied on the part of the Solicitor;
- (e) the number and importance of any documents perused;
- (f) the place where and the circumstances in which the business or any part thereof is transacted; and
- (g) the time reasonably expended thereon.

• METHOD AND TIMING OF BILLING •

Billing on the above basis is a form of value billing. Property transactions and litigation work are usually charged on a scale fee basis and an instruction fee plus item by item basis respectively. The items concerned are the individual pleadings (assessed on the basis of their length and complexity) and the various procedural steps required to bring a case to trial. Once again the instruction fee is by far the most important element.

In Ireland, as in the UK, the policy in litigation is that 'the costs follow the event', in that the unsuccessful party pays the legal costs of the successful party on what is known as a 'party and party basis'. However, the basis of assessment of 'party and party' costs is such that frequently they represent less than a full indemnity of the 'solicitor and own client' costs which are due from the successful party in the case to his own solicitor.

Barristers' fees in litigation matters depend on whether the barrister concerned is a senior counsel or a junior counsel. Traditionally, where a senior counsel and a junior counsel appear together the junior counsel obtains two-thirds of the senior counsel's fee. The 'brief fee' of a barrister in a case is negotiated on an individual basis and each barrister is entitled to charge 'what the market will bear'.

It is possible to negotiate an alternative billing arrangement. One does encounter fixed tariff billing for some smaller transactions and hourly billing is used occasionally, though rarely, as the sole basis for determining the amount of the fee. As in any jurisdiction, one should be wary of hourly billing. The firm that quotes £100 per hour can end up, through lack of experience, spending twice the amount of time to render the given services as the firm that quoted you £175 per hour.

Solicitors' fees in Ireland carry Value Added Tax or a sales tax at 21 per cent, except in the case of services provided to non-residents of Ireland, provided that the service does not relate to Irish property.

• Fee Disputes •

A client who believes he has been over-charged by his solicitor in a litigation matter may have the bill of costs assessed by the Taxing Master of the High Court.

TREATMENT OF FOREIGN NATIONALS UNDER LOCAL LAW

• Restrictions, Reports and Governmental Approvals • of Foreign Investment

Irish governments have been consistently receptive to foreign investment in Ireland and generally there are no restrictions intended to prevent foreign ownership of Irish companies or businesses, either of which may be wholly owned by overseas interests. Irish participation at shareholder or board level or in joint ventures is not normally a requirement. While most areas of economic activity are open to private enterprise, certain key functions such as the provision of telecommunications, postal services, power generation and certain transport services are generally restricted to government agencies.

This section deals with the restrictions imposed in the banking, money-lending and insurance sectors, but inevitably, specialised regulatory regimes apply to certain activities such as building societies and unit trusts. In the industrial sector, for example, mineral and offshore oil and gas exploration is a government-controlled activity for which there is separate governing legislation. Obviously, specific legal advice should be sought for any contemplated investment.

Banking

An entity may not carry on banking business in Ireland unless it is the holder of a licence granted under the Central Bank Acts 1942–1989. Banking is defined by the Central Bank Act 1989 essentially as comprising the taking of deposits and other funds. A licence to carry on banking business may be granted by the Central Bank which has a broad discretion in the exercise of its powers including, in certain circumstances, power to suspend or revoke a licence. The 1989 Act stipulates that the approval of the Central Bank will be required where a person proposes to acquire more than 10 per cent of the total shares or voting rights of a holder of a banking licence. Where the acquisition would result in 20 per cent or more of the total assets of all licenceholders in Ireland being acquired, then the Minister for Finance must consent to the acquisition.

In dealing with applications for licences, the Central Bank applies its own standards which, although they have no statutory authority, are used as practical guidelines. These guidelines were last updated in 1987 and further revision is expected to incorporate the provisions of the Central Bank Act 1989 and the EC's banking directives.

At present, an applicant wishing to establish a banking subsidiary in Ireland is required, among other things, to provide:

(a) a paid up share capital of not less than IR£5 million;
(b) an undertaking from the parent or major shareholder of a banking subsidiary that the subsidiary will be in a position to meet its liabilities; and
(c) a suitable management structure.

Money-lending

Money-lending in Ireland is governed by the Moneylenders Acts 1900–1989. It is unlawful to carry on the business of money-lending without first obtaining a licence unless the proposed lender falls within a category of enterprises excluded from the provisions of the legislation. Under the 1900 Act, s 6, as amended by the Central Bank Act 1989, the Moneylenders Acts do not apply to certain bodies, including:

- the holder of a bank licence granted under the Central Bank Act 1971;
- a company which is the holder of a certificate in respect of trading activities in the International Financial Services Centre (IFSC); or

- any person bona fide and otherwise carrying on either the business of banking or insurance or any business which does not have for its primary object the lending of money.

A person wishing to obtain a money-lending licence must first obtain a certificate from the District Court and then apply to the Department of Justice. The Moneylenders Act 1933 severely restricts a licenceholder in the conduct of his money-lending business: contracts must be in a prescribed form, there is a prohibition on the charging of compound interest and there are restrictions on communications between money-lenders and borrowers.

In order to avoid the restrictions imposed by the Moneylenders Acts, it was previously advisable for a foreign company which wished to make a loan in Ireland to obtain an exemption order, exempting it from the provisions of the Moneylenders Acts. This procedure has not been altered by the Central Bank Act 1989 which in effect provides that the Minister for Enterprise and Employment may grant exemptions to classes of businesses rather than to individual entities.

Under this provision an Order for Exemption was made on 12 September 1989 which exempts certain classes of companies from the provisions of the Moneylenders Acts. These classes include:

(1) A company providing loans for commercial purposes;
(2) A company engaged in financing the sale of goods by way of hire-purchase or deferred payment;
(3) A company engaged in the provision of loans to enable employees to acquire shares in their employing companies; and
(4) A company providing loans or other lending facilities in foreign currencies to persons not ordinarily resident in Ireland, where such a company has applied for a tax certificate in respect of trading activities to be carried on in the IFSC.

In this last case, the exemption ceases to have effect if and when a certificate is issued. The company does not then need to be exempted as the Moneylenders Acts do not apply to it and in practice this should, for the most commercial transactions, remove the administrative difficulties of seeking a specific exemption.

Insurance and reinsurance

There are a number of ways in which insurance services can be provided in Ireland. The first is through an establishment (ie head office, branch or agency) in Ireland. Up to 1991 it was unlawful for any person to carry on the business of life assurance or non-life insurance without having an establishment in Ireland authorised by the Minister for Enterprise and Employment to conduct insurance business. For insurers not authorised in a member state of the European Union it is still necessary to have an authorised establishment in Ireland.

Establishment in Ireland

In essence there are three different categories of authorisation for both life assurance and non-life insurance. These categories are:

(1) Undertakings which wish to establish a head office (which includes a subsidiary of a foreign insurer) in Ireland;

(2) Undertakings with a head office in the European Union which wish to establish a branch or agency in Ireland;

(3) Undertakings with the head office outside the European Union which wish to establish a branch or agency in Ireland.

The application procedure for each category is very similar. Each applicant is required to show that it is established in Ireland in that it has an office in Ireland and is employing at that office people qualified to issue insurance policies and settle claims. Detailed information concerning the insurer and its operations must be submitted to the Department of Enterprise and Employment including a scheme of operations containing specified information. 'Head office' insurers must maintain a minimum guarantee fund and solvency margin and all Irish established insurers must maintain certain technical reserves in Ireland.

An applicant for a branch or agency authorisation is required to demonstrate that it is authorised to carry on insurance business in its home jurisdiction and it must appoint an agent in Ireland with the broad powers to act on behalf of the insurer. An applicant from an EU member state must demonstrate that it has the required solvency margin and guarantee fund in the member state in which it is established. An applicant from a country outside the EU must maintain a solvency margin as prescribed in the governing regulations, and must maintain in Ireland certain assets representing a proportion of a guarantee fund. A proportion of the latter must be deposited with the Irish High Court.

Non-life insurance: 'large risks'/ 'mass risks'

Since June 1991 it has been possible for an insurer authorised in another EU member state to write non-life 'large-risks' insurance in Ireland. The insurer must notify the Minister for Enterprise and Employment of its intention to write such risks in Ireland. The notification must be accompanied by certain certificates from the insurer's home state regulatory authorities.

Large risks are:

(1) Marine, aviation, rail and transit insurance;

(2) Credit and suretyship insurance taken out for a commercial or professional purpose; and

(3) Fire and natural causes, other property damage, general liability and miscellaneous financial loss insurance where the customer meets certain tests based on turnover, balance sheet totals and average number of employees.

In addition, motor risks can be written subject to the customer meeting the same balance sheet, turnover and employee tests but a 'large risks' motor insurer must also appoint a claims representative in Ireland.

Apart from special rules which allow a degree of extra freedom to insurers authorised in another EU member state which have an establishment in Ireland, the remaining 'mass risks' can only be written by insurers either through an authorised establishment in Ireland or under the simplified authorisation system referred to below.

Life assurance: policyholder initiative

A life assurer authorised in another EU member state will be entitled to write life assurance for Irish policyholders where the policyholder takes the initiative in seeking insurance. Such an insurer must notify the Minister for Enterprise and Employment of its intention to provide such insurance. The notification must be accompanied by certain certificates from the insurer's home state regulatory authorities.

A policyholder will be regarded as taking the initiative where:

(1) The contract is concluded in the insurer's home state or by each of the parties in their own state and there has been no prior contact between the policyholder and insurer in the state in which the policyholder resides (whether by the insurer directly or through an intermediary or agent or a personally addressed solicitation);

(2) The policyholder approaches an independent intermediary for information or to enter into a commitment with an insurer established in another member state. The policyholder will have to sign a statement confirming these facts.

There will also be special rules allowing a degree of extra freedom to insurers authorised in another EU member state which have an establishment in Ireland.

Administrative authorisation

An insurer authorised in another EU member state can take advantage of a simplified system for obtaining an authorisation to write non-life 'mass risks' insurance and life assurance where the policyholder does not take the initiative. This involves making an application to the Minister for Enterprise and Employment and accompanying the application with certain certificates from the insurer's home state regulatory authorities and a scheme of operations containing specified information.

Further developments
From mid-1994 with the implementation of the EC Third 'Framework' Directives for both life and non-life insurance, an insurer authorised in another EU member state has much greater freedom to write insurance in the Irish market.

International Financial Services Centre (IFSC) – Dublin
In 1987 legislation was introduced to establish the IFSC in Dublin, and to introduce a special 10 per cent rate of corporation tax for business carried on in the Centre. Development of the Centre is now at an advanced stage. Over 200 major companies from around the world have established or are proposing to establish there. Companies establishing in the IFSC require a certificate from the Minister for Finance before they will be eligible for a 10 per cent tax rate on their income arising from certified trading activities.

Generally, a certificate will only issue in respect of a trading operation, provided (a) it is carried on in the IFSC and (b) the Minister is satisfied that it will contribute to the IFSC as an international financial services centre and that it falls within one or more of the following classes of trading operations:

(1) The carrying on, on behalf of persons not ordinarily resident in Ireland, of services in relation to transactions in foreign currencies, which are of a type normally provided by a bank in the ordinary course of its trade;

(2) The carrying on, on behalf of persons not ordinarily resident in Ireland, of international financial activities, including in particular:
  (a) global money management;
  (b) international dealing in foreign currencies and in futures, options, bonds, equities and similar financial assets which are denominated in foreign currencies;
  (c) insurance and related activities;
  (d) dealing in commodity futures or commodity options;

(3) The provision, for persons not ordinarily resident in Ireland of services of, or facilities for, processing, control, accountancy, communication, clearing, settlement, or information storage in relation to financial activities;

(4) The development or supply of computer software for use in the provision of services or facilities of the type referred to at (3) above or for the reprocessing, analysing or similar treatment of information in relation to financial services; or

(5) Trading operations which are similar to, or ancillary to, any of the operations described in the foregoing paragraphs, in regard to which

the Minister is of the opinion that they will contribute to the use of the IFSC as an international financial services centre.

Although the financial services provided by companies in the IFSC are intended to be provided only to non-Irish residents, it may be possible to obtain permission to provide such services to other companies trading in the IFSC or in the Shannon Free Zone.

It is to be noted that as the IFSC is not yet completed the Minister has issued certificates to companies trading elsewhere in Dublin. As a condition of these certificates, the companies must transfer their businesses to the IFSC when it is completed.

It is normally a term of a certificate that losses generated by a 10 per cent company trading in the IFSC may only be offset against profits which would otherwise be taxed at the 10 per cent rate.

In addition to the reduced rate of corporation tax, the following incentives are available:

- remission for rates (a form of property tax) for a period of ten years;
- tax allowance of double the rent actually paid for a period of ten years;
- 100 per cent allowances on capital expenditure on commercial premises in the IFSC.

Applying for a certificate

In making an application for a certificate to trade within the IFSC the following information is required:

(1) General information on the promoters, outlining size, history, performance and principal shareholders. Recent profit and loss accounts and balance sheets should also be provided. In the case of individuals and start-up operations, information should be provided on the promoters' track record in the proposed financial services activity.

(2) Details of the proposed activity/service, including a technical description of the activity for which a certificate is sought.

(3) Details of the demand for the services in proposed markets and the expected growth of these markets. Details on competitors and of the advantages the project will have over competitors. Details on the marketing plans for the project.

(4) An outline of office space requirements, whether this will be rented or purchased and details, where relevant, of interim arrangements for the period prior to transferring to the IFSC. Proposed investment in equipment (office equipment/work stations) and details of any special facilities required.

(5) Details of organisation, structure, management and special skills requirements.

(6) Details on financing requirements and how these will be funded (share capital, loans, etc).

(7) Detailed projections of profit and loss accounts and balance sheets for the first three years and of the realistic full potential of the project.

(8) Details of:
- contribution of the project to the development of the IFSC;
- potential for employment;
- demand for local services;
- other benefits of the proposed project.

All initial enquiries should be directed through the Irish Development Agency (IDA) which has been given the task of marketing the IFSC throughout the world. The Irish government is determined to ensure that the IFSC is not perceived as a 'brass plate centre', hence it is necessary for detailed proposals of projects of economic substance to be submitted. Employment is seen as an important, but not necessarily a key, factor in considering any application.

Regulation

The Central Bank Act 1989 provides that the Central Bank will perform a supervisory role over the activities of companies carrying on business within the IFSC. The legislation contemplates the establishment of self-regulatory organisations but does not attempt, unlike the UK's Financial Services Act 1986, to legislate in detail for the rules and functions of such organisations. It leaves a certain amount of flexibility to the Central Bank.

• EXCHANGE CONTROLS AND OTHER REGULATORY ISSUES •

Since 1 January 1993 exchange control has been almost entirely abolished save that the Minister for Finance under the Financial Transfers Act 1992 may impose restrictions on movements of capital or payments, in conformity with European law. To date, such restrictions have been imposed on financial transfers with Iraq and the Federal Republic of Yugoslavia (Serbia and Montenegro).

Mergers Act

The Mergers, Take-overs and Monopolies (Control) Act 1978 (as amended) (the 'Mergers Act') is designed to control mergers, take-overs and monopolies which may directly or indirectly relate to Irish businesses.

A merger or take-over is deemed to occur where two or more enterprises, at least one of which carries on business in Ireland, come under common control. Common control will exist where, for example, there is a direct acquisition of more than 25 per cent of the share capital of the target company or, in the case of an indirect acquisition, where there is no change in shareholding of the

Irish company but a change of control within the group pyramid structure, for example, by virtue of the acquisition of shares in a foreign parent company.

The Mergers Act does not apply to all mergers or take-overs but only to those where, in their most recent financial year, the value of the gross assets of each of two or more of the enterprises involved in the proposal is not less than IR£5 million, or the turnover of each of those two or more enterprises is not less than IR£10 million. It is not necessary that the Irish entity involved in the merger or take-over exceed these thresholds. All that is required is that any two enterprises involved exceed the thresholds.

Where the Mergers Act applies to a merger or take-over, a detailed notification is required to be made to the Minister for Enterprise and Employment for permission to effect such a merger or take-over. Failure to obtain ministerial approval for such a merger or take-over may render void the transfer of assets or shares and may render the enterprises involved and their officers liable to criminal prosecution.

Competition Act 1991

The Competition Act was introduced in 1991 to prohibit the prevention, restriction or distortion of, or the abuse of a dominant position in, trade in goods or services in Ireland. The Act is modelled on Arts 85 and 86 of the Treaty of Rome by which the European Economic Community was established.

Section 4(1) of the Act provides that, subject to the other provisions of s 4, all agreements, decisions and concerted practises between 'undertakings' which have as their object or effect the prevention, restriction or distortion of competition in trade in any goods or services in Ireland or any part thereof, are prohibited and void. An 'undertaking' is defined by the Act to mean a person engaged for gain in the production, supply or distribution of goods or the provision of a service.

The Act established a Competition Authority which may, in accordance with the provisions of the Act, grant a licence in respect of a matter which although on the face of it is anti-competitive nonetheless, in the opinion of the Authority:

- contributes to improving the production or distribution of goods or the provision of services; or
- promotes technical or economic progress,

while still allowing consumers a fair share of the resulting benefit and which does not impose on the undertakings concerned terms which are dispensable to the attainment of these objectives, or allow undertakings the possibility of eliminating competition in respect of a substantial part of the products or services in question. Alternatively, the Competition Authority may issue a certificate that in the opinion of the Authority, on the basis of the facts notified to it, the matter does not amount to a prevention, restriction or distortion of competition.

It is important to understand the distinction between a licence and a certificate. A licence, while in existence and while its terms are complied with, permits the doing of things which would otherwise be impermissible as anti-competitive. A certificate, however, is only a statement of the opinion of the Authority as to whether a matter notified is anti-competitive and which is given on the basis of the facts as known to the Authority at the time. It could well happen that a matter in respect of which a certificate is granted would subsequently be held by the court to be anti-competitive and therefore void under s 4 of the Act.

As a licence is not granted until after the matter has been notified to the Competition Authority, the Act provides that a licence may be granted retrospective to the date of notification.

Section 5 of the Act prohibits an abuse by one or more undertakings of a dominant position in trade for any goods or services in Ireland or any substantial part thereof. The Act does not seek to define an abuse of a dominant position but does indicate that the following matters may be regarded as such an abuse, namely:

(a) directly or indirectly imposing unfair purchase or selling prices or other unfair trading conditions;
(b) limiting production, markets or technical development to the prejudice of consumers;
(c) applying dissimilar conditions to equivalent transactions with other trading parties thereby placing them at a competitive disadvantage;
(d) making the conclusion of contracts subject to the acceptance by other parties of supplementary obligations which by their nature or according to commercial usage have no connection with the subject of such contract.

Any person who is aggrieved as a result of any agreement, decision, concerted practise or abuse which is prohibited under either ss 4 or 5 of the Act has a right of action for relief against any undertaking which is, or has at a material time been, a party to the matter complained of. If the court should find for the aggrieved person it may grant either an injunction restraining the continuance of the matter complained of or a declaration. It may also grant damages including exemplary damages.

As mentioned above, once a licence in respect of some matter has been granted by the Competition Authority such matter is, from the date of notification, no longer prohibited by s 4 of the Act and therefore there is no right of action in respect thereof during this period in which the licence is in force and its terms are complied with. The same provision does not apply in respect of a matter which the Competition Authority has certified that, in its opinion, is not anti-competitive. However, in such a case and assuming that the certificate has not been revoked, the aggrieved party is not entitled to damages in any proceedings which are commenced after the certificate has been issued where a claim is made in respect of loss suffered in respect of the period during which the certificate is or has been in force.

The provisions of the Competition Act co-exist with the provisions of the Mergers Act. However, unlike the provisions of the Mergers Act, there is no threshold below which the provisions of the Competition Act do not apply. The Competition Act has to be regarded as possibly being applicable in a case of an acquisition of one undertaking by one or more other undertakings. In the case of an acquisition of an existing Irish business, therefore, one must consider whether approval for the same needs to be obtained under the Competition Act as well as under the Mergers Act.

Business entities

The following are the more usual forms of commercial business entities found in Ireland.

Limited companies

The principal business entity in Ireland is the company. This is similar to the US corporation. The primary laws relating to companies are contained in the Companies Acts 1963 to 1990 (the 'Companies Acts'). The Companies Acts provide for the incorporation and regulation of the two most common forms of companies, namely the private limited company and the public limited company (PLC).

A limited company is a company whose shareholders' liability to contribute to the assets of the company is limited to the amount they have paid or are to pay for shares in the company allotted to them. A private company is one which restricts the right to transfer its shares, limits the number of its members to 50 and prohibits any invitation to the public to subscribe for any shares or debentures of the company.

A PLC is not subject to such restrictions, but it must have a minimum of seven shareholders and an allotted share capital in excess of IR£30,000 paid up on issue at least to the extent of 25 per cent of the nominal value of the shares allotted and 100 per cent of any share premium payable. As with any limited company, if the shares of a PLC are partly paid, the shareholders' liability extends to any unpaid amounts on shares issued to them. A PLC can have as many shareholders as it wishes provided it has a minimum of seven. There is no requirement that shareholders of Irish companies be Irish.

Prior to the passing of the Companies Act 1986 which implemented the EC Fourth Directive on company law, private limited companies were not required to file their accounts publicly. Both PLCs and private limited companies incorporated in Ireland are now obliged to file their accounts publicly each year in the Companies Registration Office. The extent of disclosure required is related to the size of the company. The larger the company, measured in terms of the balance sheet total, annual turnover and number of employees, the greater the disclosure required.

In certain circumstances, disclosure can be avoided altogether by private limited companies. At present unlimited companies, ie companies whose members have unlimited liability for the companies' debts, are not required to disclose their accounts. However, on 8 November 1990 an EC Directive was adopted extending to unlimited companies the obligation to file accounts publicly where the only members of such companies are limited companies. Ireland is obliged to implement this Directive.

The incorporation of companies is a relatively inexpensive task, comprising the lodging of two principal documents, the Memorandum of Association which contains the company's objectives and details of its share capital, and the Articles of Association which regulate the manner in which the affairs of the company are to be conducted. After receiving this documentation and details of the officers, initial shareholders and registered office of the proposed company, the Registrar of Companies issues a Certificate of Incorporation. The company comes into existence as of the date stated on the Certificate of Incorporation.

A PLC must obtain a further certificate from the Registrar of Companies, namely a certificate of entitlement to do business, before doing any business or exercising any borrowing powers. This certificate can be obtained by filing with the Registrar a statutory declaration as to the share capital of the PLC and after identifying certain preliminary expenses and promoters' remuneration.

The usual classes of shares issued by companies in Ireland are ordinary shares, preference shares with a fixed or fluctuating coupon and redeemable shares. The most common par or face value is one Irish pound, although it is possible to have shares denominated in larger or smaller amounts and in different currencies. A limited company may, in certain circumstances, purchase its own shares.

A limited company may alter its authorised but unissued share capital with little formality, but generally it may not reduce its issued share capital without the sanction of the courts.

The day to day management of companies is normally entrusted to a board of directors. Every company must have at least two directors and a secretary (who may be one of the directors). Neither the directors nor the secretary need be Irish, but for administrative reasons and indeed to assist in tax residency requirements, it is customary to appoint a local representative as a director.

The Companies Acts require that every company appoint an auditor or auditors who will report to the shareholders on the accounts prepared by the directors. Each company must hold an annual general meeting, principally to consider the accounts of the company which contain the auditors' and directors' reports. If the net asset value of either a PLC or a private limited company falls to 50 per cent or less of its called up share capital, the board of directors must convene an extraordinary general meeting of shareholders for the purpose of considering whether any, and if so what, measures should be taken to deal with the situation. The statutory form of an auditor's report must always include a statement of the auditor's opinion as to whether or not such circumstances have arisen as at the balance sheet date.

Partnership

A form of business enterprise often encountered in Ireland is the partnership. This is normally formed by a partnership deed and the principal governing legislation is the Partnership Act 1890.

There are no specific capital structure requirements for partnerships prescribed by Irish law. The Limited Partnership Act 1907 provides for a variation of this entity by permitting a limited partnership with one or more general partners to manage the firm's business who have unlimited liability and one or more limited partners who invest fixed amounts of money in the partnership, but who are not liable for its debts and obligations beyond the amount of their capital investments. Although a general partner has unlimited liability, it is possible for a limited liability company to be the general partner. Limited partnerships are relatively uncommon these days.

Branch

A popular structure with foreign investors in Ireland is the establishment of a branch of a foreign corporation. Foreign corporations which establish a place of business in Ireland (usually interpreted as a physical presence in the country) are obliged to register with the Registrar of Companies in accordance with the provisions of Part XI of the Companies Act 1963. Registration is completed by filing with the Registrar:

(a) copies of the corporation's charter and by-laws;
(b) particulars of the directors and secretary;
(c) details of the corporation's address in Ireland; and
(d) the name and address of one or more persons resident in Ireland authorised to accept service of proceedings or any notices required to be served on the corporation.

• TAX TREATMENT •

The Department of Finance, headed by the Minister for Finance, has overall responsibility for Ireland's financial affairs. However, the day to day administration and enforcement of taxing statutes is carried out by the Revenue Commissioners, a division of the Department of Finance.

The chief taxes in force in Ireland which are of direct relevance to persons considering investing in Ireland are corporation tax and income tax.

Corporation tax is payable on a company's profits, which includes income and capital gains. The principal taxing statute applicable to companies is the Corporation Tax Act 1976 as amended by the Finance Acts 1977–1992.

There is no distinction in Irish law between unlimited and limited companies or between public and private companies so far as tax law is concerned, but certain closely-controlled companies may be liable to corporation tax at a higher rate than the normal 40 per cent and certain manufacturing companies at a lower rate than 40 per cent. These exceptions will be addressed in detail below.

Territoriality

All income of an Irish resident company wherever it arises will normally be liable to Irish corporation tax. Subject to applicable double tax treaty provisions, a non-resident company carrying on business in Ireland through an agency or branch will be liable to corporation tax on all income arising through that agency or branch.

Tax residence of companies

Residence of a company for the purposes of Irish taxation is a question of fact. Unlike in the UK, mere incorporation in Ireland will not make a company automatically tax-resident. There is no statutory definition of tax residency but case law over the years has indicated that the primary criterion is the place where the management and control of the company are located. This essentially means the place where directors' and shareholders' meetings are regularly held, assuming this is where important policy decisions are taken. However, some additional factors which might be considered when seeking to determine the residence of a company are:

(a) the place where the majority of directors reside;
(b) the place where the negotiation of major contracts is undertaken;
(c) the location of the company's head office;
(d) the location of the company's books of accounts, the place where the accounts are prepared, examined and audited and the location of the company's minute books, seal and share register;
(e) the place where dividends, if any, are declared;
(f) the place where the company's profits are realised;
(g) the location of the company's bank accounts.

Just as determining residency can be a difficult exercise, so can it be difficult to determine whether a company is carrying on a business, whether it be through a branch or agency. Again, there is no statutory definition of carrying on a business, but the courts have established certain criteria such as the place of acceptance of orders and the conclusion of contracts.

The purchase of goods in itself is unlikely to constitute the carrying on of a business. Generally, the place where various terms of a contractual offer are accepted is a vital factor. It should be noted that although non-resident companies may not be liable for Irish corporation tax they may still be liable for income tax on certain income arising from Irish sources and for capital gains tax on profits arising from certain disposals.

Tax rates for companies

The standard rate of corporation tax is 40 per cent. However, a rate of 10 per cent applies for companies engaged in manufacturing. In practice, by the time capital allowances and deductions are taken into account, the effective rate of corporation tax for many companies may be less than the standard rate or manufacturing rate as the case may be.

Ten per cent 'manufacturing rate' of corporation tax

The 10 per cent rate of corporation tax was initially introduced in respect of the period from 1 January 1981 to 31 December 2000. The Finance Acts 1990 and 1991 extended this period to 31 December 2010 in the case of general manufacturing and certain other activities. This rate applies to profits derived from the sale of goods manufactured in Ireland.

There are three classes of taxpayers or 'manufacturers' entitled to the benefit of the 10 per cent rate:

(a) companies manufacturing goods within Ireland;
(b) companies selling goods which are manufactured within Ireland by a 90 per cent subsidiary, a fellow 90 per cent subsidiary or a parent company; and
(c) companies which subject goods belonging to another to a manufacturing process in Ireland.

There is no statutory definition of 'manufacture'. The broad test applied is that the final product must be distinct from the materials used in the process. Over the years, the 10 per cent rate has been extended by legislation to include a wide variety of activities which would not ordinarily constitute manufacturing. These are outlined below. Coupled with this legislative extension, the Irish courts, in a number of cases, have liberally interpreted the word 'manufacturing' for the purposes of applying the 10 per cent rate of tax.

However, some activities recognised by the courts as manufacturing have since been specifically excluded by legislation. These are:

(a) dividing, purifying, drying, mixing, sorting, packaging, branding, testing or applying any similar process to a product that is acquired in bulk so as to prepare the same for sale or distribution or any combination of the above processes;

(b) applying methods of preservation, pasteurisation or maturation or other similar treatment to any foodstuffs or any combination of such processes;

(c) cooking, baking or otherwise preparing food or drink for human consumption at or about the time at which it is prepared whether or not in the building or structure in which it is prepared or whether or not in the building to which it is delivered after being prepared;

(d) improving or altering articles or materials without imposing on them a change in their character;

(e) repairing, refurbishing, reconditioning or restoring articles or materials.

The following are the activities to which the 10 per cent rate of tax has been specifically extended by legislation:

(a) the performance in Ireland of certain professional services relating to engineering contracts executed outside the European Union;

(b) the provision of 'computer services', being:
   (i) dataprocessing services; or
   (ii) software development services; or
   (iii) technical or consultancy services which relate to either or both processing services and software development services
   where the related work is carried out in Ireland in the course of a service undertaking for which an employment grant has been provided by the IDA;

(c) the production of fish on a fish farm within Ireland;

(d) certain shipping activities;

(e) the repair of ships within Ireland;

(f) the cultivation of mushrooms in Ireland;

(g) the cultivation of plants by the process of plant biotechnology known as micropropagation or plant cloning;

(h) certain trading activities carried out in the Shannon Free Zone;

(i) certified trading activities carried out in the IFSC;

(j) the sale abroad of Irish manufactured goods by wholesale by an exporter which is a company existing solely for the purpose of carrying on a trade which consists solely of the selling of export goods. Such an exporter is deemed to manufacture the goods even though they are manufactured by a third party;

(k) the repair or maintenance of aircraft, aircraft engines or components carried on within Ireland;

(l) the production of films on a commercial basis where such films are produced for exhibition in cinemas, by way of television broadcasting or for training or documentary purposes so long as not less than 75 per cent of the work on the production of the films is carried out in Ireland;

(m) the processing of meat within Ireland in an establishment approved and inspected in accordance with the EC (Fresh Meat) Regulations 1987;

(n) the remanufacture and repair of computer equipment or of sub-assemblies where such equipment or sub-assemblies were originally manufactured by the same company or a company connected with the company carrying on the remanufacturing or repair;

(o) the selling by wholesale in the course of carrying on a trade by an agricultural or fishery society of goods purchased by it from agricultural societies or fishery societies which are its members where those members are entitled to the manufacturing relief in respect of those goods; and

(p) the sale by an agricultural society to a qualifying company of milk purchased by the society from its members.

Excluded from the benefit of the reduced rate are retail sales, agricultural goods ultimately sold to the intervention agency of the European Union, the building industry (except where manufacturing operations are concerned), mining operations which do not involve manufacturing and income from leasing even though the goods leased have been manufactured by the lessor. It should be noted that this last exclusion does not apply to a company which carries on a trade of leasing from the IFSC or Shannon Free Zone and holds a tax certificate in respect of such trade.

Only companies and not, for example, individuals, can claim the 10 per cent rate but it is not necessary for such companies to be incorporated, controlled or even resident in Ireland – for instance, an Irish branch of a foreign resident company may avail of this rate.

It is possible that some companies could have a trade consisting of the sale of both manufactured and non-manufactured goods. In this case, for the purposes of the 10 per cent corporation tax rate, the trading profits are apportioned in the ratio of the relevant sales of each category. Relief is granted on the normal tax liability to reduce the rate on the profits from manufacturing to 10 per cent. Profits from other trades and income from investment and rentals which do not involve the manufacture of goods are liable to corporation tax at the standard rate of 40 per cent. To avoid difficulties with classification, it may be advisable to ensure that separate entities carry on the sale of manufactured goods and the sale of non-manufactured goods.

The 10 per cent rate of corporation tax has been extended to 31 December 2010 in the case of profits derived from activities which constitute manufacturing in the ordinary sense of the word and in the case of profits derived from the activities listed above other than those listed at (j) above, in respect of which the 10 per cent rate will cease to be available after 31 December 2000 and other than those listed at (i) above in respect of which the 10 per cent rate will cease to be available after 31 December 2005.

Close companies

It is necessary to consider the concept of a 'close company' since, in some instances, a close company can attract a 20 per cent surcharge on undistributed investment and estate income.

A company is defined as a 'close company' where it is under the control of five or fewer participators or under the control of participators who are directors. Furthermore, a company is a close company if, on a full distribution of its distributable income, more than half of it would be paid directly or indirectly to five or fewer participators or to participators who are directors.

The legislation dealing with close companies was introduced to prevent proprietary directors and shareholders attempting to have the corporate income taxed at a lower rate than the personal rate of tax, in the hope that loans could be made or assets transferred to the participators.

If a foreign parent company would be classified as a close company applying Irish rules, then the Irish subsidiary will be treated as a close company.

There are a number of disadvantages attaching to close company status. Certain expenses incurred by a close company, if designed to bestow a benefit on a participator, may be treated as a distribution by the company and consequently fail to be deductible. In certain circumstances, interest paid over a statutory limit will again be treated as a distribution and accordingly chargeable upon the recipient.

A close company may attract a surcharge if it fails to make an adequate distribution of dividends to absorb investment and estate income. Surcharges also apply in relation to the distribution income, investment income and estate income of service companies.

Transfer-pricing

The profits and losses of commonly-controlled buyers and sellers are computed as if the goods had been sold between independent persons dealing at arm's length. Anti-avoidance transfer-pricing legislation only applies to companies qualifying for the 10 per cent rate of corporation tax. In general, the Irish Revenue Commissioners will only rely on legislation which prohibits the practice of transfer-pricing where they perceive a loss to the Irish Exchequer. Traditionally, because of the low Irish tax rates, high profit margins were taken in Ireland resulting in revenue authorities of foreign jurisdictions, rather than the Irish Revenue Commissioners, seeking to maintain that adverse transfer-pricing was occurring.

Capital allowances

The capital allowances system was restructured in the Finance Act 1988. The restructured system reflects similar changes introduced in the US to alter the emphasis of the tax system and phases out capital allowances for most companies.

Capital allowances fall into two categories of assets, namely plant and machinery and industrial buildings.

Plant and machinery

Wear and tear allowance

This is an annual allowance which may be claimed for wear and tear of plant and machinery in use wholly and exclusively for the purposes of trade, profession or employment at the end of an accounting period, and which may be claimed in respect of new or second-hand plant and machinery. In the case of plant and equipment (other than road vehicles) provided for use on or after 1 April 1992 the annual allowance is 15 per cent for the first six years and 10 per cent in the seventh year. The allowance may be increased where free depreciation or initial allowances (see below) are available. Road vehicles may be written off at 20 per cent per annum on the reducing-balance basis, although for cars, allowances are restricted to a maximum cost of IR£10,000.

Free depreciation

Accelerated wear and tear allowances of up to 100 per cent of expenditure (known as 'free depreciation') may be claimed on the cost of new plant and machinery (except road vehicles) brought into use during an accounting period where the expenditure is made by a company carrying on certified trading in the IFSC or carrying on business in the Shannon Free Zone.

Initial allowance

Where free depreciation is not claimed, an initial allowance of 100 per cent may be claimed for capital expenditure incurred on the provision of new plant and machinery (other than road vehicles) where the expenditure is made by a company trading in the IFSC or in the Shannon Free Zone. Initial allowances can be claimed where liability has been incurred for the expenditure, but the plant and machinery is not in use at the end of the accounting period. If an asset is in use at the end of the accounting period the annual wear and tear allowance may be claimed in addition to the initial allowance.

Balancing charges and balancing allowances

Any excess of sales proceeds on a disposal of plant and machinery over the tax written-down value is recovered by way of a balancing charge and any deficiency is catered for by way of a balancing allowance.

The allowances described above for plant and machinery are restricted to the net expenditure, that is, after any IDA grants. This does not apply where plant is purchased by a company to process food for human consumption. In such cases capital allowances are based on gross cost, ie the grant is ignored.

Industrial buildings

Writing-down allowances

An annual writing-down allowance may be claimed in respect of industrial buildings used for the purposes of a trade on a straight-line basis at rates of 4 per cent or 10 per cent depending on the nature of the building. For example, hotels may be depreciated at 10 per cent. Factories, docks, wharves, piers and jetties, airport runways and airport aprons used for trade consisting of the management of an airport rank as industrial buildings or structures, but offices and shops do not. Expenditure on cutting and levelling of land in the course of preparing it as a site for a factory is regarded as part of the cost of construction. Furthermore, an allowance may be claimed in respect of expenditure incurred in recreational or welfare facilities for the workforce which are regarded as part of the industrial building or structure.

Balancing charges and balancing allowances

On the sale of an industrial building for which an annual allowance has been given as described above, any 'profit' or 'loss' as compared with the tax written-down value is accounted for in the tax computation by means of a balancing charge or a balancing allowance.

Commercial buildings in urban renewal areas

Capital expenditure incurred on commercial buildings in certain areas of Dublin (including the IFSC), Cork, Galway and other cities and towns which are designated as areas of urban renewal, qualifies for allowances as if it were expenditure on an industrial building. These reliefs were available in areas outside the IFSC until 31 May 1993 (31 May 1994 where foundations were laid before 31 May 1993). They are available in the IFSC until 24 January 1997 though allowances are restricted in the final year.

One hundred per cent of capital expenditure can be claimed save in the case of capital expenditure in areas of Dublin designated as areas of urban renewal other than the IFSC, when a maximum of 50 per cent of the capital expenditure can be claimed. Companies leasing buildings in designated areas are entitled to a double rent allowance for the purpose of computing their taxable income. The allowances described above for industrial buildings are restricted to the net cost, that is after IDA grants.

Distribution, tax credits and advance corporation tax

The Corporation Tax Act 1976 introduced the imputation system of taxation for Irish resident companies and shareholders similar to the taxation of companies in the UK and France. Under this system shareholders are taxed on dividends received, but Irish residents in receipt of distributions from Irish resident companies are generally entitled to a tax credit.

The tax credit is presently 25/75ths of the amount of any distribution where the company making the distribution pays corporation tax at the standard (40 per cent) rate. It is 1/18th where the company pays tax at the reduced rate of 10 per cent. An individual resident in Ireland can offset his tax credit against his income tax liability.

Distributions received from a company resident in Ireland by a non-resident are not regarded as income of the non-resident for the purpose of the Irish income tax. Accordingly, no liability to Irish taxation will arise in respect thereof.

Companies resident in Ireland for tax purposes paying dividends and other distributions are required to pay an amount of corporation tax known as advance corporation tax (ACT). ACT is subject to the offsetting of tax credits on distributions received equal to the tax credit associated with that distribution.

ACT is due six months after the end of the accounting period in which the dividend is paid. The ACT paid is allowed as a credit against the company's mainstream corporation tax liability.

Although ACT is payable on capital dividends, it can only be set against tax on income of the company, ie it is not available to cover a charge to tax on capital gains.

Group relief is available for a company to surrender any excess ACT to another company in the group where it has paid the ACT in the accounting period and does not wish to carry it back or forward, and is also available in respect of inter-group dividends.

ACT is not payable on distributions made by 75 per cent subsidiaries of companies which are resident in the US or in another country with which Ireland has a double tax treaty.

EC Directives on direct taxation

Ireland has implemented both the Parent/Subsidiary Directive and the Mergers Directive.

The Finance Act 1991 enacted the Parent/Subsidiary Directive. Where an Irish parent receives a dividend from a company in another EU state in which it has at least a 25 per cent shareholding, credit against Irish tax will be allowed for any direct withholding, and also for underlying corporation tax charged in the other EU state, the credit being the lesser of the foreign tax and the Irish tax referable to that dividend. Similar provisions should apply in other jurisdictions within the EU in which a company which is the parent of an Irish company, pays corporate tax.

The Finance Act 1992 enacted the Mergers Directive, and provides for transferring assets in an acquisition situation by an Irish company at their tax written-down value. Furthermore, for capital gains tax purposes, the assets are treated as being acquired at the date and time at which the transferor company acquired them.

Corporation tax and capital gains tax

Corporation tax is chargeable on a company's profits which not only include income but also capital gains. Capital gains are taxed at the rate of 40 per cent of the chargeable gain. Companies effectively pay the same rates of capital gains tax as individuals.

Companies resident in Ireland for tax purposes are generally liable to capital gains tax on all capital gains, wherever the assets are located. Non-resident companies are liable to capital gains tax on the disposal of assets in Ireland which are connected with the trade carried on there through a branch or agency. The Capital Gains Tax Act 1975 sets out other instances where a non-resident company may be liable to tax on capital gains. For example, the disposal of land or minerals in Ireland or the disposal of unquoted shares in companies which derive the greater part of their value from such land or minerals is subject to capital gains tax.

In addition to indexation of base costs which will help to reduce the amount of taxable gains, there are two primary reliefs from capital gains tax. First, if a company disposes of machinery, land and buildings or goodwill and reinvests the proceeds of sale in new business assets, the liability to capital gains tax can be deferred until the new assets cease to be used for the purposes of the trade. Second, capital assets may be transferred within a 75 per cent owned group, without attracting a liability to tax. However, tax implications can arise if the subsidiary to which the assets are transferred leaves the group by, for example, ceasing to be Irish tax-resident or being sold off to an unrelated party.

Value Added Tax

Value Added Tax (VAT) is payable on goods and services supplied in Ireland by taxable persons in the course of business and on goods imported into Ireland. The rates of VAT range from 0 per cent (on exports) to 21 per cent. Generally, businesses registered for VAT are entitled to recover VAT paid on their purchases and expenses, including capital expenditure.

VAT is normally payable before imported goods are released by customs. From 1 January 1993 VAT is no longer paid at the point of entry on goods imported by Irish registered traders from another EU state but instead constitutes an 'intra-Community acquisition' precipitating a simultaneous charge and reclaim for the Irish trader. Details are given below of means of avoiding or deferring the payment of VAT on imports from non-EU countries.

A business is required to register for VAT purposes where its annual turnover exceeds IR£15,000 if the business is supplying services, and where its annual turnover exceeds IR£32,000 if the business is supplying goods.

The disposal of developed property falls within the VAT net. The following activities give rise to a charge to VAT:

(a) the development of land and buildings and the disposal of a freehold interest in them; and

(b) the development of land and buildings and the granting of a lease for them for a period of at least ten years or a disposal of a leasehold interest of such land and buildings under a lease which at the time it was created was for a term of at least ten years.

As a general rule the activities described in (a) and (b) above do not attract liability to VAT unless all of the following conditions are satisfied:

(a) the property must have been developed in whole or in part after 31 October 1972;
(b) the vendor must have a taxable interest in the property, ie either the freehold or a leasehold interest of at least ten years;
(c) the vendor must dispose of a taxable interest in the property;
(d) the disposal must be in the course or furtherance of business; and
(e) the vendor must have been entitled to a tax credit in respect of VAT on the development of the property or on the acquisition of his interest in the property.

Leases of land or buildings for a period of at least ten years attract VAT at 10 per cent on any premium, on the capitalised value of the rent reserved and on the value of the reversion.

In addition, the creation of a lease of developed property where all of the above conditions are fulfilled, except that the lease is for less than ten years, may give rise to a VAT charge of 10 per cent in relation to the first letting. This is regarded as a self-delivery and the VAT is not recoverable. However a self-delivery can be avoided if the landlord waives his VAT exemption on rents and charges VAT at the standard rate of 21 per cent to his tenants. VAT is also payable on service charges.

Avoidance and deferral of VAT

The Customs Free Airport Act 1947 provides that the importation of goods into the Shannon Free Zone is not regarded as an importation into Ireland and accordingly, no liability for payment of VAT arises.

Where goods are imported into Ireland other than into the Shannon Free Zone, payment of VAT may still be avoided where the goods are imported by a business entity carrying on manufacturing activities in Ireland. This applies where the goods being imported are imported for the purposes of manufacturing and where 75 per cent in value of the manufactured goods are exported from Ireland. It should be noted that this exemption only applies where a registered business is carrying on manufacturing in the ordinary sense of the word and not where it is carrying on a business to which the 10 per cent rate of corporation tax, the 'manufacturing rate', has been extended.

Where a business is not in a position to avoid payment of VAT on imported goods under one of the above two provisions, it may still be possible to defer payment of VAT on imported goods. Arrangements can be made with the

Revenue Commissioners to submit to them a direct debit mandate from an Irish bank, pursuant to which deferred VAT will be paid by the bank when demanded by the Revenue Commissioners. Once these arrangements have been made, goods may then be imported without payment of VAT on import. The deferred VAT is payable on the fifteenth day of the month following the month of importation.

Stamp duty

Stamp duty is a once off tax on documents implementing certain transactions. The principal act governing stamp duty is the Stamp Act 1891. The First Schedule to the Act, which has been amended over the years, sets out the transactions giving rise to a charge to duty. Under the Finance Act 1991 any instrument which is executed on or after 1 November 1991 and which relates to property situated in Ireland, or any matter or thing done or to be done in Ireland, will require to be stamped within 30 days of execution, regardless of where it is executed.

Stamp duty on the transfer of shares is payable at the rate of 1 per cent of the value of the consideration or, where the transfer constitutes a voluntary disposition, at the rate of 1 per cent of the market value of the shares.

Deeds of transfer of immovable property and 'choses in action' are subject to stamp duty at rates that are progressively variable. The maximum rate is 6 per cent of the value of the consideration where it exceeds IR£60,000 or, in the case of a voluntary disposition, 6 per cent of the market value of the property transferred.

Stamp duty is also payable on the granting of leases of property. The stamp duty is calculated under two headings. First, where any consideration is paid for the granting of the lease, then the lease will be stampable with stamp duty calculated as a percentage of the consideration. The maximum amount payable is an amount equal to 6 per cent of the consideration paid where the consideration paid exceeds IR£60,000. Second, stamp duty is payable calculated on the basis of the rent reserved by the lease. The maximum amount of stamp duty payable under this heading is an amount equal to 12 per cent of the annual amount of the rent, where the term of the lease exceeds 100 years.

Stamp duty is also payable on mortgages, debentures, bonds, etc charged over Irish property. While different rates of stamp duty are payable depending on the exact nature of the deed, stamp duty on the most usual forms of mortgages, etc has, with the passing of the Finance Act 1991, been capped at IR£500.

Capital duty

Capital duty is payable by a private limited company or a PLC where it allots shares. The amount of duty is 1 per cent of the value of the assets contributed to ᵗhe company for such shares. Capital duty is not payable by unlimited companies.

Customs and excise duties

Customs duties are EU duties which are levied on a variety of goods such as cars, textiles, televisions, VCRs and audio equipment imported from outside the EU. The rates of duty are many and varied.

Excise duties are Irish taxes which are levied on certain goods whether imported from other EU countries or from outside the EU or whether manufactured in Ireland. Once again the rates are many and varied. There are, however, various reliefs from customs and excise duties.

Inward processing scheme

Under this scheme, goods may be imported into Ireland for the purpose of being processed here and subsequently exported outside the customs territory of the EU without the payment of customs duties. There are two systems of relief available under the scheme:

(a) the suspension system under which the customs duties otherwise payable are suspended at importation; and

(b) the drawback system under which the customs duties are paid on importation and reclaimed on subsequent export of the processed goods.

The operations which can be carried on in respect of such imported goods includes fitting or assembling, adapting to other goods or repairing.

Processing under custom control

Under the provisions of this scheme, goods originating from outside the EU may be imported into Ireland on the suspension of customs duties for the purpose of undergoing certain types of processing. Unlike the inward processing scheme, the processed goods do not require to be re-exported outside the EU. Where the products arising from the processing are subsequently put into free circulation in the EU, duties are assessed as if the processed product itself had been imported rather than the original goods. This can give an advantage where the rate of customs duties payable on the processed goods is actually lower than on the goods originally imported.

Deferred customs payment

It is possible to defer payment of customs duties in the same way and on the same conditions as one may defer payment of VAT on imported goods (see above).

Taxation of employees and individuals

Foreign personnel moving to Ireland to set up a business may wish to know how the Irish tax system will affect them personally. Two fundamental concepts require consideration, namely residence and domicile.

Residence

For Irish tax purposes an individual is resident in Ireland if:

(a) he spends one day in a tax year in the country and he has a place of abode available for his use in Ireland at any time, eg if he owns a house in Ireland (this test does not apply to Irish domiciles working abroad); or

(b) he spends more than 183 days in Ireland; or

(c) he spends on average more than three months a year in Ireland, over a four or five-year period ; or

(d) he moves to Ireland with the intention of permanently residing there.

Domicile

As a matter of Irish law, an individual is domiciled in the country of his permanent home, ie the country where he regards himself as belonging. Each person is deemed to have a domicile of origin (the country where their father is domiciled when they are born) and will be regarded as domiciled in that country until a domicile of choice is acquired.

To cast off a domicile of origin a person must cease to have any further connection with that country and intend to reside permanently elsewhere. Physical presence coupled with an intention to reside permanently in a country are generally necessary to prove acquisition of a domicile of choice. Citizenship is not generally a relevant factor.

Tax implications of residence and domicile

Individuals who are both tax-resident and domiciled in Ireland are liable to income tax on their worldwide income wherever arising. Individuals resident and not domiciled in Ireland are liable to Irish income tax on Irish income, UK income and remittances of foreign income to Ireland.

A US national coming to Ireland on a temporary basis will have the opportunity of structuring his financial affairs to minimise his Irish income tax. Assuming he will be Irish resident, he could restrict Irish income arising to him from his Irish-based employer and instead arrange that he become engaged by the US parent company to render services in Ireland and elsewhere. Provided his salary is not paid in Ireland he should be able to reduce the amount of income liable to Irish tax. Any US income would only be taxable if remitted to Ireland. Remittances of capital would not be subject to income tax, and in certain instances would not be subject to capital gains tax.

Individuals who are not resident in Ireland are only liable to Irish income tax on income arising in Ireland, and are only liable to Irish capital gains tax in the same circumstances as non-resident companies.

Individuals who are resident in Ireland are liable to capital gains tax on chargeable gains on the disposal of worldwide assets. Where such individuals are not domiciled in Ireland, however, they are liable to capital gains tax on the disposal of assets situated outside Ireland and the UK only to the extent that the chargeable gains are remitted to Ireland.

In addition to availing of the above rules, US personnel based in Ireland may be compensated by, among other things, approved profit sharing schemes.

Approved profit sharing schemes

Under profit sharing schemes approved of by the Revenue Commissioners, it is possible to give employees a tax-free element of their salary package. Employees can each receive up to IR£2,000 each year in the form of shares in the company tax-free. There are certain requirements of the Revenue Commissioners concerning the exact nature of the shares, the manner of disposal of the shares and eligibility of employees to participate in the scheme, before such a scheme will be approved.

• ACCESS TO AND TREATMENT BY LOCAL COURTS •

With one exception, the Irish courts do not differentiate between Irish and foreign litigants. A foreign litigant has exactly the same access to the Irish courts as does an Irish litigant. The Irish courts have a wide discretion as to whether or not to order security for costs against a foreign plaintiff. As a general rule, the quantum of security which is likely to be granted is about one-third of the defendant's legal costs. The courts have displayed an increasing reluctance to order security for costs. It is thought that the Irish courts will display greater reluctance to order security for costs where the foreign plaintiff is domiciled in a state which is a party to the Brussels and/or Lugano Conventions.

• FOREIGN PARENT LIABILITY •

Ireland, in keeping with most common law jurisdictions, upholds the principle of separate corporate personality. Only in circumstances such as fraud or some other unlawful act can shareholders be made liable for companies' debts in excess of the financial commitment that the shareholder has agreed to pay for shares in the company. It should be noted that in the case of unlimited companies, shareholders remain liable for the total indebtedness of the company in the event of an insolvency, as such companies do not, by definition enjoy the benefits of limited liability. Similarly, in the case of partnerships, each partner will be jointly and severally liable for the debts of the partnership in the event of an insolvency.

Recently introduced into Irish law is the concept of 'shadow directors'. These are a person (such as a parent company) or persons under whose direction or instruction the Irish company's directors are accustomed to act.

Such shadow directors can, in certain circumstances, be made liable for a company's debts. In order to avoid parental liability an Irish subsidiary should be in the position to refute any allegations that it acted under directions of persons other than its board of directors.

• JURISDICTION OF LOCAL COURTS •

Where the Brussels and Lugano Conventions apply
Ireland is a contracting state for the purposes of the Brussels Convention (see Appendix) and has also ratified the 1989 Accession Convention (commonly known as the San Sebastian Convention) which came into force in Ireland in December 1993. The San Sebastian Convention amends the Brussels Convention in a number of respects. Ireland has also ratified the Lugano Convention (see Appendix) which came into force in Ireland in December 1993.

Where the Brussels Convention (as amended) and the Lugano Convention are applicable, the Irish courts are obliged to exercise jurisdiction in accordance with their provisions.

Where the Brussels and Lugano Conventions do not apply
Where the proceedings are outside the scope of the Brussels Convention (as amended) and the Lugano Convention, the Irish courts will exercise jurisdiction in accordance with Irish law. Generally, the Irish courts will exercise jurisdiction if the defendant can be properly served with the proceedings in Ireland. If the defendant cannot be served with the proceedings in Ireland, the Irish courts will exercise jurisdiction if the foreign person has submitted to the jurisdiction of the Irish courts, for example, by instructing solicitors to accept service of proceedings, or by entering an appearance to the proceedings.

The Rules of the Superior Courts enable the Irish courts to exercise jurisdiction against foreign persons in certain types of action, for example:

(1) An action brought to enforce, or otherwise affect a contract, or to recover damages or other relief for or in respect of a breach of contract:
    (a) made within the jurisdiction;
    (b) made by or through an agent trading or residing within the jurisdiction on behalf of a principal trading or residing out of the jurisdiction;
    (c) by its terms or by implication to be governed by Irish law.
(2) An action brought in respect of a breach of contract committed within the jurisdiction.
(3) An action founded on a tort committed within the jurisdiction.
(4) Any person out of the jurisdiction being a necessary or proper party to an action properly brought against some other person duly served within the jurisdiction.

(5) An injunction sought as to anything to be done within the jurisdiction, but only where the Irish courts have jurisdiction as to the substance of the matter.

Even if a cause of action falls within those specified by the Rules of Court, the Irish courts retain a discretion to refuse to exercise jurisdiction, for example, if another jurisdiction is a more convenient forum.

• FOREIGN LANGUAGE DOCUMENTS AND DOCUMENTS • GOVERNED BY FOREIGN LAW

Foreign language documents

If proceedings are brought to enforce a foreign language document, the Irish courts will undoubtedly require a translation of the document. If the parties to the litigation cannot agree the text of the translation, it will be necessary for the court to hear evidence of an appropriately-qualified translator. Subject to the foregoing, the fact that the document is in a foreign language should not present any particular difficulty.

Proof of foreign law

If a document is governed by a foreign law, the foreign law must be pleaded and proved as a fact to the satisfaction of the court. Generally, foreign law must be proved by expert evidence such as by the testimony of a judge or legal practitioner from the foreign country in question. There should be less difficulty in proving foreign law where the parties do not dispute the effect of the foreign law.

Applicability of foreign law

Where the Rome Convention applies

Ireland is a contracting state to the Rome Convention on the Law Applicable to Contractual Obligations (the 'Rome Convention'). Where the Rome Convention is applicable, the Irish courts will determine the applicable law in accordance with its provisions.

Where the Rome Convention does not apply

The Irish conflicts of law rules will apply where the contract (or a relevant part thereof) is outside the scope of the Rome Convention, or where the contract was entered into prior to 1 January 1992.

The Irish courts will generally uphold the parties' choice of law provided that the parties' intention is bona fide and legal, and there is no reason for avoiding the choice of foreign law on the grounds of public policy. The Irish courts will refuse to enforce foreign law in certain circumstances.

There are some statutory exceptions to the application of the law chosen by the parties, pursuant to the Sale of Goods and Supply of Services Act 1980.

Where there is no choice of proper law by the parties, the Irish courts will apply the law with which the transaction has its closest and most real connection.

• RECOGNITION AND ENFORCEMENT OF FOREIGN • JUDGMENTS

Convention judgments

As mentioned above, Ireland is a contracting state to the Brussels Convention (as amended), the San Sebastian Convention and the Lugano Convention. A judgment of the courts of a Convention signatory would be recognised and enforced by the courts of Ireland save that to enforce such a judgment in Ireland, it would be necessary to obtain an order of the Irish High Court. Such an Order should be granted on proper proof of the Convention signatory judgment unless it was contended that the judgment had been obtained contrary to the provisions of Arts 27 and 28 of the Convention.

Non-Convention judgments

In any proceedings taken in Ireland for the enforcement of the judgment obtained in the courts of a non-Convention state (a 'foreign judgment') the foreign judgment should be recognised and enforced by the courts of Ireland save that to enforce such a foreign judgment in Ireland it would be necessary to obtain an Order of the Irish courts. Such an Order would be granted on proper proof of the foreign judgment without any re-trial or examination of the merits of the case, subject to the following qualifications:

(a) that the foreign court had jurisdiction in view of the laws of Ireland;
(b) that the foreign judgment was not obtained by fraud;
(c) that the foreign judgment was not contrary to public policy or natural justice as understood in Irish law;
(d) that the foreign judgment is final and conclusive;
(e) that the foreign judgment is for a definite sum of money; and
(f) that the procedural rules of the court giving the foreign judgment have been observed.

Any Order of the Irish courts may be expressed in a currency other than Irish pounds in respect of an amount due and payable. However, the Order may issue out of the central office of the Irish High Court expressed in Irish pounds by reference to the official rate of exchange prevailing on the date of issue of such Order.

An Irish court has the power to stay any action where it is shown that some other forum, having competent jurisdiction, is more appropriate for the trial of the action, in which the case can be tried more suitably for the interests of all the parties and the ends of justice, and where the staying of the action is not inconsistent with the Brussels Convention as applied by virtue of the Jurisdiction of Courts and Enforcement of Judgments (European Communities) Act 1988.

•

Michael A Greene
A & L Goodbody
1 Earlsfort Centre
Hatch Street
Dublin 2
Ireland

•

——— 7 ———

ITALY

— • —

CONTENTS

•

•

7

ITALY

•

STRUCTURE OF THE LEGAL PROFESSION

The history of the legal profession in Italy had not, until a few decades ago, been one either of partnership or of specialisation. The average law firm consisted in the vast majority of cases of one practitioner and sometimes his assistant, plus a secretary. Areas of practice – courageously enough – ranged from civil and basic commercial, to criminal, family and administrative law. Depth of knowledge was perforce modest. Also because of the court system in Italy, which is comprised of 159 courts of first instance and 25 courts of appeal, besides several hundred magistrates' courts, every town – large and small alike, however remote – traditionally had its own bar, a local legal community and local traditions. The amount of business handled by each micro-practice tended to be small and eclecticism, rather than quality, was the main feature. Light years away from that tranquil, if unexciting, scene were a handful of leading counsel in Milan, Rome and two or three other cities at most, almost invariably professors, with strong personalities and a virtual monopoly over all important work.

While the 'one-man-and-his-dog' outfit remains popular, and brilliant loners are certainly not extinct, a new breed of practice made its appearance some 25 years ago in the shape of the commercially-oriented, multi-lawyer office, vaguely after the Anglo-Saxon model. The Italian version was seldom a true partnership; more frequently, it amounted to a facilities-sharing arrangement or an unequal union under the leadership of a strong founder. As a rule, it had some experience of foreign business, some understanding of foreign law and some knowledge of foreign languages. Around the mid-1970s, ten offices of this kind at the most could be counted.

There are now around 50 commercial law partnerships proper in the country, mostly, but not exclusively, in Milan, Rome and Turin, besides a few shipping law firms in Genoa. Their size ranges from a dozen to up to 40 lawyers. Knowledge of English (and other languages) is more than adequate.

Understanding of foreign, notably UK and US, law systems is reasonably widespread, if not always profound, and representation of foreign clients is common.

While the size of the Italian law firm comes nowhere near Wall Street or City of London standards, and there is far less specialisation in consequence, the degree of experience and technical sophistication of the internationally-minded office will in most cases prove entirely satisfactory. The foreign client will find that the larger partnership in a major city is able (allowing for smaller scale) to render a service fundamentally comparable to that of a City firm. If the case is located in the province the lawyer instructed in the first place will as a rule retain a local man, and keep dealing with and reporting to the foreign client.

Milan and Rome commercial partnerships virtually all deal regularly in company, contract, property and sometimes intellectual property cases, besides commercial litigation. A few are informed on EU matters, and the competition practice is developing, partly as a result of the recent coming into force of full fledged domestic anti-trust legislation. There is no real split profession in Italy, and the *avvocato* combines the functions of barrister and solicitor.

HOW TO FIND A SUITABLE LAWYER

• RECOMMENDATIONS •

The sources that are likely to prove the most promising are personal recommendations from the candidate's current or former clients, or from other foreign lawyers who have had previous dealings with the firm. When the circumstances allow, more recommendations should be obtained, ideally from different sources, followed by a visit and personal interview. Whenever possible, one should insist that a specified partner be recommended, and make sure that the main field of practice of the candidate is at large what one seeks.

• BAR ASSOCIATIONS •

Bar associations will, in principle, respond to enquiries. However, being supposed to observe impartiality towards their members, the foreign client will never obtain ratings, or even recommendations based on skill. Rather, lists of names will be supplied and, as a rule, no indication of specialisations will be given.

• LEGAL DIRECTORIES •

Taking out an entry in an international directory, such as *Martindale-Hubbell* or *Kime's International Law Directory*, is akin to advertising but fundamentally on the right side of etiquette. However, directories being no longer particularly selective, to appear listed will in itself not mean much more than fair linguistic abilities and past experience with foreign clients.

• ADVERTISING •

Advertising is traditionally thought not befitting the status and image of the liberal professions in Italy, and most professions indeed still regard any form of self-promotion by their members as ethically improper, besides being in bad taste. This is notably the case for the legal profession, and anything that aims at attracting custom by addressing non-clients – let alone outright advertising – is frowned upon, and may have disciplinary consequences for the culprit. While the aversion of the Bar for visible promotion is probably slowly relaxing, it is a fact that the leading counsel or professor, or the upper-echelon law firm, will not advertise in Italy, and rather make a point of not needing to do so. What comes nearest to acceptable promotion is writing articles and books, giving speeches and leading seminars, none of which is likely to supply much guidance to the foreign client's quest for legal assistance in Italy. Conversely, the few members of the profession who feel bold or desperate enough to depart from this unwritten rule, and possibly weather the rigours of their bar associations, are invariably not top league, and will rarely prove an ideal choice. Hence, advertising should hardly be considered a way to identify a suitable lawyer in Italy.

• CHAMBERS OF COMMERCE AND EMPLOYERS' CONFEDERATIONS •

Bilateral chambers of commerce (ie Anglo-Italian, Italy-US, etc) in the larger cities will sometimes provide recommendations; these normally indicate that the person recommended is known to the chamber and has both a fair knowledge of the foreign language and a fair ability to handle average commercial cases. The leading members of the profession will, however, seldom be approached through so unselective a source. Foreign consulates and trade representations may also assist in identifying lawyers willing to deal with straightforward commercial cases, divorce and family relations cases, small estates, simple property matters, etc. This is sometimes useful if one needs help outside the large cities, where a foreign client's chance to find a reliable person through other sources is more remote. However, the recommendation is unlikely to imply more than average ability to communicate and basic honesty and competence. It is not usual in Italy for employers' confederations to provide recommendations to non-members, and they are unlikely to assist one's selection process. On the whole, one is unlikely to draw much comfort from recommendations emanating from institutions.

FACTORS IN CHOOSING A SUITABLE LAWYER

There are a number of factors which, in an ideal world, should all carry weight in one's selection process. However, the range of candidates from within which to make one's choice being normally finite, one should necessarily set oneself priorities.

• PROFESSIONAL QUALIFICATIONS •

The legal profession in Italy is nominally split between *procuratori legali*, who can represent clients and plead within the district of the court of appeal they reside in, and *avvocati*, who can plead anywhere in the country. However, in practice, one would not plead alone in another court of appeal's district, but always together with a local man. Therefore, the more senior title (*avvocato*) just means greater experience. In fact one becomes an *avvocato* simply through the passage of time (six years after enrolling as *procuratore*). A special breed of *avvocati cassazionisti* enrolled in a special register is mandated for representation in the Supreme Court, the Constitutional Court and other central jurisdictions, the access to the special register again being gained with time (eight years after enrolling as an *avvocato*). Most senior lawyers are enrolled. However, the choice of *avvocato cassazionista* may prove critical to a Supreme Court case, where oral pleadings and recognised standing in the environment carry weight. Leaving Supreme Court cases aside, professional qualifications are unlikely to play too much of a role as far as the foreign client is concerned.

• LANGUAGE ABILITY •

In the author's view, language ability is a top priority. English as a working language is claimed by legions, but only small numbers will survive such tests as a full day's negotiation or the drafting of a contract in accomplished legal English. There are naturally various degrees of language ability needed and, for instance, a domestic litigation will tend to require less fluency than will discussing a transaction strategy in a large meeting, and still less linguistic command and elegance than is required when drawing up a formal opinion. However, if the candidate cannot communicate and write in good English without the need of a translator, the brightest of legal intellects may well not get the expected results either because he is confronted with opponents who have a good command of the language, or simply because he does not succeed in fully communicating his thoughts to his client.

• FAMILIARITY WITH OVERSEAS CONTRACT TYPES •

A factor which is bound to carry increasing weight, at present and in the years to come, is doubtless knowledge of European Union law on the part of the candidate. Familiarity with things European tends to be claimed by growing numbers of practitioners in Italy. However, the pace at which Union law progresses, the sheer bulk of the implementing legislation at member states' level, and the changes that are introduced almost daily into the domestic systems, are so great that it is a major effort to keep acceptably well-informed and be able to advise one's clients correctly in consequence. The attention that the legal profession in Italy has devoted to Union law has in the past been sadly inadequate, and there are areas of the law – such as intellectual property, pharmaceuticals, securities, banking, insurance or consumer protection – in which the candidate's insufficient grasp of the European side of the case may prove a disappointment, if not an outright handicap.

• SPECIALISATION IN TOPICS •

Claims to topical specialisation should also be handled with caution. The average Italian law office is not large, and the chances of coming across the degree of departmentalisation and specialised knowledge that is common in the UK or the US (such as the financial derivatives specialist who does nothing else in his life, or the litigator who just defends non-insured liability actions, etc) is remote. Those members of the legal profession who boast specialisations usually tend to claim too many of them and one is likely to be disappointed.

The true specialist will, in the vast majority of cases, be a leading professor and his specialisation a full branch of the law (eg intellectual property law, administrative law, etc) or, in fewer cases, a niche practitioner (such as the copyright or the building law expert). This breed of specialist will be retained rather by other lawyers, and his strengths will not necessarily be foreign languages or how to deal with foreign clients. It is probably more productive for such specialists to be consulted by the general practice office retained in the first place, for instance, to seek a formal opinion or to join forces in a complex litigation, than for the average foreign client itself to weather the inevitable difficulties in communication and differences in mentality, that are bound to be encountered if the specialist is instructed directly.

To sum up on specialisation, the large enough general practice office located in Milan or Rome, with proven language ability, familiarity with English format contract-types and prior experience in transactions or litigations involving foreign parties or foreign laws, is probably all that one should aim at. Of course, if the case presented objective features of specialisation – such as a chemical patent case, a commercial paper programme, a double taxation question, etc – the candidate should be asked if he has that ability and experience available in-house. The reply that it might be beneficial for outside special counsel, typically a professor, to be also retained is not necessarily a bad sign, provided the client retains a degree of control over the selection of the expert and the cost associated with it.

• ASSOCIATE OFFICES IN BRUSSELS •

It may also be important, whenever a degree of liaison or dialogue with European institutions is required, to engage a firm familiar with Brussels. There are very few Italian law firms with their own real office in Brussels. Claimed Brussels outfits, associations and alliances should always be verified, and one should not be embarrassed to ask specific questions.

• CLIENT CONFLICTS •

Since the number of largish commercial law firms engaging in international practice in Italy is limited, conflicts of interest are not infrequent. Again, one should not hesitate to request one's candidate to confirm that, for instance, he does not represent certain other parties, even before telling too much of the case. To represent or advise a client in a conflicts of interest situation is a disciplinary offence, and may even constitute a criminal offence. The bar associations are competent to deal with the disciplinary side, and tend to take a rather strict view. In summary:

(1) A lawyer cannot take a new client or a new case if there is a conflict of interests with a current client or a current case;

(2) A lawyer cannot use information acquired from an ex-client in a subsequent case involving the ex-client as an adversary;

(3) A lawyer cannot represent both parties and if he happens to be instructed on the same deal or case by two existing clients, he will be expected to step down and represent and advise neither.

Such being the rule, not all lawyers may be equally keen or prompt in perceiving a conflict scenario; hence, again, the need to ask specific questions and obtain specific answers in advance. In a doubtful case, it will always be preferable not to accept a spurious arrangement and clear the potential conflict from the outset, even if this involves the inconvenience of a fresh selection.

COMMERCIAL ARRANGEMENTS WHEN INSTRUCTING COUNSEL

Having made its selection, the foreign client will generally want to address commercial arrangements before completing the instruction process.

• FEE STRUCTURE •

Italy has a professional tariff of traditional structure which lays down in detail a catalogue of activities, both judicial (eg studying or preparing evidence, drafting a writ, reviewing an adversary brief, conducting an oral pleading, etc) and extrajudicial (eg preparing an opinion, drafting a contract, attending a conference, etc). The activity is related basically to two variables, ie the rank of the lawyer concerned (trainee, *procuratore*, *avvocato*) and the value of the case.

The combined results of these variables are tables of fees, which range fairly widely between a minimum and a maximum. Every single activity is traced to an item of the tariff and a fee value is attached to it. The aggregate of the fee figures applicable to each activity performed is the fee payable. Disbursements are separately accounted for and recharged.

Contingency and results-related charging is not permitted. Outright *ad valorem* charges (ie unrelated to the actual quantity and quality of activity performed) are allowed in extremely limited instances, such as estate administrations. It is considered unethical (as being unfairly competitive towards one's colleagues) to charge less than the tariff minimum.

The tariff system will not, in practice, be followed by:

(a) the larger commercial firms, who tend to charge by time (see below);
(b) the very leading specialist or professor, who, usually being very much in demand, will in essence charge what he pleases.

However, if the bill is contested, the fee charged will in either case be 'reconstructed' based on the tariff, with a view to the requisite opinion being obtained from the relevant bar association (see below). The tariff is also compulsorily used when submitting one's legal costs for an award in a litigation. The courts enjoy a wide discretion in awarding and taxing legal costs, based on the general principle that the winner recovers and the loser pays. In practice, their approach is less than generous, and what is recovered even in case of a complete victory is invariably but a fraction of the actual costs incurred.

Finally, the tariff will be resorted to in all other instances when the lawyer retained is neither an internationally-oriented commercial firm, nor a top league loner, and no express agreement was made to remunerate the lawyer's services (which is perfectly permissible, albeit slightly unusual). Payment must never be less than the tariff minimum.

•   RETAINER   •

Retainers, estimates and flat fees negotiated in advance unrelated to time share a common problem. The commercially-minded law firm used to charging on the basis of time will be reluctant to make commitments beforehand, where the time that may be at stake is unknown or difficult to quantify. Hence, if the lawyer is pressed by the client to do this, the figure given will invariably be on the high side. The result may be far from ideal for client and lawyer alike for the following reasons:

(a) it is unlikely that less than the amount estimated will be charged, even if the time spent was less than predicted;

(b) the constraint of the estimate supplied may work against the quality of the service, as the lawyer will be inclined to stop deploying billable time on the safe side of the ceiling;

(c) if the lawyer is not instructed because the client considers the figure too high, an otherwise good choice may not be made, without real good reason, as a result.

Therefore, if the selection is right on most counts regarding the honesty of the candidate and the faith placed by the client in the accuracy of the time billed, departing from the time charge will introduce undesirable factors of strain. If the selection was made subject to reservations because, for instance, the client was not fully convinced of the chosen candidate's honesty, then the insistence on a binding estimate or flat charge is only likely to expose the problem further, without the selection becoming a better one in consequence. Retainers as such are relatively uncommon among top league commercial firms, unless the client is a new one, or the case involves an exceptional amount of up-front time or disbursements.

•   METHOD AND TIMING OF BILLING   •

While most lawyers of the traditional cast charge by the tariff, and their clients on average find this acceptable, the foreign client should be slightly more cautious for the following reasons:

(a) each single activity triggers a fee item (regardless of the time deployed);

(b) there are relatively numerous variables that contribute to produce the final fee figure, which follow mechanics with which the foreign client will inevitably be unfamiliar and hard-put to appreciate in full;

164

(c) the foreign client, foreign language feature will, as a rule, be utilised as grounds to apply the top of the bracket.

The end product of this complex process may prove altogether unpredictable and sometimes result in a higher fee figure than a straight billing based on time spent would have generated.

As indicated, there is no legal reason why client and lawyer should not decide by agreement between them what the remuneration for the lawyer's service will be, thereby making the subsequent resort to the tariff unnecessary. That remuneration could be a flat fee regardless of all circumstances, a fee charged on the basis of the time employed or a combination of both.

The flat fee formula is not common and, with few exceptions (such as, for instance, formal opinions in repetitive transactions), the large commercial firm in Italy will seldom expect such a proposition from the client.

Time charging is fairly generally in use, and is expected by most internationally-oriented practices. Virtually all offices which charge on the basis of time are computerised, and will basically load time units by client, case and lawyer to produce time aggregates which may or may not be immediately translated into a fee figure. Lawyers' rates are by the hour and are, as a rule, diversified within the firm to account for seniority and individual ability. Senior partner rates will currently range from Lire 300,000 to Lire 400,000 per hour. Rates get updated from time to time, albeit not too frequently.

Some law firms will bill strictly by the computer, while others will retain a discretion to override the arithmetic and adjust the computer-generated fee upwards or downwards according to circumstances (eg difficulty, value, financial result, degree of success, client's satisfaction, etc). While the foreign client, and the US client in particular, will be instinctively nervous of the resulting uncertainty, an insistence to rule out that discretion may not necessarily work in the client's favour.

Disbursements and costs are also loaded on the computer, and will be shown on the bill. Italian law firms do not usually charge paralegal time, wordprocessing time or secretarial overtime. An overhead recharge on disbursements is sometimes shown.

All in all, the information that appears on the computer printout which originates the bill of an Italian law firm will not look too different from that given in the UK or the US, and the foreign client used to being charged by time will feel on familiar ground.

There are various degrees of detail, and especially of billing frequency, that may be required by a large foreign client. While detail requirements will in most instances be satisfied, most Italian law firms will resist an exceedingly frequent billing, which is felt to place too much pressure on the firm's administration and accounting structures. As a result, promises of punctual monthly billings are likely, in fact, to be dishonoured, good intentions notwithstanding .

The author's suggestion is that the client should enquire as to what the lawyer's existing structure is in reality capable of delivering, in terms of both detail of information and frequency, and attempt to live with this. Solemn promises to change one's billing procedures to please an important client tend to be forgotten as promptly as they are given. One should also bear in mind that, unless it was agreed with the client beforehand to submit the computer printout along with the summary of the bill, the printout will normally not be sent, unless specifically asked for. Asking for details or the printout after receiving the bill is likely to be taken as criticism of the bill or a sign of mistrust.

• FEE DISPUTES •

If the amount charged was not previously agreed and is contested by the client, the lawyer may apply to the bar association to which he belongs for an opinion. Bar associations tend to be fairly generous in approving fees, and the opinion is often little more than a rubber stamping of the bill. The bill accompanied by the bar association's opinion enables the lawyer to seek a summary judgment for monies owed. The client may oppose the summary judgment by ordinary summons, and the court will in that case adjudge the fairness of the fee charged in relation to both quality and quantity of the service rendered, on the basis of the tariff but without restrictions. Of course, the lawyer may refrain from choosing the summary judgment route, which is more aggressive, but more costly and less elegant, and sue the client by ordinary proceedings instead. All in all, Italian lawyers seldom and reluctantly take legal action against clients or ex-clients, and tend to consider doing so vaguely unbecoming. The seeking of an opinion from the bar association is slightly more frequent, and the fee sometimes gets paid to the extent approved without proceedings being instituted (and the client is naturally lost).

• LEVEL OF EXPERIENCE NEEDED •

Another feature to bear in mind is the level of experience of the lawyers within the firm who will actually be performing the work. The dilemma is the usual one of cost versus quality versus efficiency. The author's advice is that the client should refrain from having too strong a say in the composition of the team. If the chosen candidate is appropriately busy, the more senior partners will also be healthily occupied and not keen nor able to deploy too much top-rate time on files which could be adequately dealt with by less senior persons. If this proves not to be the case, this means that the chosen firm's structure is top-heavy and the selection probably not right in the first place. Conversely, if the chosen firm is well-organised and responsibly run, the junior persons will do most of the research, preparation and drafting work, but the senior person will always shape strategy and review the end product. Again, if the more seasoned partner never shows up, and the client feels that the junior he deals with seems to be given an unnaturally broad leeway, this will indicate too lean a set up and, again, a structural problem.

Summing up, the foreign client should, in the author's view:

(1) Unhesitatingly head for billing on the basis of time, this being the system with more in-built checks and balances than any other;

(2) Enquire beforehand as to the lawyers' hourly rates applied, and ask to be told in advance when they are changed;

(3) If special details of hours or the full printouts are required, say so beforehand;

(4) Not impose on the lawyer's reporting requirements or billing frequencies that are not in line with the lawyer's existing organisation and which are, therefore, unlikely to be observed;

(5) Not interfere unduly, once the partner in charge of the case is identified, with the distribution and organisation of the work and the composition of the team within the firm;

(6) Refrain from pressing too much for binding estimates, if it is perceived that the lawyer is loath to work in that way.

Clearly, for the client to be persuaded to live with all the above, there must subsist a relation of trust with the chosen candidate. If such trust is absent, there is no clever billing arrangement that will turn a poor choice into a good one.

TREATMENT OF FOREIGN NATIONALS UNDER LOCAL LAW

Italy has been traditionally liberal towards foreign nationals and entities, even prior to the days of the European Union. While reciprocity of treatment is theoretically a condition of the recognition of the legal capacity of foreign persons, this has been applied only in a handful of instances, or not applied at all, even where reciprocity was clearly absent. However, with the Single Market having become a reality in Europe, and the four liberties:

- of movement of goods;
- of movement of capital;
- of movement and establishment of persons; and
- of rendering of services

being virtually implemented in nearly all fields, a distinction needs to be drawn, dependent on whether the foreign national or entity belongs to a European Union member state, or a non-Union country.

In the former case, the foreign national or entity is in essentially all respects placed on an equal footing with Italian nationals as regards the investment of capital, the ownership of real property, the right to acquire and run a business, etc. However, the entry of non-Union nationals in certain sectors of the economy, such as insurance, financial services, banking, transports, publishing, media and public procurement may be restricted or subject to conditions. No such restrictions or conditions may be imposed on Union persons, except under the usual safeguard clauses (eg national defence or security, public policy, stability of the currency) or in the extremely few cases in which the intra-Union liberalisation is not yet a full reality (for instance, in the financial services area, as to which the Italian nationality of the vehicle – not the Italian control of its capital – is currently prescribed).

• RESTRICTIONS, REPORTS AND GOVERNMENTAL APPROVALS • OF FOREIGN INVESTMENT

Foreign investments in Italy are entirely liberalised and are not subject to any governmental reportings or approvals. Naturally, in those areas where Italian nationals are required to secure a licence or permit (such as the obtaining of a pharmaceutical or refining family licence, a Central Bank approval to acquire a stake in a bank, a building permit, etc) the foreign national or entity will equally need to comply. In numerous instances, the proposition will remain theoretical, as the foreign national or entity wishing to engage in business in Italy will almost invariably create an Italian corporate vehicle to that end.

Essentially, it is only in those few sectors referred to above that the non-Union ownership or control of the vehicle's capital, or the non-Union nationality of the components of its constituent bodies, may amount to a disqualification from engaging in business, or make the engaging in business by it subject to conditions or approvals. However, in the vast majority of cases, the foreign, even non-Union, nationality of those concerned, is virtually irrelevant.

• EXCHANGE CONTROLS AND OTHER REGULATORY ISSUES •

Italy repealed all exchange controls in 1990, regardless of whether the foreign country of origin or destination of the monies, securities, etc is an EU member state or a non-Union country.

Other features that still indirectly affect foreign investments are:

(1) Anti money laundering legislation requiring funds, securities, valuables, etc above certain minimum thresholds to be channelled through the banking system, and furthermore requiring banks and financial intermediaries to collect and report certain information on their customers.

(2) Tax legislation, to the extent that certain withholdings apply to payments of dividends, capital gains, interest, royalties, etc and furthermore to the extent of making it necessary in a number of instances for the foreign-resident entity or person to secure an Italian taxpayer number or to appoint a tax representative in Italy.

(3) Statistical requirements, which mandate the filing of certain forms or the reporting of certain particulars, for instance, upon remitting abroad or receiving from abroad funds above certain thresholds, upon importing or exporting goods, etc.

(4) The need for the foreign national or entity concerned to secure beforehand, or prior to commencing operations, certain specific accomplishments or approvals. These may apply regardless of the foreign nationality (such as in connection with an anti-trust filing, or the filing of a public offering), or because of the foreign, non-Union nationality (eg with respect to seeking a banking or an insurance licence) of the person or entity concerned.

• TAX TREATMENT •

As regards the taxation of income, personal as well as corporate, the basic criteria are the residence or deemed residence of the taxpayer and the worldwide revenue received or accrued in the tax year, subject to credit being given for taxation paid abroad.

Double tax treaties

Italy is a party to a large number of bilateral treaties against the double taxation of income (besides those dealing with income derived from shipping, air transport and estates). The treaties which address the taxation of income (of which there exists the largest number) normally define what constitutes tax residence and what constitutes a taxable permanent establishment. In certain instances, the objective nature of the income triggers an absolute presumption of residence of the recipient as far as the taxation of that income is concerned, for instance:

(a) the possession of real property in Italy entails the payment of income tax on the cadastral income, regardless of the residence or nationality of the owner, and regardless of whether the property is let or unlet;

(b) capital gains realised from the disposition of certain Italian securities may be taxable again regardless of the residence or nationality of the person or entity having realised the gain.

In other instances, a recipient of such income (such as dividends, interest, royalties, etc) who is a foreign resident is subject to a withholding tax. If a double tax treaty is in force with the country of residence of the recipient, the rate of the withholding tax cannot be in excess of the treaty rate.

Indirect taxation
VAT is now procedurally unified in the European Union as far as phase one goes, if not with respect to rates. VAT is or is not applicable essentially regardless of the nationality or residence of the person or entity liable. However, non-residents may need to appoint a tax representative in Italy in order to comply with the VAT laws, file returns, make payments, seek refunds, etc.

Other indirect taxation, such as registration tax on the sale of property or a money judgment, stamp duty on transfers of shares, etc as a rule applies equally to Italians and foreign nationals, residents and non-residents alike.

Finally, estate duties and gift tax are levied on the worldwide estate of the deceased and the full gift received from the donor, respectively, if the deceased or the donor was an Italian resident (again, with credit being allowed in whole or in part towards taxation suffered abroad), but only on the estate assets or donated assets situated in Italy if the deceased or the donor was a foreign resident.

Allowing for margins of inconsistency (which remain relatively frequent owing to the extreme, largely unnecessary complexity of the tax system in Italy), it is fair to say that there is no detrimental tax treatment which is a consequence of the foreign nationality of the taxpayer.

• ACCESS TO AND TREATMENT BY LOCAL COURTS •

Italy grants to foreign nationals a full right of access to its courts, on an equal footing with its citizens. Representation by counsel is in practice necessary for Italian citizens and foreign persons alike. The representation of a foreign plaintiff or defendant will need to be documented by a power of attorney, duly authenticated and legalised if made outside Italy. There are no restrictions or limitations whatsoever affecting the constitutional right to bring and defend legal actions in the Italian courts.

Similarly, the treatment of foreign parties by the Italian courts is generally in no way less favourable than that of Italian nationals. However, in summary pre-trial proceedings, the fact that the defendant is a foreign resident – his nationality is irrelevant – and has no assets in Italy, may carry some weight in persuading the court to grant the relief sought. By contrast, the foreign nationality or residence of the defendant in other instances rather entails a more favourable treatment, out of concern that distance, language and communication barriers, and the greater difficulty in taking proper care of one's interests that inevitably follow, should not result in an objective hindrance to the right of defence. To exemplify:

- no *ex parte* summary money judgment is permissible against a defendant who does not have a domicile or a domicile of choice in Italy;
- the deadlines allowed for entering appearance in a legal action are increased with distance if the defendant resides or is domiciled abroad;
- if service of process is to be made outside Italy, a sworn translation of the papers served in the language of the recipient is prescribed;
- if there is no positive proof that the service of process abroad was successful, the court will almost invariably order the repetition of service before proceeding by default;
- if a foreign national is to give evidence as a witness in an Italian court, he will be entitled to an official translator.

• FOREIGN PARENT LIABILITY •

Under Italian law, if a stock company or a partnership limited by shares has or remains with a single member (as opposed to a plurality thereof) and the company becomes insolvent, the single member is unlimitedly liable for the company's obligations having arisen when the entirety of the company's capital was held by him. However, limited companies (not stock companies or partnerships limited by shares) can, from 1993, have a single shareholder following the implementation of EC Directive 667/1989. Subject to the various conditions and accomplishments prescribed by the implementing legislation being observed, the privilege of limited liability will in that event be preserved. When the single member is unlimitedly liable, this applies regardless of his nationality, residence or domicile.

Leaving the specific issue of the liability of the single member aside, the principle of the separate legal personality of bodies corporate is recognised, and foreign and non-resident parents will not be held liable in Italy for the actions and the debts of their subsidiaries unless, for instance, they have issued a guarantee or have voluntarily undertaken a joint and several obligation. However, again in certain specified areas such as banking, insurance, securities, etc the explicit undertaking of certain direct responsibilities, or the making available to the subsidiary or branch of assets by a foreign parent, may be a necessary condition for the granting of consent to the commencement of the subsidiary's operations. In anti-trust matters, where a group concept applies, a parent company may be directly liable for the illegal actions of its subsidiary in Italy, even where it is not the single shareholder thereof.

• JURISDICTION OF LOCAL COURTS •

Italy is a party to the Brussels Convention (see Appendix) on jurisdiction. Italy is also a party to the Lugano Convention (see Appendix) which largely extends the system of the Brussels Convention to the EFTA countries, and which has very recently also come into force. Where either Convention applies, the jurisdiction of the Italian courts will, in judicial relationships with nationals (and essentially residents as well) of the country concerned, be determined exclusively on the basis of the criteria laid down thereby, and the domestic jurisdictional rules will not apply.

Outside the systems of the Brussels and Lugano Conventions, jurisdiction will continue to be determined in accordance with the domestic criteria. In a nutshell, the Italian courts will retain jurisdiction over a foreign national if:

(a) the defendant has his residence, a domicile or a domicile of choice in Italy;

(b) the defendant has a general representative in Italy;

(c) the defendant has submitted to or has accepted the Italian jurisdiction (except in matters where real property situated abroad is at stake);

(d) the action concerns property situated in Italy, or an estate opened in Italy, or obligations having arisen or to be performed in Italy;

(e) the action is connected with another action which is pending in Italy, or has as its object preliminary or cautionary relief sought to be obtained in Italy or relative to matters over which the Italian courts have jurisdiction;

(f) in the reciprocal case, if the foreign court has jurisdiction over an Italian national.

Special criteria apply in shipping, admiralty and intellectual property actions. The foreign defendant may always contest the jurisdiction of the Italian courts, provided he has not purely and simply defended the action on the merits or asserted counterclaims (in which event he may be deemed to have accepted the jurisdiction). Until the case is decided on the merits in the first instance, all parties (thus, including the foreign defendant) may petition the Supreme Court for a preliminary binding ruling on jurisdiction. In this event, the merits case in the court below is stayed until a determination is made by the Supreme Court.

• FOREIGN LANGUAGE DOCUMENTS AND DOCUMENTS •
GOVERNED BY FOREIGN LAW

Documents drawn up in a foreign language are enforceable in Italy, but a translation into Italian will, as a rule (but not necessarily always), need to be tendered if the document is produced in court or in administrative proceedings or is filed with a notary public in Italy. The translation may need to be sworn to or certified, sometimes (but again not necessarily always) by an official translator. Subject to translation requirements being observed, there are no legal reasons why, for instance, a contract between an Italian and a foreign party (or even between Italians), a will, etc should not be drawn up in a foreign language. However, it will in certain instances prove more expedient for the document to be drawn up in Italian and be accompanied by a translation into the foreign language, than the other way round. Documents in which both languages are designated equally binding are not, as a rule, recommended.

Italy is a party to a large number of uniform laws and private international conventions which aim either at regulating substantively in a uniform way situations in which the parties are not of the same nationality or are not domiciled in the same country, or at identifying by objective criteria the domestic substantive law which is to apply if the parties have failed to elect one (for instance, in a contract), or in cases where no such election could be made (for instance, in family relations matters). Among these, of particular interest to the foreign client will be, for instance:

- the 1980 Vienna Convention on the international sale of movables;
- the 1980 Rome Convention on private international law in contractual matters;
- virtually all shipping and air law conventions, etc.

If one remains outside the ambit of a private international law or uniform law convention, the Italian courts will apply the national rules of conflict. These provide for a variety of connecting factors, which will be looked at by the court in its process of identification of the substantive law that is to govern cases which are not, or not entirely, domestic in nature. In a nutshell, these are:

- the nationality of the person concerned as to question of legal capacity, personal and family relations, estates, successions and gifts;
- the place where the property was situated;
- the place where the obligation arose or the contract was made.

Italy will (subject to certain exceptions, eg in employment matters) recognise the election by the parties of a foreign law as the proper law of the contract, except that a foreign law may not be recognised (in contractual and non-contractual matters alike) if this is contrary to Italian public policy. The concept of public policy is very cautiously resorted to in this connection, and Italian courts do not often deny recognition to a foreign law on these grounds.

Italy does not accept the doctrine of *renvoi*. As a result, only the foreign substantive law will be applied, not the foreign private international law. The provisions of foreign law are not proved as matters of fact in proceedings and the Italian courts may acquire knowledge thereof outside the ambit of the rules of evidence. However, it will in principle be in the interests of the party which invokes the application of a foreign law to supply the court with appropriate sources of information, such as, for instance, affidavits, expert opinions, certified copies of the statutes accompanied by Italian translations, precedents and interpretation by the foreign courts, etc.

If an international convention is applicable, the domestic private international law is overridden and will not apply.

• RECOGNITION AND ENFORCEMENT OF FOREIGN • JUDGMENTS

The Brussels Convention (as amended) and the Lugano Convention (see Appendix) also contain a uniform system of recognition and enforcement of foreign judgments, which applies to the judicial relationships between Italy and the countries concerned. The Italian courts have a long record of applying the Brussels Convention, and the recognition and enforcement of foreign judgments on that basis may be expected to be entirely in line with the case law of the European Court of Justice.

Moreover, Italy has for decades been a party to the 1958 New York Convention on the recognition and enforcement of arbitral awards, and is and has been a party to numerous bilateral conventions on the recognition and enforcement of both judgments and arbitral awards which are in force with a variety of countries all over the world.

If the Brussels, Lugano or New York Conventions, or those of a specific bilateral convention apply, the domestic rules of recognition and enforcement of foreign judgments and awards will not apply.

If no multilateral or bilateral convention is applicable, the foreign judgment or award will nonetheless be capable of recognition and enforcement in accordance with the domestic rules, which are ordinarily fairly generously applied by the courts. The recognition and enforcement are accorded either principally by judgment of the competent court of appeals in ordinary proceedings, or *incidenter tantum* by any other court who is seized of a different claim or action, if:

(a) the foreign court had jurisdiction according to the criteria prevailing in Italy, ie if there was substantial identity between the two jurisdictional systems concerned;

(b) the summons was duly served and a reasonable period of time to enter appearance was allowed;

(c) the parties duly entered appearance, or their default was duly ascertained and declared;

(d) the foreign judgment has become final;

(e) the foreign judgment is not in conflict with the judgment of an Italian court;

(f) there is not pending in an Italian court between the same parties an action having the same object having been previously instituted;

(g) the foreign judgment is not contrary to the Italian public policy.

Unless the foreign judgment was made by default (and leaving aside an extremely limited number of other exceptions) the Italian courts will strictly confine themselves to adjudging the fulfilment of those requisites and conditions, and will not review the merits of the case having resulted in the foreign judgment sought to be recognised or enforced. If recognition and enforcement are granted, the foreign judgment accompanied by the Italian judgment granting the same will constitute title for, typically, the levying of execution over assets situated in Italy.

•

Roberto Jacchia
De Berti & Jacchia
Foro Buonaparte 20
Milan 20121
Italy

•

8

JAPAN

•

CONTENTS

•

•

8

JAPAN

•

STRUCTURE OF THE LEGAL PROFESSION

Influences on the present structure of the Japanese legal profession can be traced to as far back as the 8th century, when Chinese legal doctrine had a strong influence on the nascent Japanese legal profession. However, the modern structure of the Japanese legal profession was shaped for the most part after the Meiji Restoration in 1868 when Japan introduced a Western legal system, and in the early post-World War II period when the Japanese Diet approved the present Constitution (shaped largely by the Allied Forces) and passed legislation resulting in two major changes with respect to the Bar.

First, almost all of the power to regulate the Bar was taken from the Ministry of Justice and given to the Japan Federation of Bar Associations (*Nichibenren*), a non-governmental self-regulatory organisation. Japanese practicing attorneys (*bengoshi*) are free from government control. It is compulsory, however, that *bengoshi* and Foreign Law Solicitors (see below) be members of the local bar association and the *Nichibenren*, and subject to their control.

The second major change wrought by the Diet was the introduction of a unified and systematic training system for *bengoshi*, judges and public prosecutors. This system, still in effect, begins with enrolment in an undergraduate university's faculty of law. There, the student's first two years will consist of general education, with the second two years devoted to acquiring a broad general knowledge of law. Generally speaking, those students who wish to pursue a legal career after graduating from the faculty of law must first pass the notoriously difficult National Legal Examination, which traditionally has had a pass rate of approximately 2 per cent. The few students (500 in 1991, 600 in 1992 and 700 in 1993) who do pass the exam then enter the Legal Training and Research Institute for two years of study as apprentices, during which time they receive a government salary, take numerous courses in legal theory and practice and are seconded to civil and criminal courts, to a prosecutor's office

179

and to a local bar association. After passing a final examination, apprentices are eligible to become *bengoshi*, assistant judges or public prosecutors.

In any discussion of the Japanese Bar, mention must be made of its small size – there are about 15,000 practising attorneys from a population of over 125 million. Without further explanation, this figure is slightly misleading, because many functions performed by attorneys in other countries are performed in Japan by legally-trained individuals (discussed below) who are nevertheless not qualified to practise as *bengoshi*. Even accounting for such differences, however, the Japanese Bar is undoubtedly far smaller than its European, and certainly its US counterparts.

Foreign lawyers generally practice in Japan as *gaikokuho jimu bengoshi*, or Foreign Law Solicitors (FLSs), and have been permitted to enter Japan in this capacity under special conditions since 1987. FLSs face a number of restrictions on the scope of their practice, the most significant of which is that they may not advise on any laws of a country other than that in which they originally qualified as a lawyer. Nor can FLSs open offices or advertise in the name of their firms; rather, the firm name must be subordinate to the name of the local FLS. However, this rule is now scheduled to be abolished along with certain other restrictions on FLSs, except the prohibition of hiring *bengoshi* and entering into partnership agreements with *bengoshi*. There are approximately 80 FLSs currently practising in Japan, mainly in Tokyo.

HOW TO FIND A SUITABLE LAWYER

• RECOMMENDATIONS •

Because lawyers are largely proscribed from advertising their services (see below), Japanese firms hoping to generate new clients rely heavily on recommendations. By way of example, approximately 95 per cent of the new clients of this author's firm (Hamada & Matsumoto) came to the firm via referral. Again, because what advertising exists is heavily circumscribed, those seeking counsel in Japan would do well to consult people or companies that already have had such experience.

• LOCAL LAW SOCIETY OR BAR ASSOCIATION •

There are a number of local bar associations in Japan that offer regular legal counselling to foreign nationals at a reasonable hourly rate. For individuals seeking Japanese legal advice regarding their personal affairs, a call to one or several of these associations might be useful. Those in Tokyo are:

(1) Tokyo Bar Association (tel 3581-2201);
(2) DaiIchi Bar Association (tel 3581-2136); and
(3) DaiNi Bar Association (tel 3581-2255).

In addition, the consular section of the US Embassy maintains an annually updated list of *bengoshi* who are interested in representing US citizens.

• LEGAL DIRECTORIES •

Approximately 100 Japanese law firms pay for listings in *Martindale-Hubbell* and some are also listed in *Kime's International Law Directory*. However, depending on the information given, the listing may violate *Nichibenren* regulations (see below).

• ADVERTISING •

Lawyers in Japan are permitted to advertise only specified items such as the name, address and telephone number of the lawyer and his or her office, the bar association of which he or she is a member, the date he or she registered as a *bengoshi*, and information on academic degrees, scope of practice, business hours and the billing rate stipulated by the member bar association. Photographs, family histories, lists of publications and foreign languages spoken are all permissible only in school alumni publications or lawyers' directories for which no fee is paid for the listing.

Probably the best source of information on a given lawyer or firm is a *bengoshi*'s office brochure, which can describe the office's history (with the exception of the names of clients who pay a retainer), introduce members of the office, describe in detail the services provided and discuss any recent office developments. Because *bengoshi* are permitted to distribute office brochures only upon a prospective client's specific request, the individual seeking Japanese counsel should contact a prospective firm and ask for one.

Because the *Nichibenren*'s regulations, including those on advertising, are primarily established by *bengoshi* who are not involved in international legal practice, the rules are in reality drawn rather narrowly from the standpoint of the international practitioner. For example, the Japanese law firms that pay for listings in international law directories – clearly an essential practice for international lawyers – may, depending on the information given therein, be in violation of *Nichibenren* regulations if and when published in Japan. The *Nichibenren* announced recently that *bengoshi* are prohibited from mentioning their offices outside Japan. The author is now seeking the co-operation of other listed offices in attempting to have such overly-narrow rules modified, but because listed offices are only a minority in *Nichibenren*, the changes may take some time.

• LOCAL VISITS AND PERSONAL INTERVIEWS •

Some foreign clients, especially large organisations, may send a representative to Japan to visit a number of law firms to interview partners and/or to conduct a 'beauty contest' before choosing their Japanese legal counsel.

FACTORS IN CHOOSING A SUITABLE LAWYER

• PROFESSIONAL QUALIFICATIONS •

All Japanese lawyers must have passed the highly competitive National Bar Legal Examination and have graduated from the Legal Training and Research Institute, or must have more than five years' experience as a national law school faculty professor and the special approval of a local bar association. All must be registered with a local bar association (one of which is found in each district court jurisdiction, except in Tokyo, where there are three) and the *Nichibenren*, which entitles them to practise throughout Japan.

• LANGUAGE ABILITY •

Although all Japanese have studied English extensively in school, most members of the Japanese Bar cannot communicate in English effectively for business purposes. This is because most Japanese *bengoshi* concentrate on domestic disputes where English is not used, and because preparation for the National Legal Examination often consumes nearly eight years of a lawyer's time – an interval sufficient to forget any English learned. However, a small number (probably less than 5 per cent) of Japanese lawyers do spend a few years in the UK or the US to obtain an LLM or comparable degree and/or to work at a UK or US law firm. These lawyers generally return to Japan to work at large Japanese firms, almost all of which are listed in either the *Martindale-Hubbell* or *Kime's* legal directories, with a notation indicating the individual lawyer's academic history and language proficiency. The excellence of these *bengoshi* is evident in that many of them pass the New York bar examination after one year of LLM study.

· TYPE OF TRANSACTION ·

Because many functions performed by attorneys in other countries are performed in Japan by other legally-trained individuals, the person seeking a lawyer in Japan must pay particular attention to the nature of the task at hand. In addition to lawyers in private practice called *bengoshi*, the following legal professions are practised in Japan:

Notary publics (*koshonin*) handle notarial matters such as certifying or notarising deeds, attesting a variety of private documents and attesting articles of incorporation. Notaries are supervised by the Ministry of Justice, which establishes a schedule of fees which must be paid by the client upon performance of the work.

Patent attorneys (*benrishi*) handle applications for patents, trademarks and other industrial property rights to be filed with the Patent Office of Japan, and related matters. Patent attorneys are permitted to litigate in courts with *bengoshi*.

Tax attorneys (*zeirishi*) handle tax filings and other tax matters. Tax attorneys are entitled to advise, draft and file tax returns, and represent clients in complaint procedures within the Tax Office. Unlike patent attorneys, however, they are not permitted to handle litigation in courts.

Judicial scriveners (*shihoshoshi*) handle company and real estate registrations such as registering transfers of real estate and the incorporation of a company in a registration bureau.

Administrative scriveners (*gyosei shoshi*) draft documents for submission to government or public offices, the drafting of which is not otherwise restricted by law. Their work consists largely of drafting and filing licence applications for small businesses and other legal work relating to such enterprises.

Except for notarial matters, *bengoshi* may handle all the legal matters mentioned above, although a *bengoshi* must be registered as a patent attorney or tax attorney to work in those respective fields; otherwise, the specified areas are reserved for each profession, subject to a registration requirement with each profession's self-regulatory body and subject to supervision by the relevant government authority.

From the above-mentioned specialist fields, foreign clients are probably most interested in patent attorneys. There are approximately 2,000 patent attorneys' offices in Japan, of which roughly half deal with foreign clients. There is no usable patent attorneys' directory in English, but free consultation by patent attorneys is offered every day at the Japan Patent Attorneys'

Association in Tokyo (tel 3581-1211), where schedules of charges for foreign clients are also available.

• FAMILIARITY WITH OVERSEAS CONTRACT TYPES •

As indicated above, a small number of *bengoshi* are familiar with overseas contracts, including UK/US contracts.

• SPECIALISATION IN TOPICS •

Generally, corporate matters including licensing and joint ventures are handled by in-house law faculty graduates who have not passed the National Legal Examination and so are not qualified as *bengoshi*. Specialist areas such as financing, patent, tax, insurance claims, litigation and complex corporate matters are handled by Japanese law firms. In contrast to the common law system of the UK and the US, which requires specialisation of attorneys in those countries, Japan's rigid but simpler continental legal system enables a capable and hard-working Japanese lawyer to handle all fields of practice. Consequently, a single such *bengoshi* can render comprehensive and efficient legal services on a project involving various fields of law.

• ASSOCIATE OFFICES IN BRUSSELS •

There are no Japanese law firms with associate offices in Brussels.

• CLIENT CONFLICTS •

Following the model of the *Nichibenren*, each bar association adopts an ethical code of conduct, violations of which are strictly monitored by a committee that includes non-bar member observers and which can be punished by an order to suspend business or disbarment.

• RIGHTS OF AUDIENCE IN LOCAL COURTS •

Generally speaking, any litigant can represent himself in person or through *bengoshi*.

COMMERCIAL ARRANGEMENTS WHEN INSTRUCTING COUNSEL

• TIME CONTRAINTS AND DEADLINES •

This is a matter to be discussed on a case by case basis, and will necessarily be a function both of the particular client's needs and of the particular lawyer's experience. Obviously, a lawyer who has already extensively researched a given issue will be in a better position to answer questions swiftly regarding that issue than would a lawyer who is facing such questions for the first time. It is probably best, therefore, to approach a more senior partner first who, having the most thorough acquaintance with the firm's experience, will be in the best position to estimate the amount of time a case will require.

• FEE STRUCTURE •

Nichibenren regulations (which are also basically reflected in the regulations of each local bar association) provide that an attorney's fees in Japan will consist of an initial fee and a success fee for litigation and dispute settlement, a service fee, a legal counselling fee, a legal opinion fee, a regular retainer fee and a daily allowance. The *Nichibenren* and the local bar regulations provide for lawyers' fees in great detail, even including permissible ranges of fluctuation, and in theory no deviation from these rates is permitted. In practice, however, figures are somewhat negotiable.

For litigation, the initial fee is payable when an attorney takes a case and is based on the economic value of the subject matter. The success fee is payable upon the accomplishment of the assignment and is based on the economic value of the benefit secured for the client. Other fees are payable in accordance with various provisions of the *Nichibenren* regulations.

In civil cases, the standard initial fee (to be received at the outset) for litigation involving 500,000 yen or less is 15 per cent of the monetary amount involved, with a success fee of equal proportions. Fee scales provide decreasing percentages for each increment of the litigation's monetary value and the benefit derived therefrom, with a 2 per cent initial and 2 per cent success fee for the litigated value and the benefit derived therefrom in excess of one billion yen. A deviation of 30 per cent upward or downward from the standard fees is permissible, depending on the circumstances of the case.

The fee schedules provided for by the *Nichibenren* are mainly concerned with litigation and dispute settlement. Fees for non-litigation matters, which will probably be the primary concern of the foreign client seeking counsel in Japan, commonly involve hourly rates, and these will vary with the level of experience and language ability of the lawyer involved. The *Nichibenren* rules establish a fee of 5,000 yen or more per 30 minutes, but Japanese law firms engaged in international business set their own rates for each *bengoshi*, which can vary somewhat depending on the experience of the attorney and the complexity of the matter. Because *Nichibenren* rates are based on counselling in Japanese, the rates for counselling in foreign languages with practical knowledge of differences between the Japanese and the client's country's legal system and the business involved are normally set higher, generally in the range of 7,000 yen to 10,000 yen per hour. For corporate clients, a retainer fee is sometimes used, but if more time is spent on the case than was originally anticipated, a time charge is ordinarily added.

The present *Nichibenren* fee schedule has been criticised as being overly complex and is currently being reviewed.

When negotiating a fee, it is best to obtain an estimate beforehand, even if the estimate includes some flexibility for contingencies. Requesting details of the time spent on a matter by each individual attorney who worked on the case is not common practice. The time a firm requires will depend on whether it has handled such a matter before; if so, the firm involved will have many of the necessary materials to hand, for which it will charge an appropriate premium. A firm that has not handled a given matter before will not be so advantageously positioned and will need more time, for which an appropriate discount will be made. Generally speaking, as in the West, good Japanese law firms give top priority to their reputation which will be evaluated by each client on the basis of the quality and cost of the work.

• METHOD AND TIMING OF BILLING •

Generally, Japanese attorneys follow the UK/US practice, and it is common to send the client the bill (fee plus out-of-pocket expenses) after a project is completed.

• LEVEL OF EXPERIENCE NEEDED •

In contrast to the usual practice of big law firms in the UK and the US, in Japan the client can ordinarily specify the particular lawyer he wishes to take on an assignment. Of course, this does not preclude a senior lawyer who has been so specified from receiving assistance from more junior members of the firm. After working with a particular firm on a number of matters, a client will sometimes become acquainted with the more junior members there, and will then be in a position to specify a particular *bengoshi* with whom he is especially comfortable.

TREATMENT OF FOREIGN NATIONALS UNDER LOCAL LAW

• RESTRICTIONS, REPORTS AND GOVERNMENTAL APPROVALS •
OF FOREIGN INVESTMENT

Foreign investment in Japan is governed by the Foreign Exchange and Foreign Trade Control Law which defines a foreign investor as one of the following:

(1) A non-resident for exchange control purposes;
(2) A corporation or other organisation formed in accordance with foreign laws or having a principle office located in a foreign country;
(3) A Japanese corporation with 50 per cent or more of its shares or interest owned directly by (1) and/or (2) above; or
(4) A corporation or other organisation with a majority of directors who are exchange non-resident individuals.

Procedures required of foreign investors vary depending on the category of investment, with foreign investment generally categorised as either a direct inward investment or as a capital transaction.

Direct inward investments
Direct inward investments, which generally include:

- acquisitions of interest in a non-listed corporation;
- acquisitions of (in the aggregate) 10 per cent or more of the total issued shares of a listed corporation;
- changes in the objectives of certain foreign owned corporations;
- establishment of certain branch offices; and
- certain large loans made to corporations formed in Japan

must be notified to the Minister of Finance and other relevant ministers in charge of the relevant industries, usually one month before the date of the proposed investment.

After a prior notice is submitted, there is usually a 30-day waiting period during which the government investigates the prior notice. The 30-day period can be shortened or extended in certain circumstances; afterwards, the government will either approve the investment or recommend that it be modified or suspended. Direct inward investments in industries concerned with national safety such as aerospace and arms, or in other important industries such as agriculture, forestry, oil and leather, may entail a longer waiting period for examination.

Technology transfers, or licences from a non-resident to a resident, however, require prior notice by both parties to the Minister of Finance and other relevant ministers in charge of the relevant industries. Such transactions must be notified at least one month prior to the date of the relevant agreement. After the notice is submitted, the procedures applicable to direct inward investments apply.

Capital transactions
Requirements for capital transactions vary with the nature of the transaction involved. Possible requirements include various combinations of prior notice, prior permission and government investigation. More specifically, capital transactions consist of:

(1) Transactions that require prior permission, such as deposit or trust contracts between a resident and a non-resident, and the issue of yen-denominated securities abroad by a non-resident;

(2) Transactions that require prior notice and investigation, such as a resident's loan granted by a non-resident;

(3) Transactions that require prior notice but no investigation, such as a non-resident's loan granted by a resident, foreign currency portfolio investments acquired from a non-resident by a resident, or portfolio investments in any currency acquired from a resident by a non-resident;

(4) Transactions that do not require prior notification, such as certain portfolio transactions in which one party is a security company designated by the Ministry of Finance; and

(5) Transactions controlled by the Ministry of International Trade and Industry (MITI) that involve import or export and that require prior notice, an investigation, a recommendation and an order, including certain offsets with import or export considerations.

• EXCHANGE CONTROLS AND OTHER REGULATORY ISSUES •

Japan has two generally-applicable sets of restrictions – one for peacetime and the other for emergencies.

Peacetime controls apply to the following areas:

(1) Investments that would threaten public or national safety. Applicable areas include aerospace, weapons, nuclear power and certain sectors of the medical industry;

(2) Investments that would seriously affect an existing key industry specifically or the Japanese economy generally. Applicable areas include forestries, fisheries, mining, petroleum and leather; and

(3) Investments in areas where there is no reciprocity or international agreement on direct investment between Japan and the investor's country.

Emergency control restrictions will be instituted if the Ministry of Finance deems that Japan's international balance of payments, the yen's foreign exchange rate or the country's financial or capital markets are likely to be adversely affected by the proposed investment. While peacetime controls are aimed at specific investments, emergency restrictions apply to foreign investment generally.

It is worth mentioning in the context of restrictions on foreign investment that, generally speaking, all Japanese industry is heavily regulated. However, internal and external pressure for some relaxation of the regulatory regime has been showing increasing success.

• TAX TREATMENT •

In assessing its tax liability, a foreign corporation must make several inquiries:

(1) Whether the corporation has a fixed place of business in Japan;
(2) What are the sources of the corporation's income; and
(3) Whether a tax treaty between Japan and the corporation's home country alters the application of Japan's corporation tax law.

Fixed place of business
Generally speaking, a foreign corporation must have a fixed place of business in Japan in order to be subject to Japanese corporate income tax. Japanese domestic tax law provides that fixed places of business include the following:

(1) Branches, offices, factories, warehouses, mines, quarries and similar places;
(2) Construction, installation and assembly activities or the provision of personal services for the supervision of such activities in Japan for over one year; and
(3) The presence of a person who:
    (a) is authorised to and regularly concludes contracts on behalf of a foreign corporation;
    (b) maintains stock from which customer orders are regularly filled; or
    (c) solicits orders or regularly performs other important activities to conclude contracts almost exclusively on behalf of the foreign corporation.

Note that most tax treaties provide a more favourable definition of fixed place of business than the one outlined above.

Offices of a foreign corporation that perform only liaison and research for the corporation, or offices used only to store the corporation's merchandise, or buying offices that ship only to overseas offices of the foreign corporation, will not be considered as fixed places of business.

Even in the absence of a fixed place of business, a foreign corporation will be subject to tax on the following, subject to the provisions of any applicable tax treaty:

- income derived from assets located in Japan;
- income derived from the transfer of real property or rights thereto located in Japan;
- income derived from personal services;
- income derived from immovable property located in Japan;
- income derived from prizes or donation of assets located in Japan;
- interest or dividends earned from Japanese stocks, bonds and loans; and
- income derived from certain transfers of shares.

Tax treaties
A foreign corporation with a fixed place of business in Japan will, in principle, be subject to Japanese corporate income taxes on its income from all sources within Japan: in theory, there need not be a connection between the fixed place of business and the source of the income. In the interest of avoiding double taxation, however, Japan has entered into tax treaties with a number of countries, including the US and most of the countries of the European Union, which generally provide that a foreign corporation's income will be taxed only if it is attributable to a fixed place of business in Japan. That is to say, tax treaties typically require a nexus between fixed place of business and source of income, rendering corporation income not effectively connected with the corporation's fixed place of business in Japan not subject to Japanese corporate income taxes.

• ACCESS TO AND TREATMENT BY LOCAL COURTS •

Article 32 of the Constitution provides that no person shall be deprived of access to the courts, guaranteeing (theoretically at least) that foreign nationals will have access to Japanese courts. With regard to suing the state, however, the breadth of Art 32 is circumscribed by the State Compensation Act, which requires reciprocity in the ability of a foreign national to sue the sovereign.

• FOREIGN PARENT LIABILITY •

Jurisdiction over corporations is determined by the location of the company's principal office or principal place of business or by the domicile of the principal person in charge of the company's affairs. Maintaining a branch office or other place of business in Japan will subject a foreign corporation to Japanese jurisdiction regardless of whether the particular cause of action arose in Japan in connection with the operation of the branch office.

In this regard, foreign corporations seeking to do business continuously in Japan are required to establish an office or place of business in Japan and to register the address of the office and name of the representative. However, failure to do so will not preclude a Japanese court from finding jurisdiction where the company does have a physically recognisable office in Japan. In the absence of such a physically recognisable office or place of business, Japanese courts are generally reluctant to assume jurisdiction, unless Japan has some other connection with the matter. A subsidiary or joint venture established in Japan by a foreign corporation is not itself necessarily an office or place of business of a foreign corporation.

• JURISDICTION OF LOCAL COURTS •

The fundamental Japanese jurisdictional principle is that a suit should be brought before the court sitting at the defendant's domicile (*jusho*). Domicile generally refers to the central place of a person's life, as determined by the person's own attitude towards the place, his or her actions there and other factors. Residence (*kyosho*), a less stringent requirement than that of domicile in that a few months' sojourn can be sufficient to establish the former, will also render a defendant amenable to the jurisdiction of a Japanese court of that site.

A Japanese court will also assume jurisdiction based on (among other things) the place of performance of a contract, the place of a tort (either where the misconduct took place or where the injury occurred, should these be different), and the location of the property or other assets.

• RECOGNITION AND ENFORCEMENT OF FOREIGN • JUDGMENTS

Article 200 of the Japanese Code of Civil Procedure provides that a final and binding foreign judgment will be enforceable in Japan upon four conditions. These are:

(1) The jurisdiction of the foreign court is not otherwise disallowed by law or treaty;
(2) If the defendant is a Japanese national, he or she must have received service of process other than by public notice;
(3) The judgment of the foreign court must not be repugnant to the public order or morals of Japan; and
(4) The foreign jurisdiction must reciprocally recognise the judgments of Japanese courts.

A foreign judgment that is entitled to recognition under Art 200 is also entitled to enforcement. To have the judgment enforced, however, the plaintiff must obtain an execution judgment which carries out the foreign judgment without inquiring into its merits.

Only decisions rendered by foreign courts are entitled to recognition; decisions of administrative tribunals are ineligible. Where a contract specifies that disputes will be settled by arbitration, however, in or outside Japan, Japanese courts will honour the arbitration provision and will dismiss a suit brought in violation thereof.

•

Keiji Matsumoto
Hamada & Matsumoto Law Firm
Sankyu Building
6-14 Kasumigaseki 3-chome
Chiyoda-ku
Tokyo 100
Japan

•

—— 9 ——

LUXEMBOURG

• —

CONTENTS

•

LUXEMBOURG

•

9

LUXEMBOURG

•

STRUCTURE OF THE LEGAL PROFESSION

Luxembourg has an independent legal profession which has been newly organised by a law enacted on 10 August 1991 (*Loi du 10 aout 1991 sur la profession d'avocat, Mémorial A-58 of 27 August 1991*). This Law provides for important aspects of the legal profession, like the Bar Association, admission to the Bar, disciplinary measures and rights and duties of the attorney. The Law has granted a monopoly to licensed attorneys to represent clients in court, and also for the giving of legal advice (Art 2). The Law also provides, as far as confidentiality is concerned, for an absolute duty of secrecy regarding all attorney/client communications (Art 35). Article 458 of the Penal Code applies to the lawyer's duty of confidentiality. To this extent, a breach of such duty would carry criminal sanctions.

Until recently, nearly all Luxembourg law firms were involved in general practice. A recent trend is spreading in the Luxembourg law environment for the concentration of certain law firms in the business law area. This includes banking law, corporate law, commercial arbitration and financial law. The law firms involved are also the largest ones in the city, although there are a limited number of them (not more than five or six).

The qualification of expert in a field of the law is limited to those who have obtained special university degrees or who have concentrated their practice in a particular area of law.

• ADMISSION TO THE BAR •

Since Luxembourg has no university (only a first year in legal studies is offered), the foreign (generally French or Belgian) diploma first has to be recognised by the competent authorities. The candidate then has to attend four months of courses on Luxembourg law. After successful completion of these courses, the candidate is eligible to be sworn in. This is followed by a

195

three-year training period which may be reduced under certain conditions to two years. At the completion of the latter period there is a final examination.

• BAR ASSOCIATIONS •

There are two Bar Associations (*Barreaux*) in the Grand Duchy, one in the judicial district of Luxembourg and the other in the judicial district of Diekirch. There is also a single Administrative and Disciplinary Council (*Conseil Disciplinaire et Administratif*) for the whole profession and the two Bar Associations.

Each of the two Bar Associations has its own structure, and each is governed by its own Bar Council (*Conseil de l'Ordre*). The President of each of the Bar Associations (*le Batonnier*) has a duty to allocate young lawyers as *pro bono* lawyers to clients earning less than a minimum amount, as well as to clients who are unable to find a lawyer. The *pro bono* procedure is soon to be subjected to a Grand-ducal regulation which will be registered with the Parliament very soon.

• BAR COUNCILS •

Each Bar Council has several self-regulatory duties, which include the enactment of rules governing professional responsibility, professional secrecy, legal fees, information to the public about the legal profession and the protection of interests of clients and third parties (Art 19). Each of the two Bar Councils uses their regulatory power to draft internal regulations (*règlements d'ordre intérieur*), which are applicable to the lawyers registered in the respective district.

The Bar Councils also have the duty of examining complaints filed by clients or colleagues against a lawyer. A report is drawn up and the Council decides whether the matter has to be referred to the Administrative and Disciplinary Council for further examination and disciplinary procedure.

HOW TO FIND A SUITABLE LAWYER

• RECOMMENDATIONS •

The best method of identifying a suitable lawyer is to rely on the recommendation of another person or corporation who has used a Luxembourg lawyer's services in the past. New corporations coming to Luxembourg indeed often ask the management of other corporations coming from the same home country about whom they should see for legal advice. Of course, it should be ascertained whether the other corporation from which the recommendation is sought needed legal advice in the same area of the law.

• BAR ASSOCIATIONS •

The Bar Associations (*Ordres des Avocats*) may also indicate names of lawyers specialising in a particular area of the law. However, the Bar Associations may not recommend a specific lawyer and the list of specialised lawyers upon which they rely is not always up-to-date, as many lawyers do not inform the Bars of the specialisation under which they wish to be listed.

• LEGAL DIRECTORIES •

One may also look for a suitable lawyer in a lawyer's directory. There are many of these (all international) with different degrees of reliability. The US Law Directory *Martindale-Hubbell* and *Kime's International Law Directory* are considered to be most useful.

• ADVERTISING •

As already mentioned, the Bar Associations (*Ordres des Avocats*) are the self-regulating bodies of the legal profession for their respective jurisdictions. They decide, within the framework of the Law of 1991, on important issues such as advertising. Advertising has always been very strictly regulated. The only form of advertisement allowed is a listing in professional legal directories. Appearance at conferences, publication of legal articles or monographs is also permitted. It is, therefore, fairly common to see articles in specialised law reviews or periodicals written by Luxembourg attorneys. Participation in panels and congresses is also common among Luxembourg lawyers. The rules might in the near future be somewhat loosened.

The law is silent on the use by attorneys on their letterhead or business cards of specific professional qualifications, specialty in an area of the law, or university degrees. However, in the above-mentioned circular on advertising, the Bar Associations regulate the qualifications, specialisations and degrees that an attorney can include on his stationery and office sign. In particular, the qualification of *avocat*, *avocat-avoué* and *avocat à la cour*, indicating membership of the Bar, the title obtained through a university degree, and the admission to a foreign Bar can be mentioned.

FACTORS IN CHOOSING A SUITABLE LAWYER

• LANGUAGE ABILITY •

When choosing a lawyer, one should consider his ability to work in several languages. If this is applicable worldwide, it is especially important in Luxembourg. With three languages spoken in the country (Luxembourgish, French and German) and many nationalities represented in the business community, Luxembourg is one of the most polyglot countries. The choice of a lawyer will thus depend greatly on the country from which the potential client comes. Most lawyers, but not all, speak English. This should be verified, of course, by anyone anticipating cross-border transactions involving an Anglo-Saxon country, or simply needing English-speakers, before retaining counsel.

• FAMILIARITY WITH OVERSEAS CONTRACT TYPES •

Luxembourg attorneys are allowed to give advice only on Luxembourg law. In a transaction involving aspects of foreign law, collaboration with foreign counsel will be necessary. Nevertheless, some law firms are more accustomed than others to work on cross-border deals involving the application of foreign law. This is especially true with UK and US contracts. Concerning the latter, it should be noted that more and more foreign lawyers are travelling to the UK or to the US to complete their legal education with a Master's degree, and even sometimes with practical training and/or admission to the local bar. Again, the firms involved in financial law are most prepared to handle these matters. A few of the firms involved mainly in business law have recently entered into co-operation agreements with leading Belgian law firms and, by the same token, have access to a complete European network of law firms. Because they offer a 'total service' throughout Europe, these firms are certainly the best prepared in handling matters involving aspects of law of different European countries.

• CLIENT CONFLICTS •

Law firms in Luxembourg remain fairly small, with the result that in practice client conflicts almost never arise. Should this happen, however, even in the absence of regulations on the matter, the lawyers will withdraw from representing the party to the conflict which last retained their services.

• RIGHTS OF AUDIENCE IN LOCAL COURTS •

All lawyers admitted to the Bar in Luxembourg are fully licensed to appear in front of all courts, with one exception: to appear in front of the highest court in Luxembourg, an *avocat* must be assisted by an *avocat avoué*, although this results in a formality, since it is accepted that a signature by an *avocat avoué* affixed to the brief suffices.

COMMERCIAL ARRANGEMENTS WHEN INSTRUCTING COUNSEL

• FEE STRUCTURE •

Luxembourg prohibits contingency fee agreements. An agreement between counsel and client, whereby a client assigns a fixed percentage of the value of the case to his counsel if the latter is successful, would be void.

Lump-sum agreements, whereby a counsel agrees to take over a case for a fixed sum of money, are very rare in practice.

• RETAINER •

In the litigation area, charging a retainer is common.

• METHOD AND TIMING OF BILLING •

Luxembourg attorneys are increasingly calculating their fees on an hourly basis, taking into account the seniority of the lawyer actually in charge of the case, his experience, the difficulty of the subject matter and the importance of the case. Most lawyers who are acting for clients on a regular basis will issue quarterly statements of fees.

• FEE DISPUTES •

Another important duty of the Bar Councils is the special procedure which allows clients to ask for a review of the legal fees charged by an attorney. This procedure, called 'taxation', allows the client who feels that he has been charged too much to refer the dispute to the relevant Bar Council (Art 19). The Council, in its decision, takes into consideration the length and difficulty of the case and the time spent on it by the lawyer.

TREATMENT OF FOREIGN NATIONALS UNDER LOCAL LAW

• RESTRICTIONS, REPORTS AND GOVERNMENTAL APPROVALS • OF FOREIGN INVESTMENT

With regard to inward investment, there is no restriction on foreign owner-ship in Luxembourg, nor is there any restriction on foreign investments.

• EXCHANGE CONTROLS AND OTHER REGULATORY ISSUES •

Transfers to Luxembourg can be made in foreign currency. There are no registration requirements for foreign capital and technology of any type. There are restrictions neither on non-resident currency accounts nor on the repatria-tion of capital or earnings.

• TAX TREATMENT •

Foreign non-resident persons are only taxable on certain Luxembourg source items of income. Withholding taxes are applied to dividend income, income from employment and pension income irrespective of the foreign or national status of the person earning such income. Luxembourg tax law generally does not discriminate between foreign and national taxpayers.

By request to the tax authorities, banks can apply for special allowances for foreign personnel temporarily assigned to Luxembourg. The persons eligible must be either foreign managers of newly-created banks (ie banks established for less than ten years in Luxembourg) or foreign experts hired for their special knowledge in the banking area in the case of a shortage of qualified domestic experts. The application of this special tax regime enables the foreign taxpayer to deduct a supplementary allowance against his income. The benefit of this special allowance is, however, limited to a maximum period of 60 months.

• ACCESS TO AND TREATMENT BY LOCAL COURTS •

Foreign persons are granted access to Luxembourg courts. However, according to Art 16 of the Civil Code and Art 166 of the Code of Civil Procedure, in all except commercial matters foreign plaintiffs may be required to give security for legal costs, unless their home country has a treaty with Luxembourg exempting them from this obligation.

• JURISDICTION OF LOCAL COURTS •

Subject to the rules of conflicts of jurisdiction, Luxembourg courts have jurisdiction over Luxembourg nationals and foreign nationals alike.

• FOREIGN LANGUAGE DOCUMENTS •

In Luxembourg, the official languages are Luxembourgish, French and German. Foreign language documents submitted to a Luxembourg court will have to be translated by a sworn translator into one of the official languages.

• RECOGNITION AND ENFORCEMENT OF FOREIGN • JUDGMENTS

For the recognition of foreign judgments, Art 546 of the Code of Civil Procedure, and Arts 2123 and 2128 of the Civil Code contain the rules which apply generally to all foreign judgments (unless an international treaty is applicable). For judgments of courts of European Union member states different rules apply, as laid down in the Brussels Convention (as amended) (see Appendix).

This Convention does not cover judgments dealing with:

- the status or legal capacity of natural persons;
- rights in property arising out of a matrimonial relationship;
- wills and succession;
- bankruptcy proceedings relating to the winding-up of insolvent companies or other legal entities;
- judicial arrangements, compositions and analoguous proceedings;
- social security and arbitration matters.

For judgments that are not covered by the Brussels Convention, the Luxembourg judge, before granting recognition or enforcement, ascertains whether:

- (a) the decision has become enforceable in the country where it was given;
- (b) the foreign judge has jurisdiction;
- (c) the law that was applicable according to Luxembourg rules of conflict of laws has in fact been applied;
- (d) the foreign rules of procedure have been observed;
- (e) there has been due process;
- (f) it is not contrary to Luxembourg public policy;
- (g) the application of a foreign law was not the result of a fraud (*fraude à la loi*).

Under the Brussels Convention, recognition and enforcement may only be refused:

(1) If such recognition is contrary to public policy in the state in which recognition is sought;

(2) Where the judgment was given in default of appearance, if the defendant was not duly served with the document which instituted the proceedings or with an equivalent document in sufficient time to enable him to arrange for his defence;

(3) If the judgment is irreconcilable with a judgment given in a dispute between the same parties in the state in which recognition is sought;

(4) If the court of the state in which the judgment was given, in order to arrive at its judgment, has decided a preliminary question concerning the status or legal capacity of persons, rights in property arising out of a matrimonial relationship, wills or succession, in a way that conflicts with a rule of the private international law of the state in which the recognition is sought, unless the same result would have been reached by the application of the rules of private international law of that state;

(5) If the judgment is irreconcilable with an earlier judgment given in a non-contracting state involving the same cause of action and between the same parties, provided that this latter judgment fulfils the conditions necessary for its recognition in the state addressed.

In addition, the judgment must not conflict with certain rules on jurisdiction laid down in the Convention.

Judgments of foreign courts are recognised and enforced by a judgment of *exequatur* of a Luxembourg court. Proceedings must be brought in the same way as in all other normal civil matters. A certified copy of the foreign judgment, together with an official translation when required, must be submitted to the court. There are no specific regulations as to the transmission of foreign judgments. The foreign judgment is ordinarily sent by the party wishing to have it enforced in Luxembourg to an attorney who will then submit it to the court.

Judgments concerning the capacity and legal status of persons are effective without a judgment of *exequatur*, but may not be enforced without one.

For judgments that benefit from the Brussels Convention, recognition is automatic and a simplified procedure is applicable. For enforcement a judgment of *exequatur* is also necessary, but the procedure to obtain it has been simplified by the Convention and may be commenced by application to the presiding judge of the district court.

The following documents must be produced:

(a) a copy of the judgment which satisfies the conditions necessary to establish its authenticity;

(b) in the case of a judgment given in default, the original or a certified copy of the document which establishes that the party in default was served with the document instituting the proceedings, or an equivalent document;

(c) documents which establish that, according to the law of the state in which it has been given, the judgment is enforceable and has been served;

(d) when appropriate, a document showing that the applicant is in receipt of legal aid in the state in which the judgment was given.

A certified translation of the documents will have to be produced if the court so requires.

•

Alex Schmitt
Bonn & Schmitt
62 Avenue Guillaume
BP 522
L-2015
Luxembourg

•

---- 10 ----

THE NETHERLANDS

•

CONTENTS

•

THE NETHERLANDS

--- 10 ---

THE NETHERLANDS

——— • ———

STRUCTURE OF THE LEGAL PROFESSION

The legal profession in the Netherlands consists of two specific categories. The first and numerically largest category is *advocaten* (advocates), who are general attorneys at law. The second smaller category is *notaries* (notaries), who are civil law notaries, appointed by the Crown to perform specifically-defined legal services. A third group, *belastingadviseurs*, while not as a general rule legal professionals (although they may be), render advice and assistance with respect to tax matters.

Historically, advocates and notaries have formed separate firms, although not technically required to do so. In recent years, however, the trend has been for advocates and notaries to merge their practices while maintaining the distinction between the different services each group offers. Moreover, most of the larger Dutch law firms have now developed tax practices.

• ADVOCATES •

Advocates are permitted generally to practise in all areas of legal work, with the exception of those services which may only be rendered by notaries. Today those areas consist of, among other things, corporate law, patent and trademark law, anti-trust, employment, bankruptcy and administrative law and litigation. Advocates are also the only practitioners who may appear before most of the higher courts in the Netherlands (ie the District Court, Court of Appeals, Supreme Court).

Advocates are admitted to the Bar in one of the 19 jurisdictional districts of the Netherlands, if they meet the requirements for admission. (Once admitted, however, they may practise anywhere in the Netherlands.) These requirements include, among other things, academic training, which takes four to six years. The professional career of an advocate begins with a three-year apprenticeship during which he or she is supervised by a senior attorney and must, in addition, complete a mandatory professional education course.

All advocates collectively constitute the *Nederlandse Orde van Advocaten*. This is a professional body established by the Act on Advocaten of 1952. This Act subjects advocates to a system of disciplinary law in respect of any act or omission in breach of the duty of care which an advocate has to observe in regard to those whose interest he serves or ought to serve. While only the provisions of the Act determine the scope of the disciplinary review of the activities of advocates, the duty of care and other obligations of advocates are set forth in more detail in the Rules of Conduct published by the *Nederlandse Orde van Advocaten* in 1980. These rules provide, among other things, for the confidentiality of communications between counsel and client and between counsel of opposing parties.

As of December 1993, approximately 7,600 advocates were admitted to the Bar. Approximately 40 per cent of these advocates practise in firms with less than six attorneys. Approximately 28 firms maintain offices with more than 20 advocates. A limited number of these 20 firms maintain foreign (representative) offices. A few firms are part of cross-border partnerships.

• NOTARIES •

Notaries are appointed by the Crown and their number is strictly limited by law. Among the requirements for their professional qualification is an academic law degree, although their course of study varies to some extent from that of advocates. Only notaries are allowed to, among other things, incorporate public and private limited corporations, to enact trusts and wills and to convey real property. Notaries are also subject to a system of disciplinary law, similar to that applicable to advocates, pursuant to the Act on Notaries of 1838.

As of February 1994 approximately 1,140 notaries were appointed, who in turn employed approximately 1,380 assistant notaries. Approximately 10 per cent of the notaries work within law firms. The other notaries have their own firms, which employ, on average, three notaries and assistant notaries.

• TAX ATTORNEYS •

Some law firms also maintain a tax department. As opposed to the tax advisers of the accounting and tax firms, these tax attorneys are advocates and have the same privileges and are subject to the same disciplinary rules as advocates who practise in other areas of law.

• *BELASTINGADVISEURS* •

While the law firms – particularly those with civil law notaries and tax attorneys – provide advice in all areas of law, other professions and businesses such as civil law notaries, accounting firms, tax advisers, process-servers and collection agencies, each provide legal advice in specific areas, sometimes in addition to their other not legally-oriented activities. These other professions and businesses are not discussed in detail here, as their areas of activity are not limited to legal advice or are concentrated on a limited area of legal advice.

HOW TO FIND A SUITABLE LAWYER

• RECOMMENDATIONS •

The best way to find a suitable lawyer is obviously to rely on recommendations of business acquaintances having satisfactory dealings with Dutch law firms. One should consider, however, that each firm is not equally suitable for each problem. Generally speaking, the large firms in the Netherlands are best equipped to deal with complicated problems or problems having cross-border aspects. Of a total of approximately 7,600 lawyers (as per 31 December 1993) 12 firms (mainly based in Amsterdam, Rotterdam and The Hague) employ over 60 lawyers, of which five firms employ over 130 lawyers. The largest firms generally have offices abroad in, for example, New York, London, Paris and Brussels. To approach these offices is an efficient way to be referred to a specific Dutch lawyer who specialises in the problem for which the client seeks advice.

Another way to find a suitable lawyer is to rely on the experience that the client's local counsel may have had with a Dutch law firm. He will probably be able to estimate the nature, complexity and relevant practice areas of the client's problem and therefore the specific knowledge the Dutch counsel will need.

• LOCAL LAW SOCIETY OR BAR ASSOCIATION •

Although it is not a common way to find a suitable lawyer, one could contact the local law society or bar association to obtain a referral to a suitable lawyer.

• ADVERTISING •

It is now a couple of years since Dutch law firms have been allowed to advertise, although few have actually engaged in advertising. Most of the largest firms, however, distribute newsletters, firm's resumés and similar brochures. Obviously one can only hope that the law firm one approaches from an advertisement is competent to deal with the specific problems the client may have.

• CHAMBERS OF COMMERCE AND EMPLOYERS' • CONFEDERATIONS

To approach local chambers of commerce and employers' confederations is an unusual way to find a suitable lawyer. These institutions are not specifically qualified to judge the nature or complexity of the client's problem.

• LOCAL VISITS AND PERSONAL INTERVIEWS •

There is certainly a trend towards personally interviewing a law firm that may potentially handle the client's case. This way one can find out whether the lawyer's approach suits the client and whether the estimated costs are acceptable. Especially when one foresees a longer lasting client/lawyer re-lationship, it is obviously very important that the lawyer's approach matches the client's expectations.

FACTORS IN CHOOSING A SUITABLE LAWYER

• PROFESSIONAL QUALIFICATIONS •

To be admitted to the Bar, the requesting person should have graduated from one of the Dutch university law schools. Admission to the Bar is conditional upon passing some exams and successfully concluding a mandatory education programme within a three-year period. In general, academic standards are high and, as such, are not really an issue in the choice of a suitable lawyer.

• LANGUAGE ABILITY •

When dealing with Dutch lawyers, language problems are not usually an issue either. Although the quality may vary, Dutch lawyers generally speak several languages, including English, German and French. English is widely spoken and written and when dealing specifically with business lawyers, communica-tion in English should not be a problem. You will even find quite a few lawyers who speak Spanish, Italian and other languages.

• TYPE OF TRANSACTION •

The choice of lawyer should be highly influenced by the type of problem the client has. If the problem is solely governed by Dutch law and does not have any cross-border aspects or if the problem is limited to only one legal aspect, a client could select any well-established Dutch firm or a 'boutique' law firm, specialising in one specific field.

However, when the problem is more complex, ie when more than one jurisdiction or several legal aspects are involved, the client may need a more specialised lawyer or a firm that is able to generate more manpower if the problem is time-consuming. In this case, it might be advisable to choose a large firm that has specialised know-how and manpower in several areas of law and that is able to co-operate with its offices abroad which have experience in the foreign law aspects. When the transaction involves buying or selling of real estate or incorporating companies, it is advisable to choose a law firm that also has in-house civil law notaries, since only civil law notaries can execute deeds which are required to convey real estate, incorporate companies or amend companies' bylaws.

• FAMILIARITY WITH OVERSEAS CONTRACT TYPES •

The Netherlands has a rather homogeneous legal system which is uniform for the whole of the country, and therefore the domicile of the law firm does not affect its ability to be consulted regarding any place in the Netherlands or abroad or for one of its lawyers to appear in a Dutch court outside its domicile.

The larger law firms in particular have considerable experience with international transactions and have thorough knowledge of international contract types and foreign law. Since these firms often have offices abroad, time and costs may be saved because specific questions can be referred to these foreign offices.

• SPECIALISATION IN TOPICS •

In the Netherlands the small and medium-sized firms often have a general practice, meaning that they handle cases in several practice areas. The large firms usually have departments of lawyers concentrating on specific areas of the legal practice such as litigation, finance, corporations, labour law, taxation, intellectual property, real property, administrative law, insurance law and bankruptcy. Particularly when the client needs to relate to several practice areas, it is useful to employ a large firm that can deal with all the problems involved, often through several departments. As mentioned before, when the problem is less complex and limited to one practice area, it might be less costly to make use of a medium-sized or small firm.

• ASSOCIATE OFFICES IN BRUSSELS •

Only the largest firms in the Netherlands have offices in Brussels, where extensive knowledge of European law is concentrated. Some other Dutch firms have ties with networks including a Brussels' law firm.

• CLIENT CONFLICTS •

As a general rule, Dutch lawyers are not allowed to handle the case of two or more parties if the interests of these parties conflict or are likely to conflict. If a lawyer handles the case of several parties, he is obliged to withdraw from the case altogether as soon as a conflict of interest arises. These rules apply not only to the individual lawyer but also to any lawyer in one firm.

• RIGHTS OF AUDIENCE IN LOCAL COURTS •

To a large extent Dutch proceedings are conducted in writing. The court, however, does not have the discretion to refuse oral pleadings. As mentioned before, any lawyer in the Netherlands can perform these actions in any Dutch court, if necessary accompanied by another attorney if the action takes place outside his own domicile.

COMMERCIAL ARRANGEMENTS WHEN INSTRUCTING COUNSEL

• TIME CONSTRAINTS AND DEADLINES •

The foreign attorney or client will generally find Dutch advocates and notaries willing and able to work within short time constraints and deadlines. Most law firms now have wordprocessing systems and other forms of automated support technology. However, wherever possible, it is advisable to tell the Dutch counsel in advance the applicable time constraints and deadlines, as Dutch law firms frequently charge special premium rates for work that needs to be done at short notice.

• FEE STRUCTURE •

General rule
The fee structure and retainer is in principle freely negotiable between advocate and client. There is, however, one exception. As opposed to the

situation in the US, professional rules of conduct prohibit an advocate to enter into contingency fee arrangements, unless the case is a debt collection matter and is handled on the basis of the collection rate discussed below.

Guidelines

In the absence of specific arrangements the fees will, in general, be calculated in accordance with the guidelines adopted by the *Nederlandse Orde van Advocaten*. Pursuant to these guidelines, the fee is determined on the basis of the standard hourly rate, the number of hours devoted to the case and certain special factors. Generally, the fee is calculated as follows:

Fee = basic hourly rate × number of hours devoted to the case × special factors

The basic hourly rate as of 1 January 1993 is Dfl 265. This rate is revised annually by the *Nederlandse Orde van Advocaten* and published as soon as possible after 1 January of every year. The basic hourly rate includes general office expenses such as the costs of accommodation, equipment and personnel.

The special factors which affect the basic hourly rate include the financial interest of the case, specialised knowledge needed for the case, the urgency of the case, the experience of the lawyer concerned and – if a case is handled for an individual instead of a company – the ability of the client to pay.

The financial interest of the case is defined as the amount of money at issue in the case. Depending on that amount, the basic hourly rate is multiplied by the following factor:

Financial interest					Factor
Less than	Dfl	7,500			0.7
Between	Dfl	7,500	and Dfl	15,000	0.8
Between	Dfl	15,000	and Dfl	30,000	0.9
Between	Dfl	30,000	and Dfl	150,000	1.0*
Between	Dfl	150,000	and Dfl	300,000	1.5
Between	Dfl	300,000	and Dfl	750,000	2.0
More than	Dfl	750,000			2.5

* This factor is also applied to cases in which the financial interest cannot be determined.

In cases in which specialised knowledge is needed, and in urgent cases, a factor of 1.5 is applied.

Depending on the level of experience of the lawyer involved the following factors apply:

Experience	Factor
Case handled by an apprentice lawyer (generally, less than three years' practical experience)	0.6
Case handled by a lawyer with less than five years' experience	0.8
Case handled by a lawyer with more than five years' experience	1.0

For individual clients with moderate financial means, a factor of 0.7 may apply. Certain clients with a low income may be eligible for services on the basis of a government-paid legal aid scheme. In that case the guidelines of the *Nederlandse Orde van Advocaten* do not apply.

The amount of the fees is calculated as follows:

- all factors which apply to the case are multiplied by each other;
- the final result is multiplied by the basic hourly rate; and
- this sum is multiplied by the total number of hours devoted to the case.

In addition to the fee, an invoice may include disbursements and, to the extent that it applies, Value Added Tax on the fee and/or disbursements at a rate of 17.5 per cent. Generally, VAT will not be charged on the fee for services rendered to a business which is located outside the Netherlands.

The disbursements will include such charges as court fees, bailiff costs and travel and accommodation expenses. For expenses that are difficult to specify – such as postage, telephone, fax and photocopying expenses – a lawyer will generally charge a fixed percentage of the fee, which may not exceed 5 per cent.

As the rules outlined above constitute a guideline only, the lawyer may and sometimes should deviate from these rules, for instance, if they lead to an unreasonably low or unreasonably high invoice. This applies particularly to cases which do not turn out as favourably as originally expected.

Collection rate

For cases involving the collection of money a lawyer may, if agreed in advance with the client, charge his fee on the basis of the 'collection rate'. The collection rate is calculated on the collected amount according to the table below:

Over the first	Dfl 6,500	15%
Over the amount above that up to	Dfl 13,000	10%
Over the amount above that up to	Dfl 32,500	8%
Over the amount above that up to	Dfl 130,000	5%
Over the amount above	Dfl 130,000	3%

In addition to his fee, the lawyer may charge disbursements and VAT as outlined above.

• RETAINER •

Retainers are freely negotiable between advocate and client.

• METHOD AND TIMING OF BILLING •

Although there are no specific rules on the method and timing of billing, most of the large firms invoice on a regular basis – for instance, once every three months – and will include a description of the services rendered in their invoices. If the description contained therein does not satisfy the client that the invoice is commensurate with the agreed fee structure, the client may ask for a statement indicating in more detail the time spent, the rates charged as well as the disbursements.

Lawyers are required to record the time spent on a case as well as the nature of their services. The large law firms maintain a time record system and are therefore able to produce more detailed statements on the time spent and the nature of their services. Arrangements to provide more detailed descriptions regularly with the invoice can, of course, be made in advance.

If a dispute arises over the invoice and cannot be resolved amicably, the Act on Advocaten of 1952 provides for a specific procedure to establish the amount due by the client.

• LEVEL OF EXPERIENCE NEEDED •

Generally, within the scope determined by the legal assistance sought by the client, a client will allow the attorney to seek the assistance of other attorneys within his firm. It is not customary to make arrangements on the number or areas of experience of the attorneys rendering the required advice. These arrangements can, however, be made and are sometimes made in larger cases.

TREATMENT OF FOREIGN NATIONALS UNDER LOCAL LAW

• RESTRICTIONS, REPORTS AND GOVERNMENTAL APPROVALS • OF FOREIGN INVESTMENT

Investments by Dutch nationals and foreign nationals are treated identically. Consequently, there are no laws or regulations which prohibit or limit foreign investment in the Netherlands.

• EXCHANGE CONTROLS AND OTHER REGULATORY ISSUES •

The foreign exchange control is based on the Act on Financial Relations with Foreign Countries (*Wet Financiële betrekkingen buitenland*). Pursuant to this Act, there are no limits on the import of short and long-term capital unless the financial transaction is related to a transaction in 'strategic goods' (ie military and military-related technology).

Residents are required only to supply the central bank with certain information, including information on payments and receipts of amounts exceeding Dfl 25,000.

• TAX TREATMENT •

Foreign non-resident individual taxpayers
With respect to a foreign individual taxpayer, the following sources of income, enumerated in the Individual Income Tax Act (IITA), are taxable:

(1) Profits from a business enterprise conducted through a permanent establishment (branch) in the Netherlands;

(2) Net income derived from existing or previous employment in the Netherlands;

(3) Net income from real estate located in the Netherlands;

(4) Net income from rights to profits from a Dutch business enterprise, other than through securities;

(5) Net income from shares, profit shares, bonds and claims received from a Dutch company in which the payee has a substantial interest;

(6) Net income from certain annuities or periodic payments;

(7) Net income from periodic payments or allowances made by Dutch public entities;

(8) Profits, including capital gains, from a substantial interest in a Dutch company, if the shares do not belong to the assets of the payee's business enterprise.

Income from other sources, such as dividends or interest paid by a Dutch company in which the foreign person does not hold a substantial interest, is not subject to Dutch individual income tax (though dividend withholding tax – which is discussed below – may be due). Other investment income from Dutch sources, including royalties, is presently not taxed in the hands of non-residents.

Itemised deductions are basically not available for non-resident taxpayers, whereas only the lowest personal exemption can be applied. The tax rate on the first bracket is 25 per cent and does not include social security premiums. The rates on the next brackets are equal to those for resident taxpayers (ie 50 per cent and 60 per cent).

For present purposes, only the items (1), (2), (5) and (8) above need to be discussed in somewhat more detail.

Profits from a business enterprise

Non-resident entrepreneurs are subject to Dutch taxation only if some part of their business is conducted through a permanent establishment or a permanent representative in the Netherlands. In practice, the term basically covers the permanent establishment concept which conforms to the OECD model income tax treaties. For unilateral tax purposes, however, real property belonging to the assets of a business enterprise is always deemed to constitute a permanent establishment or branch.

Taxable business profits consist of all income that is derived from an enterprise. Capital gains form part of the concept of 'business profits' and thus are currently subject to taxation. No special tax rate is applicable to capital gains.

The computation of annual taxable business profits is based on the principle of 'sound business practice'. Although this term as such is not defined by law, its scope has been developed and defined in Dutch case law, regulations and public and private rulings.

Once a method for computing taxable income is chosen, it must be used consistently. In practice, any method in accordance with generally-accepted accounting principles may be chosen, unless legal provisions or case law provide otherwise.

Employment and services income

This source of income includes labour income as defined in the Wage Tax Act of 1964, ie all income derived from private or public employment, including salaries, directors' fees, fringe benefits and pensions. The wage tax is a prepayment of individual income tax due.

In the majority of cases, employment income is subject to Dutch wage tax withholding by the employer at the progressive rates for the individual income tax. With respect to employees or members of a board of directors or supervisory board living abroad this is, in principle, also true as long as the activities concerned are performed within the Netherlands. Tax treaties may alter the aforementioned tax liability.

If the employer is not a resident of the Netherlands, wage tax withholding is only required if the employer maintains a permanent establishment or permanent representative in this country.

As regards employees who are assigned to the Netherlands within an international group of companies, favourable tax treatment may be obtained under the 35 per cent ruling. This ruling provides for a tax free expense-reimbursement in an amount of up to 35 per cent of gross employment income. 'Gross employment income' includes any reimbursement of expenses that is related to the personal life of the employee concerned ('mixed' expenses).

Purely business expenses are not included in gross employment income and may (in addition to the 35 per cent lump sum reimbursement) be reimbursed in the usual course of business without incurring any additional tax liability, or may be deducted from taxable income.

With respect to non-employment income, the employee is (upon request) deemed to be a non-resident of the Netherlands for a maximum period of four years. In principle, the 35 per cent ruling may be applied for an eight-year period. However, an interim test is applied after the first four-year period to ascertain whether the conditions imposed in the ruling are still met. These conditions include, ie that the employee has highly-specialised education or offers skills that are not readily available in the Netherlands.

Income and profits from a substantial interest

Generally, a substantial interest is deemed to exist if the shareholder (alone or together with his spouse and close relatives) directly or indirectly holds or has held at any time during the preceding five years shares representing, together with the shares held by close relatives, at least one-third (or together with the shares held by the spouse more than 7 per cent) of the company's nominal paid-in capital (per different class of shares, if any).

The taxable capital gain (or loss) is the difference between the value received for the shares concerned and their acquisition price, but in neither case may the value applied be less than the average amount paid-in on the shares.

It should be noted that, in general, the Netherlands does not levy any individual income tax on capital gains derived from personal property and investments. The taxation of capital gains on the alienation of shares belonging to a substantial interest is the exception rather than the rule.

Since the gain represents a one-off event, the applicable tax rate is reduced to a flat 20 per cent. Accordingly, 20 per cent of the losses can be credited against regular income tax due.

In addition, foreign taxpayers are subject to Dutch income tax with respect to income derived from shares, profit shares, bonds and claims received from a Dutch company in which they have a substantial interest. In this case, the applicable rates are the regular, progressive ones.

Foreign non-resident corporate taxpayers

The Dutch taxable income of foreign corporate taxpayers is determined in accordance with the rules for non-resident individuals. Apart from this, the main difference as compared to a resident company is that a foreign taxpayer is not deemed to commit the total of its capital to a business enterprise. Therefore, a non-resident entity may be taxed in the Netherlands even on non-business income derived from Dutch sources, such as profits from a substantial interest. Business income is taxable only if derived through a Dutch permanent establishment (branch) or permanent representative.

In general, the principal features of the Dutch corporate income tax system and the rules for determining the taxable income of companies are the same as those for individual entrepreneurs discussed above. However, for corporate taxpayers, the computation of taxable income is also based on the principle of sound business practice. Unless otherwise specified in the Corporate Income Tax Act (CITA), or unless the nature of a corporate taxpayer requires otherwise, the rules of the IITA governing the 'profits derived from a business enterprise' are equally applicable.

Formal and informal shareholder contributions to the capital of a company do not influence its taxable income, nor do repayments of share capital, including those out of a capital surplus account that is recognised for tax purposes. Dividend distributions, in any form whatsoever, are not deductible.

The current corporate income tax rate (for resident and non-resident taxpayers) is 35 per cent for taxable income exceeding Dfl 250,000 and 40 per cent for the first Dfl 250,000 of taxable income. The repatriation of Dutch branch profits to the foreign home country is not subject to Dutch withholding tax.

Losses may be carried back to the three preceding taxable years. The loss carry-forward period is eight years. Start-up losses may be compensated indefinitely.

As opposed to many other countries, the Netherlands employs the 'classical system' in taxing corporate profits. This means that shareholders receiving a dividend are not entitled to any tax credit or imputed credit against underlying taxes paid by the distributing company. As regards Dutch corporate share-holders, double taxation is generally avoided by the tax exemption of distributed profits under the participation exemption.

The participation exemption applies to all positive and negative income derived from qualifying shareholdings and ignores such income for corporate income tax purposes. Basically, the exclusion from taxable income relates not only to dividends (including bonus shares and claims), but also to capital gains (including currency gains) and losses in connection with the participation. An exception is made only for losses incurred upon a completed formal liquidation of the subsidiary, provided certain additional requirements are met.

A shareholding qualifying for application of the participation exemption exists if:

- over 5 per cent of the paid-in share capital of a company is held; and
- the shares are not held as 'stock on hand';

and, where the shareholding is in foreign companies, if:

- the shares are not held as a mere portfolio investment; and
- the company concerned is subject to tax on its profits levied by the country in which it is resident for tax purposes.

If the participation exemption applies, costs incurred in connection with foreign participations are generally not deductible for Dutch tax purposes.

In principle, the rules regarding the participation exemption are equally applicable to Dutch branches of foreign corporate taxpayers, provided that the share participation concerned is attributable to the branch's assets.

Dutch withholding tax
Under the Dividend Tax Act of 1965, all income derived from shares, profit sharing rights and other profit sharing securities, such as bonds or notes, issued by Dutch limited companies, private companies or Dutch open limited liability partnerships, is subject to Dutch dividend withholding tax at the rate of 25 per cent. The rate on distributions to foreign, corporate substantial shareholders is, under most tax treaties concluded by the Netherlands, reduced from 25 per cent to 0 per cent or 5 per cent.

The dividend tax withheld may be credited against the individual or corporate income tax due. Any excess credit is refundable. If the foreign payee is not a substantial interest holder, Dutch investment income does not usually trigger any Dutch income tax liability, so that the tax constitutes a final tax.

For tax purposes, the definition of dividend comprises a wide range of income and includes any amount transferred to a shareholder in his capacity as shareholder, such as bonus shares (except those issued against the surplus capital account), claims, hidden distributions and liquidation payments, as long as the amount transferred does not constitute an officially recorded repayment of capital.

The Netherlands does not levy any withholding tax on other interest payments or on royalties.

• ACCESS TO AND TREATMENT BY LOCAL COURTS •

Foreign companies and individuals may institute litigation in Dutch courts against Dutch nationals, provided that the court has jurisdiction over these nationals. Generally, the court will have jurisdiction if the Dutch national is domiciled within the court district.

Foreign plaintiffs are treated the same as Dutch plaintiffs, with one exception. The foreign plaintiff will, at the request of the defendant, be required to post security for the costs of litigation to be paid to the defendant should the defendant prevail. This security may not be required if a treaty between the Netherlands and the country of the plaintiff so provides. Such a treaty exists between the Netherlands, the other EU countries and Japan, but does not exist between the Netherlands and the US. Consequently, US plaintiffs may be required to post the above-mentioned security.

The parties to court proceedings will be represented by local counsel. While the client and local counsel may be assisted by the foreign counsel of the client, only Dutch lawyers have the right to appear in most of the higher courts of the Netherlands — the District Court, Courts of Appeal and the Supreme Court. A foreign counsel from one of the EU countries may appear in court in conjunction with, and having been introduced to the court by, a local lawyer. The court procedure will always be conducted in Dutch. Other languages may be spoken if the court grants permission. The court may then require that the services of an interpreter be used.

• FOREIGN PARENT LIABILITY •

As a general rule, a shareholder of a corporation is not liable for debts of the corporation beyond the obligation to make the agreed contributions in cash or in kind on shares. In a limited number of circumstances, exceptions to this rule apply.

First, a parent company may be held liable for certain debts of its subsidiary if the parent has filed a statement with the Trade Register that it accepts liability for debts arising out of legal acts, such as the execution of agreements and the making and acceptance of offers of its subsidiary. The parent will file such a statement if it wishes to exempt its subsidiary from the requirement to make the mandatory public filing of its annual accounts with the Trade Register. This result can only be achieved if other requirements are met as well, which requirements include that the parent company has to adopt consolidated annual accounts to which the Seventh EC Directive on company law applies.

Second, a parent company may be held liable to creditors of the subsidiary on the basis of a tort claim if it abused its power as the controlling shareholder of the subsidiary. Case law indicates that, under specific circumstances, a parent can be held liable if it was actively involved in the management of the affairs of the subsidiary and allowed its subsidiary to incur debts while it knew that creditors of the subsidiary would remain unpaid.

Finally, a parent company may be held liable for all or part of the deficit in the bankruptcy of the subsidiary if it was the managing director of the subsidiary or, in fact, acted as such. This liability for actual management may only be incurred if the management tasks were apparently neglected and if this mismanagement is an important cause of the bankruptcy.

• JURISDICTION OF LOCAL COURTS •

Pursuant to the Dutch Code of Civil Procedure, a Dutch court will have jurisdiction over any foreign national in litigation instituted by a plaintiff with domicile in the Netherlands. This will not be the case if the parties have accepted the exclusive jurisdiction of another court, of arbitrators, or if a treaty applies that overrules this provision of Dutch national law.

The main treaties that override this provision are the Brussels and Lugano Conventions (see Appendix). These Conventions provide that a party with domicile in a country which belongs to the EU or the European Free Trade Association (EFTA) (the members of which are Austria, Finland, Iceland, Norway, Sweden and Switzerland) can only be sued before a Dutch court if the Dutch court has jurisdiction pursuant to the Brussels or the Lugano Conventions. As the Conventions do not govern the relationship between residents of Japan and the US and the Netherlands, they do not affect the jurisdiction of Dutch courts over Japanese and US residents.

Generally, the Brussels and Lugano Conventions require a plaintiff to sue a party domiciled in another EU or EFTA state before the court of that EU or EFTA state. However, a foreign party may be sued before a Dutch court if:

(a) the action involves a contractual obligation to be performed in the Netherlands;
(b) the action involves a tort committed in the Netherlands;
(c) the action involves real estate located in the Netherlands;
(d) the foreign party agreed to the exclusive jurisdiction of the Dutch court.

• FOREIGN LANGUAGE DOCUMENTS AND DOCUMENTS • GOVERNED BY FOREIGN LAW

Dutch law does not as such distinguish between documents in the Dutch language or in a foreign language. Documents in a foreign language are enforceable.

With respect to the governing law, it is a generally accepted principle of Dutch case law that the parties to an international contract may stipulate the law pursuant to which the contract is to be governed. This rule is also laid down in the EC Convention on the Law Applicable to Contractual Obligations. Consequently, Dutch courts will generally enforce documents governed by foreign law, provided of course that these documents are enforceable pursuant to the law by which they are governed.

There are, however, some exceptions to this rule. First, the parties may not override a special choice of law rule of national law or a treaty that by its nature excludes a choice of law by the parties. This exception prevents, for instance, the parties electing that the foreign law applies on the transfer of title to real estate, which can only occur with the assistance of a civil law notary.

Second, Dutch courts may refuse to apply a rule of foreign substantive law if such a rule is incompatible with the public policy of the Netherlands. An appeal on rules of public policy is, however, almost never recognised by the Dutch courts.

Finally, Dutch courts may apply certain Dutch rules of an internationally mandatory nature that govern the relationship of the parties regardless of the law by which that relationship itself is governed. The mere fact that certain rules are mandatory in a Dutch internal context does not make these rules mandatory in an international context. These rules of an international mandatory nature are therefore exceptional as well. One of the few examples in case law of internationally mandatory rules is the provision in the Decree on Labour Relations that an employment agreement cannot generally be terminated without the prior permission of the regional director of labour relations. This rule also applies on labour agreements governed by foreign law if the interests of the Dutch labour market are affected by the employment agreement.

• RECOGNITION AND ENFORCEMENT OF FOREIGN • JUDGMENTS

As a general rule, foreign judgments cannot be enforced in the Netherlands unless a treaty in force in the Netherlands provides otherwise. The main treaties that provide for the enforcement of foreign judgments in the Netherlands are the Brussels and Lugano Conventions (see Appendix).

Pursuant to these Conventions, judgments of courts of EU or EFTA countries must, as a rule, be recognised and enforced in the Netherlands. The Dutch court is not allowed to review such a judgment on its merits. However, EU or EFTA judgments will not, among other things, be recognised and enforced, if:

- the foreign court had no jurisdiction pursuant to the Convention;
- the defendant did not receive the documents initiating the litigation in time to allow him to defend himself properly;
- the judgment is contrary to the public policy of the Netherlands.

Dutch law provides for a simple procedure in which it can be established that an EU or EFTA judgment can be enforced in the Netherlands.

In the absence of a treaty, the parties will generally be required to re-litigate their case before the Dutch court. Case law indicates that a Dutch court may, nevertheless, be prepared to recognise a foreign judgment in the absence of a treaty if:

(a) the foreign court that rendered the judgment had jurisdiction according to internationally accepted standards, for instance, because the dispute was subject to the jurisdiction of the foreign court pursuant to a clause in the agreement between the parties;

(b) the foreign judgment was rendered after proceedings which meet requirements of due process, such as fair notice and fair hearing;

(c) the foreign judgment is not contrary to Dutch public policy.

This case law may be relevant for those judgments as to which the Brussels or Lugano Conventions do not apply, ie in areas outside the scope of the Conventions or for judgments obtained in the US and Japan.

•

Allard C Metzelaar and J Maurits van den Wall Bake
Stibbe Simont Monahan Duhot
Stibbe Tower
Strawinskylaan 2001
PO Box 75640
1070 AP Amsterdam
The Netherlands

•

11

PORTUGAL

•

CONTENTS

•

11

PORTUGAL

•

STRUCTURE OF THE LEGAL PROFESSION

• REGULATION •

The legal profession is regulated by the lengthy Decree-Law No 84/84 of 16 March which comprises 176 articles. The first part of the Decree-Law sets out the organisational structure of the Bar Association (*Ordem does Advogados*) which governs lawyers in Portugal, and the second part deals with the conduct of the legal profession.

According to the Decree-Law, only lawyers and trainee lawyers duly registered with the Bar Association may, throughout the whole of the national territory, carry out acts which pertain to the legal profession, namely the legal representation of clients or legal consultation, as a remunerated, independent profession.

However, this rule admits of a number of exceptions, which are as follows:

(1) Holders of a university degree in law who are either civil servants or employees may engage in legal consultation without being registered with the Bar Association;

(2) Junior legal clerks (locally called *solicitadores*), if registered with their respective association, may carry out minor functions in the field of client representation and legal consultation;

(3) Law professors and assistants may give legal opinions in writing without the need to be registered with the Bar Association.

The exercise of a legal mandate and the representation of a client by a lawyer, for the defence of rights and assistance in legal disputes, is always admitted and may never be refused by any administration, authority or public entity.

As an independent profession which has a supportive role in the pursuit of justice, the law recognises certain privileges and grants certain guarantees to lawyers. Lawyers may freely choose whether or not to take certain cases and the client may always freely choose the lawyer he wishes to represent him at any moment. Where lawyers are employed by a private or public entity, this employment relationship may in no way affect the technical and professional independence of the lawyer.

All authorities are obliged to treat lawyers in accordance with the dignity of their profession. Lawyers enjoy the right to consult non-secret documents in any court or governmental agency and may request the issue of certificates verbally. They also enjoy a right of access to areas usually reserved for employees in any public buildings, including courts. Furthermore, lawyers are entitled, according to the terms of the Decree-Law, to communicate personally and in private with clients, even when they are imprisoned.

In order to further protect and guarantee the proper exercise of his professional duties, documents may not be seized in a lawyer's office if they relate to the exercise of his profession. Any records of his office or the seizure of such documents can only take place after having been authorised by a judge, and must be carried out in the presence of the lawyer, a representative of the Bar Association and the authorising judge himself.

Since 1980, the incorporation of lawyers' firms has been allowed provided their articles were previously approved by the Bar Association. Once authorised, a legal firm is entitled to carry on the profession on the same basis and with the same guarantees as those afforded to individual lawyers.

Foreign individuals holding a law degree issued by a Portuguese university may register with the Bar Association on the same terms as Portuguese nationals, provided their country of origin grants reciprocal rights to Portuguese nationals. Brazilians, holding either a Brazilian or a Portuguese degree, may register with the Portuguese Bar Association.

Residents of other EU member states who wish to practise law in Portugal on a permanent basis will be admitted to the Bar Association provided all of the following requirements are met:

- proof of being a lawyer in his country of origin;
- documents evidencing reciprocity with his country for Portuguese lawyers;
- that he be resident in Portugal.

Those wishing to carry out sporadic activities as lawyers should notify the Bar Association in advance that they wish to handle a specific case, which must be duly identified, and indicate a sponsor who must be a Portuguese lawyer. The appearance of the foreign lawyer in court in these cases will only be authorised when he is accompanied by the said sponsor.

• ORGANISATION •

Many Portuguese lawyers operate as sole practitioners. Where firms have been established, it is common for there to be a small number, eg four or five, equity partners who effectively own the business and a number of other partners who are in effect salaried partners or associates. There will also be other more junior lawyers as well as trainees. Trainee lawyers undergo an 18-month training period following their law degree.

On qualifying, it is common for lawyers to be given significant responsibility particularly in respect of matters relating to the courts. However, it would be normal for there to be supervision of a newly-qualified lawyer dealing with any matter involving a private client.

• *SOLICITADOR* AND NOTARY •

There are two further branches of the legal profession in Portugal: the *solicitador* and the notary. The Portuguese *solicitador* should not be confused with the English solicitor. A *solicitador* has a similar role to the English legal executive but usually operates independently from firms of lawyers. He is generally not a law graduate but has an important function in dealing with the many administrative procedures in Portugal in the courts and elsewhere, compliance with which is essential to the successful completion of many matters. As such, his assistance and co-operation is often crucial.

One of the principal administrative procedures in Portugal is the practice of notarising many of the documents produced in Portugal. For this purpose there are many notaries, again operating independently of lawyers' offices, carrying out this function. Notaries are, currently, public officers and are required to be law graduates. Notarising involves payment to the notary for certification of a range of matters whether of a signature of a document or of the powers of representation claimed by managers of a Portuguese company.

HOW TO FIND A SUITABLE LAWYER

• RECOMMENDATIONS •

The legal and financial community in Portugal is still a relatively small one and consequently recommendations can often be a reliable source of information when trying to find a suitable lawyer. The main citizens in this community are normally well-known to each other and so a recommendation from such a Portuguese person is likely to be well-informed. In the same way, many of the main UK, US and other northern European transactions involving a Portuguese element will often have been dealt with by a small number of the principal Lisbon law firms which have established some expertise in such matters. Consequently, the recommendation of somebody who has dealt with a particular Portuguese lawyer or firm of Portuguese lawyers on such a transaction may well be a reliable reference.

Many UK firms, which are significantly larger than their continental counterparts, have gone through or are in the process of establishing relationships with Portuguese and other European law firms, and have built up profiles of these lawyers and their specialisations. As such, a company's UK lawyers may prove a useful source of information for business people or in-house lawyers seeking direct representation abroad.

The embassy or consulate of a country is often regarded as a good source of information on local professionals and indeed the British Embassy in Lisbon and Consulate in Oporto have details of lawyers practising in particular fields with knowledge of English which they will provide to casual enquirers.

• LOCAL LAW SOCIETY OR BAR ASSOCIATION •

Common sources of local information on foreign lawyers such as the local law society appear to be of little assistance when seeking a Portuguese lawyer. The Bar Association does not provide details of or information on Portuguese lawyers and would not, in any case, make recommendations.

• LEGAL DIRECTORIES •

The details of several Portuguese firms are included in *Martindale-Hubbell* and *Kime's International Law Directory*.

• ADVERTISING •

Under the professional rules governing their conduct, lawyers in Portugal are still not permitted to advertise their services although, as mentioned above, details of several firms are included in legal directories.

• CHAMBERS OF COMMERCE AND EMPLOYERS' CONFEDERATIONS

The various chambers of commerce and industry throughout Portugal (*Câmara de Comércio e Indústria*) do not provide information on lawyers to foreign nationals although its members may well have access to such information. There are various employers' confederations throughout Portugal but again these are unlikely to provide such information to foreign nationals making casual enquiries. Actual recommendations from any of these bodies are even less likely.

• LOCAL VISITS AND PERSONAL INTERVIEWS •

As part of a general movement towards greater association between lawyers in Europe, several law firms, at least in Lisbon, will be familiar with conducting personal interviews with visitors looking for suitable representation in Portugal and with firms of foreign lawyers looking for standing associations for themselves and their clients with one or more local law firms.

As a more direct way of establishing the compatibility of personalities and, in particular, the standard of English spoken, a visit to a local law firm can be a more reliable source of information than a simple recommendation. Such a meeting also gives a clearer impression of the facilities available and an opportunity to discuss the basis upon which it is anticipated that dealings will be conducted.

Often the firm will be accustomed to providing standard information regarding its specialities and background of its lawyers for use in internal reference systems of potential clients, and in some cases may have its own brochure or other materials for publicity purposes.

Many lawyers in Portugal are still practising alone. Where firms of lawyers have been established these firms are made up of much smaller numbers of partners than their UK, US or other northern European counterparts. Clearly, adequate warning of such a visit should be given so that the appropriate partners are available who have the authority to establish any specific arrangements, financial or otherwise, with a potential client and so that the visitor can meet the people who are likely to be responsible for any future matter.

FACTORS IN CHOOSING A SUITABLE LAWYER

• PROFESSIONAL QUALIFICATIONS •

A Portuguese lawyer will normally have completed a five-year law degree course followed by an 18-month training period which is spent in the employment of a lawyer but also involves attendance at training courses. The technical title of a lawyer during this 18-month training period is *advogado-estagiario*. After the 18 months this shortens to *advogado*.

• LANGUAGE ABILITY •

It is unlikely that many people involved in a matter with a Portuguese element will speak any Portuguese. Consequently, dealing with Portuguese lawyers with a good command of spoken and written English will often be of paramount importance.

Many Portuguese commercial lawyers, at least those practising in Lisbon and Oporto, will speak and write good English; this is particularly true of younger lawyers. The degree of importance attached to written and, in particular, technical or legal English will, of course, depend upon the extent to which any documentation will need to be prepared in Portugal or detailed written advice provided. Where only general information is required, for example, as to Portuguese practice in a given area, fluency in English may be less crucial.

As well as English, Portuguese commercial lawyers will often speak Spanish and, particularly in the case of older lawyers, French.

• TYPE OF TRANSACTION •

The role of the Portuguese lawyer will vary greatly depending upon the Portuguese element in the transaction. This is, therefore, something which should be considered and established at the outset. Where a matter involves various jurisdictions it is sensible to establish, before foreign lawyers are appointed, basic matters such as the law which will govern the transaction and the parties who will be responsible for drafting the documentation and giving any legal opinions.

Where a matter or transaction is to be governed by Portuguese law, clearly the role of the Portuguese lawyer will be significant and the client should choose a firm with the necessary back-up and expertise to conduct the transaction. The converse situation, where only advice on an aspect of Portuguese law or practice is required and where account will simply be taken of this information, is quite different.

To illustrate this difference, take for instance the acquisition by an English company of a Portuguese subsidiary from its English parent. The acquisition will be documented by English lawyers and governed in all probability by English law. However, advice would no doubt be required from Portuguese lawyers on a range of issues relating to the Portuguese company to be acquired, including the effect on that company of the acquisition and any Portuguese tax effects of the transaction. In this case, the role of the Portuguese lawyers would be limited to advising on these particular issues.

As against this there is the situation where the parent company is itself Portuguese and the agreement is likely to be governed by Portuguese law. The Portuguese lawyers would then have a much more significant role in the transaction, probably drafting, negotiating and advising the English acquirer on the terms of the acquisition agreement as well as advising on the matters affecting the target company as discussed above.

If litigation is being undertaken in Portugal, the role of the Portuguese lawyer will be significant and his choice will merit more careful consideration.

• FAMILIARITY WITH OVERSEAS CONTRACT TYPES •

There are often significant differences in the approach of lawyers in different jurisdictions to the drafting of documents and in the usual contents of those documents. The degree to which a Portuguese lawyer is familiar with the normal forms of, in particular, UK and US documentation may be a relevant factor when choosing representation.

The way in which a Portuguese lawyer addresses the drafting of a contract is often quite different from the common UK/US type of contract. Portuguese law implies many provisions into most contracts and consequently it is common practice either to cross-refer to legal provisions or to omit reference to a particular matter altogether on the basis that Portuguese law already provides for the situation in question. This approach is rarely acceptable to UK and US clients (even when assured of the effect of Portuguese law) who generally wish to address matters expressly in the documentation, invariably in detail.

A number of Lisbon firms now have considerable experience in dealing with significant UK/US transactions and are familiar with the usual form and contents of the related documentation. This familiarity may be an important factor in choosing a lawyer where UK/US style documentation is to be used.

• SPECIALISATION IN TOPICS •

The make-up of a Portuguese law firm is quite different from its UK or US counterpart. As mentioned above, the sole practitioner is still the most common way for lawyers to operate in Portugal. However, commercial lawyers increasingly operate in partnerships (although often on a shared expenses rather than shared profits basis) but these formations, even in the largest firms, are not on the same scale as UK, US or some northern European commercial firms. Lawyers are much less specialised and are more likely to address all aspects of law.

At the same time some of the firms will have built up expertise in specific areas such as banking and tax and this should be established, where relevant. There are now lawyers in certain firms specialising in these type of areas and devoting most of their time to their speciality. A number of the larger firms in

Lisbon also have experience of dealing with sophisticated financial instruments and placing methods for the UK or US market such as American Depositary Receipts (ADR) or bond issues which are still rare in Portugal.

• ASSOCIATE OFFICES IN BRUSSELS •

It is most unlikely that any Portuguese firm would have an office in Brussels but, given the importance of the European market, a firm may well have an association with a firm which has such an office and this may be useful where a client is not already represented there.

• CLIENT CONFLICTS •

It is helpful when instructing a Portuguese lawyer to have an idea of the accepted behaviour in a situation where the lawyer has or encounters some conflict in representing his foreign client. The conduct of a Portuguese lawyer in a conflict situation is governed by the requirements of the Bar Association. The rules state that a lawyer must refuse to act where he is already involved in the matter in some other capacity, or where he represents or has represented one of the other parties or where action is being taken against an existing client.

• RIGHTS OF AUDIENCE IN LOCAL COURTS •

A Portuguese lawyer has rights of audience in all lower Portuguese courts and, ten years after qualifying, also in the Supreme Court. During the 18-month training period, referred to above, a trainee lawyer may represent clients in the lower courts on matters involving amounts of up to Esc 500,000. As matters stand, foreign lawyers, even from other EU member states, do not generally have rights of audience before the Portuguese courts unless registered with the Portuguese Bar Association.

COMMERCIAL ARRANGEMENTS WHEN INSTRUCTING COUNSEL

• TIME CONSTRAINTS AND DEADLINES •

It is important to establish at the outset what time constraints or other determining factors, such as deadlines for tax clearances, financial year-ends, etc exist. It is then advisable to settle the timing of the transaction since perceptions of how the matter is to be conducted may well vary. (In Portugal, for instance, most companies' financial year-ends are on the same date, namely 31 December, and so the potential existence of a different year-end may not be apparent.) In particular, the following practical factors may affect the perceived timing of a transaction.

Business hours

Portuguese lawyers tend to start and end the normal business day later than their UK or US counterparts, often starting around 10 am and finishing around 7 pm. Lunch tends to take one and a half hours and is normally taken between 1.30 pm and 3 pm when switchboards are not always manned.

When planning a single day's journey to Portugal for meetings, it is worth bearing in mind that it is normal to break up meetings for lunch outside the office although discussions may continue over lunch.

Holidays

Bank holidays will not always coincide and it is unlikely that an office would have the capability or even the inclination to open and operate on a holiday. It is usual for offices either to close or to work with much reduced staff during August when holidays are commonly taken.

Courts

The Portuguese courts close at Christmas and Easter and for some two months between mid-July and mid-September except for very restricted categories of emergency hearings. Portuguese lawyers are not empowered to serve documents. Service must be effected through the courts which can be a slow process affecting the perceived timing of litigation.

Notarising

The requirement for the notarisation of many documents produced in or outside Portugal but for use in Portugal may well come as a surprise at the end of a matter and cause delay in completing the matter as well as adding to the costs.

Documents, such as the resignation of directors from the board of a Portuguese subsidiary (which may well be signed abroad), will require notarisation in order to be effective in Portugal. Since notarisation of a signature may require the presence of the signatory before a notary, this process can create an unwelcome delay unless anticipated. Documents likely to require notarising should be established at the outset, as should the likely whereabouts of any signatory and a notary outside Portugal, should it prove necessary to use one.

Finally, the absence of a reply from a Portuguese lawyer should not be taken as an indication that an item of correspondence has not been received or is not being acted upon since it is not usual to send any form of acknowledgment.

• FEE STRUCTURE •

Although the time spent on a matter is not usually the overriding factor for a Portuguese lawyer when billing, the principal firms will generally have specific hourly rates for work carried out by their lawyers. These rates will, of course, vary from trainee lawyers to the most senior partner and account will be taken of the value of this work when billing a client. Similarly, at least in the larger firms, it is usual to keep recorded details of the time spent on any matter. Details of hourly rates charged for different categories of lawyers and of time recorded on a matter are not generally made public.

• RETAINER •

The many sole practitioners in Portugal would invariably request a retainer when acting for a client and commonly require periodical payments on account of the final bill. However, firms acting for large international clients would not operate on the same basis. A large international client would not be asked to pay a retainer and its bill is more likely to be based on time spent and the outcome of the matter than on the traditional criteria for billing referred to below.

• METHOD AND TIMING OF BILLING •

Under the rules of the Bar Association, a lawyer should have regard to a number of specified factors when billing his client. These factors include the time spent on a matter, the difficulty of the work, the outcome of the case and the client's financial standing. He is expressly prohibited from agreeing a percentage fee on the basis of the outcome of the matter, whether it be litigation or other business.

It is possible and permissible for a lawyer to ask for an amount in advance on account of the ultimate fees or to request periodical payments on account of these fees. Where continuous services are likely to be required, for example, by a company with continuing interests in Portugal, some firms may be willing to provide these services on a permanent basis for a fixed monthly payment, irrespective of the amount of work which turns out to be involved excluding exceptional matters such as commencing litigation.

It is usual for firms to bill their clients on a quarterly basis in respect of work carried out during that quarter. Firms will commonly itemise a bill in detail specifying correspondence sent, papers reviewed and documents drafted. However, since practice varies in this respect, where a detailed and itemised bill is required this should be established with the firm at the outset so that adequate records are kept.

• FEE DISPUTES •

If a dispute arises over the amount of fees charged by a Portuguese lawyer, one of the ways in which the matter may be resolved is by referring it for an opinion to a division of the Bar Association. An opinion can be obtained from this division as to the fairness or otherwise of the bill delivered and although this opinion is not, in itself, binding upon the lawyer or his client or upon the court in any subsequent litigation, it can be a useful way to settle what might otherwise be a costly dispute.

• LEVEL OF EXPERIENCE NEEDED •

It is probably true to say that Portuguese firms are still of a size and at a stage of developing specialisations that a partner would normally be directly involved in a matter, particularly where a foreign client is involved in view of any unanticipated complications. However, where the continuous involvement of a partner is considered important the fact should be established at the outset. Of course, when specifying the continuous involvement of a partner or other senior lawyer, naturally that person's services will be more expensive than those of a more junior lawyer. There may be aspects of a transaction which can quite properly be dealt with by a more junior lawyer without supervision.

TREATMENT OF FOREIGN NATIONALS UNDER LOCAL LAW

• RESTRICTIONS, REPORTS AND GOVERNMENTAL APPROVALS • OF FOREIGN INVESTMENT

The matter of restrictions and regulations concerning foreign investment in Portugal is one which is in the course of changing as a consequence of the timetable negotiated with the European Union upon Portugal's accession.

As regards direct foreign investments, these are still subject to a prior declaration to be filed with a governmental agency called ICEP which issues an investment prior declaration statement within some three to five months of application. Upon sale of the direct foreign investment the vendor has to complete a form which is sent to the Bank of Portugal for statistical purposes.

Generally speaking, there is no discrimination in the law regarding foreign investors. Some sectors of the economy are still closed to private investment but these restrictions concern foreign nationals and residents alike. An important exception to the above concerns the privatisation programme, implemented over the last couple of years, in which the government has always limited the percentage of equity which may be purchased by foreign nationals. Though this is a clear case of discrimination in breach of the Treaty of Rome, the Portuguese government has maintained, so far successfully, that France and the UK did the same in their privatisation programmes.

Once a foreign investor has obtained ICEP's prior declaration he becomes entitled to remit any dividends, royalties and other charges without restrictions provided the taxes due have been paid. Investors may likewise repatriate the proceeds of the sale of their investment together with any capital gains thereon, again without restriction. Upon conversion of the escudos proceeds into foreign currencies, there is a 9/1000 (nine per thousand) stamp tax payable.

• EXCHANGE CONTROLS AND OTHER REGULATORY ISSUES •

Portugal, prior to joining the European Union, had an array of strict foreign exchange controls which it has been dismantling progressively. As things stand today, the Portuguese government has lifted entirely the exchange controls on financial markets, and now Portuguese-based companies may freely lend, borrow and issue guarantees in relation to non-resident entities.

• TAX TREATMENT •

Personal income tax
Non-resident individuals are subject to withholding taxes on their several sources of income obtained in Portugal which includes income from employment, bank deposit interest, income from shares and securities, commissions and royalties. The withholding tax rates vary between 15 per cent and 25 per cent. These withholding taxes are definitive and income does not need to be declared, except income from immovable property (eg rentals) which must be declared by filing a tax return and paying the amount of tax due, the general rates of which vary between 15 per cent and 40 per cent.

An individual is considered resident in Portugal for tax purposes if he stays in Portugal for a period in excess of 183 days, consecutive or not, within a one-year period.

Corporate income tax
Non-resident companies are subject to corporate income tax on income obtained in Portugal.

Non-resident companies without a permanent establishment are subject to definitive withholding taxes, the rates of which vary between 15 per cent and 25 per cent depending on the source of income. Income from immovable property must be declared by filing a tax return and paying the amount of tax due at a rate of 25 per cent.

A non-resident company is considered as having a permanent establishment in Portugal if it carries on business in Portugal through:

- fixed premises or permanent representation;
- employees or other personnel employed for such purposes for a period of at least 120 days, whether or not consecutive, within a one-year period.

A permanent establishment of a foreign company is subject to corporate income tax in the same way as a Portuguese company, and is therefore subject to the standard corporate income tax of 36 per cent. A municipal surcharge of 10 per cent on the amount of corporate income tax is also payable, bringing the actual rate to 39.6 per cent.

There is no withholding tax on the remittance of profits from a branch to its foreign parent company.

Property transfer tax

This tax is payable by the purchaser (individual or company) of immovable property and calculated on the basis of the purchase price. The tax rate is 10 per cent for building and land for construction and 8 per cent for land.

The purchase of property for residential purposes is exempt from property transfer tax up to an amount of Esc 8,100,000, subject to progressive rates up to Esc 24,200,000 and to 10 per cent thereafter.

Municipal property tax

This tax is payable on a yearly basis by the owner of immovable property on its registered value.

• ACCESS TO AND TREATMENT BY LOCAL COURTS •

Foreign persons have access to Portuguese courts without any discrimination due to their nationality. The court's jurisdiction derives from various criteria set out in the Civil Procedural Code, none of which concerns a party's nationality. The criteria of residence of the parties and of the location of the asset under dispute are the main criteria.

Depositions and testimonial evidence produced before a Portuguese court have to be in the Portuguese language and, if required, the court may order a translator to be present. Equally, documents written in a foreign language have to be translated into Portuguese and such translation legalised under oath by a Notary Public. Otherwise, if anything, Portuguese courts discriminate in favour of foreign nationals having any business to transact before them, taking into consideration the incremental inconvenience associated either with travelling or with a lack of prior experience of local courts.

• Foreign Parent Liability •

According to the Portuguese Companies Act of 1986, it is clear that a foreign parent is not liable for actions undertaken by a local subsidiary except in the case of the existence of a specific guarantee or commitment given by the foreign parent.

However, where the foreign parent may – by itself or together with others related to it by means of a shareholders agreement – elect or appoint a member of the board of a subsidiary or a member of its supervisory counsel, without the other shareholders having a right to vote on such matter, it is jointly liable to the subsidiary for acts caused by such appointed elected officer and is also liable to the subsidiary if the choice of such person was made negligently or for a fraudulent purpose and such person himself acted in breach of his duties. The regime of parent/subsidiary liability is different where both have their head office in Portugal, in which case there are various situations of statutory joint liability to third parties.

• Jurisdiction of Local Courts •

As explained above, local courts have in many circumstances jurisdiction over foreign nationals provided this jurisdiction results from specific rules of competence. (As regards the applicable law, the nationality of an individual is relevant in cases of matters which, because of their very personal nature, the law considers should be regulated by the law of the nationality of the individual. This is, for instance, the case concerning the capacity to celebrate marriage, the contents and effects of any marital contracts regarding the ownership of property and the regime of inheritance on death.)

• Foreign Language Documents and Documents • Governed by Foreign Law

As stated above, no court or Notary Public may enforce or act upon any document which is not in Portuguese.

Among the parties, however, nothing prevents a private agreement being executed in a foreign language and the obligations contained therein are valid and enforceable upon the parties. Translation is only required upon its presentation to court. In the case of documents drawn up abroad which would have been liable to stamp tax if executed in Portugal, these are liable to stamp tax upon presentation to the Portuguese authorities as if they had been executed in Portugal.

In the cases where the rules of competence of Portuguese law so allow, documents may be governed by foreign law. However, Portuguese law and Portuguese courts will always have exclusive jurisdiction where the dispute concerns real property located in Portugal and labour matters concerning a Portuguese employee.

• RECOGNITION AND ENFORCEMENT OF FOREIGN •
JUDGMENTS

As regards the recognition of foreign judgments in Portugal, these will first have to be revised and confirmed by a local court of appeal. This procedure of revision does not entail re-litigation of the merits of the case but will basically check certain formal aspects regarding the formal foreign judgments:

- its authenticity;
- that it is final;
- that the writ was duly served

and the court will then ensure that the revised judgments contain no provisions contrary to Portuguese public order.

For judgments originating in judicial courts of EU member states, the revision procedure referred to above is not required as a separate procedure, as Portugal has now become a signatury to the Brussels Convention (see Appendix). For all other cases, including arbitration decisions, the regime of revision and confirmation remains applicable.

•

Professor Andre Gonçalves Pereira
Gonçalves Pereira, Vinhas, Castelo Branco e Associados
Praça Marguês De Pombal
Nr 1-8th Floor
1200 Lisbon
Portugal

•

—— 12 ——

SPAIN

•

CONTENTS

•

•

•

SPAIN

•

STRUCTURE OF THE LEGAL PROFESSION

The legal profession in Spain is presently structured and organised around a basic rule, the General Statute for the Legal Profession passed by Royal Decree 2,090 of 24 July 1982.

• BAR ASSOCIATIONS •

The governing bodies of the legal profession are the bar associations, which are in turn co-ordinated and represented by the General Council of the Legal Profession. There is a bar association for each province, competent within its territorial scope.

The essential purpose of the bar associations is to organise the practice of the profession and represent it exclusively, to defend the professional interests of their members, to co-operate with and promote justice, etc.

• LAWYERS •

The profession is composed of practising lawyers. These are Bachelors at Law who join the relevant bar association as practising lawyers and who, having a professional office, engage in the defence of the legal interests of others. In order to practise as a lawyer, in addition to being a Bachelor at Law it is necessary:

- to be a Spanish citizen;
- to be of age;
- to be without a disqualifying criminal record;
- to pay the bar association membership fee;

- to pay the contribution to the Mutual Aid Society; and
- to register with the Tax Licence.

Foreign lawyers

Special provisions apply to foreign lawyers who are citizens of other member states of the European Union. Here it is necessary to differentiate between such lawyers who are non-resident in Spain, but wish to provide legal services in Spain on a temporary basis (such as representation of their client in a particular piece of litigation in the Spanish courts), and such lawyers who wish to establish themselves in Spain to practise law on a permanent basis.

So far as the first category is concerned, in accordance with European law, any such lawyer who is properly qualified under the law of the member state where he is established in legal practice can offer legal services on a temporary basis in Spain, and will enjoy the privileges and be subject to the duties which apply to Spanish lawyers. This follows from the implementation in Spain of EC Council Directive 77/249. The Directive does not provide for mutual recognition of qualifications but merely sets up a system so that services rendered, provided that the provisions of the Directive are respected, may be carried out on the basis of possession of the qualifications of the member state where the lawyer has his permanent establishment.

The Directive is very short. Its main aspects are as follows:

(1) All member states will recognise as lawyers the lawyers established in another member state.
(2) Lawyers rendering services in a member state other than the state where they are established cannot be obliged to join the bar association of the state in which the service is rendered or to reside in that state. Nevertheless, they must respect the ethical standards of that state.
(3) Lawyers may represent and defend their clients before the courts or public authorities of the host state, observing the same rules as the lawyers established in that state. For this purpose, the member states may impose the following restrictions:
    (a) the lawyer should introduce himself to the president of the court and as appropriate to the dean of the competent bar association of the host state;
    (b) the lawyer should act together with a lawyer practising before the court in question, who will assume liability before that court if necessary, or with a court solicitor acting before that court.

As concerns the permanent establishment in Spain of foreign lawyers from other member states, Spain applies EC Regulation 89/48 relating to the general system of mutual recognition of law degrees granted in higher education. However, even where the relevant qualifications are possessed, the lawyer concerned must have undergone professional training in Spain of at least three years' duration.

Lawyers who are members of a bar association may form a group for professional practice. A lawyer who is a member of a group practice is prohibited from having an office independent from that practice. When a group practice is organised, it must be recorded on the register kept by the bar association to which it belongs. A group practice is not deemed to exist merely because associates or trainees co-exist with a lawyer in the same office, or because lawyers acting with independent organisation and having no association between them share the same premises.

Finally, anyone with the status of lawyer is authorised both to render legal advice of any kind and to defend and represent his clients before the courts; there is no additional qualification required for this latter duty.

HOW TO FIND A SUITABLE LAWYER

• RECOMMENDATIONS •

The most reliable way of finding a suitable lawyer is through direct recommendation. The person seeking a lawyer contacts companies in his area with experience of similar matters, requesting the names of firms able to assist him. The advantage of this is that it makes it possible to contact someone who is probably already experienced in the sector in which the client operates.

Reference to specialised publications is another reliable form of search, as the main firms together with their most representative clients often appear in them. Another efficient method of reference is to ask contacts with law firms in the client's country for their knowledge of and possible contacts with a given country. In most cases, law firms are in a position to refer the client to one or more local firms with which they have had direct contact and which they trust, from among which the appropriate choice may be made for the matter in question.

• BAR ASSOCIATIONS •

It is unlikely that a bar association will recommend specific lawyers since the association is really at the service of the group as a whole.

• ADVERTISING •

It is not possible for lawyers in Spain to advertise. The General Statute of the Legal Profession referred to in the preceding section (see above) prohibits lawyers from advertising or publicising their services either directly or through the media.

• CHAMBERS OF COMMERCE •

In Spain it is not usual to have recourse to chambers of commerce for recommendations. In certain cases, consulates may be a satisfactory solution, although they are usually advised by their own lawyers and do not necessarily have the experience in a specific matter to provide information of this kind.

• LOCAL VISITS AND PERSONAL INTERVIEWS •

Whatever the formula followed to find a lawyer, it is advisable to supplement it by becoming personally acquainted in a meeting, if the urgency of the matter so allows. This enables the lawyer to explain to the client how the office selected operates, his experience and his speciality, and of course the lawyer in turn makes the acquaintance of his potential client. From this interview and personal acquaintance, including comparison between various firms if interviews are arranged with different firms, the necessary information will be obtained in order to evaluate with little risk of error the lawyers who, in the light of their attitudes, means, specialisation and overall services, may best meet the requirements of the client needing assistance in a foreign country. This will undoubtedly help to ensure that the selection made is correct.

FACTORS IN CHOOSING A SUITABLE LAWYER

• LANGUAGE ABILITY •

The knowledge of languages other than the mother tongue is of decisive influence in ensuring adequate communication with the client. This skill also indicates the lawyer's inclination towards and experience in international transactions.

• TYPE OF TRANSACTION •

It is perhaps helpful to remember that most of the cases placed before a lawyer are not of a single kind but rather of a complex and diverse nature, arising from the structure of the transaction itself. In fact, any transaction proposed by a large undertaking usually has various viewpoints, all of great importance, which have to be appropriately combined so that the proposed transaction is completed satisfactorily. Most of such transactions have commercial, labour, tax, competition and exchange control aspects, etc all of which must be properly known and harmonised.

The chosen firm should have the capacity to co-operate with lawyers from other countries in trans-national operations. A typical example of this would be the purchase of a holding company with subsidiaries in various countries. On the one hand, the purchase agreement would be subject to the law of the purchaser or the seller, but on the other, an entire range of legislation affecting the transaction would have to be taken into account when it is carried out, namely the laws governing the subsidiaries.

This leads us to consider that the most important factor in the choice of the appropriate lawyer is the chosen firm's capacity to furnish integrated services to the client.

• FAMILIARITY WITH OVERSEAS CONTRACT TYPES •

Familiarity with Anglo-Saxon and US agreements is another factor that can be taken into account in the choice of a lawyer. The fact is that in Spain, the number of transactions in which Anglo-Saxon forms of contract are applicable is growing steadily, naturally adapting them to Spanish legislation. Today, no-one is surprised by a purchase and sale transaction in which an entire battery of representations and warranties applicable to it are set out, together with numerous attachments giving the smallest details of the subject-matter of the transaction, or by the performance of the respective legal and financial audits.

• SPECIALISATION IN TOPICS •

In order to furnish integrated services to the client, the firm should be specialised according to fields of law (a requirement ever more essential in a world that is progressively more complex) and should provide the necessary human element, the high professional capacity of each of the specialists participating in the project. Care in the selection of human resources in a law firm is, in the author's opinion, an essential factor to ensure that optimum services are rendered to the client.

The above means that constant training and specialisation must be under-taken and knowledge must be permanently updated both through experience and by the study and analysis of legal texts, case law, attendance at seminars, etc. In addition, the lawyers should be able to communicate fluently with the client in his own language or at least in a language internationally accepted in trade.

Together with human resources, technical means are of enormous impor-tance in providing the maximum quality of service to the client. Undoubtedly a properly-computerised law firm with appropriate means of communication and supported by documentation, accounting and translation services, etc will be more efficient in resolving the problems arising within the mechanics of any transaction.

Therefore, the overall capacity of a law firm to deal with the various problems arising in any operation, combining the appropriate specialists and material means, is a factor of prime importance to be considered when selecting a lawyer.

• ASSOCIATE OFFICES IN BRUSSELS •

From the standpoint of the European Union, where most transactions performed come under European Union legislation with the specialisation and precautions that this entails, an office in Brussels is another factor of great importance when choosing a lawyer. The existence of such an office is a clear sign of the firm's international vocation, of its specialisation in issues of a complex nature and its capacity to be actively present in the suitable forum.

When choosing the firm, it is also of interest to check whether it has a presence in other international forums. It may have offices in various countries or may belong to and take a leading role in lawyers' alliances and organisations.

• CLIENT CONFLICTS •

The lawyer must always place his client's lawful interest before any other. This means that he must at all times procure the best advice for his client through a twofold approach: to do and to refrain from doing. By doing, he has to guide the client in the direction suitable to resolve his problem, advising him on the action to be taken at each stage including, for example, the reasonable settlement of litigation even though there are possibilities of success for the client and its continuation would mean larger fees for the lawyer. By refraining from doing, the lawyer should refrain from advising or co-operating in fraudulent strategies intended to provide the client with unfair enrichment through fraud on the law. The legal profession's responsibility and its main purpose of assisting justice strongly requires advice against participation in such actions to be given even where they could produce a large immediate profit. In the long term, conduct of this kind has catastrophic consequences for those adopting it.

A significant pointer to the ethical conduct of a law firm is the firm's permanence in time. It is unlikely that a firm whose conduct towards its clients and towards society in general is disloyal will remain in existence over many years.

Closely connected with the ethical conduct of a law firm is the problem of how to deal with and resolve conflicts of interest. The Spanish Criminal Code refers to this question, imposing penalties of special disqualification and fining the lawyer who, on undertaking the defence or representation of a given client, afterwards defends, represents or advises the opposite party in the same transaction without the first client's consent.

Regardless of whether or not this conduct is punishable, if a conflict of interests arises, even if it does not fall strictly within the bounds of the Criminal Code, the lawyer should inform the parties of it and resolve the question in such a way that no one is damaged. In the case of doubt, loyalty to the client of longest standing should be the criterion governing disputes of this kind.

COMMERCIAL ARRANGEMENTS WHEN INSTRUCTING COUNSEL

• FEE STRUCTURE •

The bar associations provide a list of standard fees as a guideline for billing. They lay down policies both according to topics, setting out the minimum percentages and amounts that should be charged according to the type of matter in question, and according to the system of billing by time. These fee guidelines are usually followed by law firms in procedural and real estate matters. Lawyers do not have a tariff that regulates their fees.

• RETAINER •

The annual retainer system means that whatever the service rendered, or even if the lawyer's services are not required, the client will pay a certain fixed amount per annum. This mode is often agreed with a variant, setting a fixed amount for what can be considered customary legal services, such as secretary-ship, powers of attorney, preparation of simple documents, etc and billing separately work of a less regular nature such as purchases and sales, mergers, labour restructuring, etc.

This system is in general used less frequently than the hourly billing system (see below), due to the imbalance it creates. On the one hand, the client is obliged to pay a greater or lesser amount even though he may not have used the lawyer's services, or may have done so only superficially, while on the other hand the lawyer may find himself burdened with a heavy workload with the agreed retainer hardly covering his expenses. In the long term, this system usually gives rise to situations that are unsatisfactory for one or other of the parties.

• METHOD OF BILLING •

First, it is recommended that the client sit down with the lawyer in order to ascertain the lawyer's billing system, state his preferences and thereby reach an agreement satisfactory to both parties, not only with regard to given professional fees for a specific transaction, but also with regard to the manner in which the client wishes to be billed in a relationship extending over a period of time. These flexible relations will prevent any disagreeable surprises arising later between the lawyer and the client.

Although there are various systems by which lawyers set their fees, the two basic systems followed are the annual retainer (see above) and the hourly tariff where the lawyer bills the client accordingly to the time devoted to his affairs.

Naturally, hourly tariffs vary according to the category of lawyer entrusted with the matter. Obviously, the cost of an hour of a senior partner is not the same as that of a trainee.

In Spain, large firms use unit sheets or work sheets per client. The lawyer notes the time devoted to the matter daily on the client's sheet, breaking it down into items. With a suitable computer system and a strict time control, the lawyer is thus able to state the number of hours or actions devoted to, for example, an agreement, a memorandum, a meeting, keeping minutes, a telephone conversation, etc.

In this hourly system, basic hourly rates are usually fixed. As a general rule, they may vary between approximately 4,000 pesetas for a trainee to approximately 35,000 pesetas for a senior partner. These hourly tariffs are usually the base. This means that they may be varied in the light of certain factors:

- the place where a meeting is held;
- the need to travel or otherwise;
- the complexity of the matter;
- creativity; or
- urgency

are factors that may mean that the final amount invoiced is not the precise result of multiplying the number of hours by the hourly tariff offered.

As stated above, one of the factors to be remembered when preparing the bill is the urgency with which the service is requested. Deadlines frequently exist today in the preparation of work or the closing of a transaction. These deadlines imply efforts and work that generally require the hourly tariff applied to be amended.

Fixed fees
There are other forms of billing. Sometimes client and lawyer agree on closed and unchangeable fees for a given transaction. These fees will then remain

fixed, regardless of the time that the proposed transaction takes or its complexity.

Contingency fees

Another form of fee is known as the *pacto cuota litis* or contingency fee. Where the contingency fee is agreed, the lawyer assumes the risk and venture of the transaction. If the transaction is not closed, the lawyer is not paid, and conversely, if the transaction is performed, the lawyer collects a percentage of it, which in practice is usually considerably higher than the amount he would have collected had a regular billing system been used. It must be clearly stated that the contingency fee is absolutely forbidden by the code of professional conduct in Spain.

Litigation fees

Because of the complexity of court actions, the time they take and their particular nature, in practice fees for litigation lawyers are usually set according to the size of the sum which is the subject of the litigation and the level of the court reached by the proceedings. It follows that they will be less if the matter is resolved at first instance, or if a settlement is reached before judgment has been passed at any level of court, than if it is necessary to exhaust all the court channels until obtaining a decision from the Supreme Court. Generally, a litigation lawyer invoices the client at the end of each stage in the proceedings.

Provision of funds

A lawyer may request the client to furnish a provision of funds to cover the expenses generated during the transaction. Such expenses may be of the most diverse nature, although they usually cover expenses generated with third parties, such as public authorities for filing of documents, tax payments, notaries, registries, transactions and other fees of official agencies. Other expenses may be due to constant communication with the client necessary in any transaction, such as telephone, fax, travel and accommodation in other cities, etc. These are usually advanced by the law firm and billed to the client together with the professional fees that accrue. The request for a provision of funds is customary practice. Naturally, the use of these funds is carefully accounted for when settling up with the clients and if any balance exists it is refunded.

Advance payment on account

Similar to provisions of this kind are payments requested in advance on account of professional fees. Provisions of this kind are not widely employed by large firms. In most cases, a continuous relationship of trust exists between the client and lawyer so that the lawyer rarely requests the client for an advance payment on account of his fees. However, it must be stated that both provisions of funds and advance payments on account are quite legal and the lawyer may request them or not at his discretion. Requests to cover fees are seldom made except in questions of litigation, although there is a tendency for them to increase in times of crisis with the risk of bad debts.

Negotiating the bill in advance

It is always possible to negotiate the bill in advance, and this is advisable in major transactions. Agreement can be reached on a fixed amount to be billed for a given transaction. This system can be advantageous for both parties. It benefits the client, because even when the firm selected follows a system of hourly billing, the complexity of the transaction may make it hard to forecast its duration, complexity and ramifications. This means the client, once involved in the transaction, may be obliged to meet legal costs exceeding his initial budget. If the amount is fixed, even with certain maximum deviations, this allows him to know very nearly the amount of his legal expenses, and therefore to keep the figures of his investment within the limits he may reasonably have foreseen.

For the lawyer, the system is advantageous as it allows him to be certain of collecting fees in an amount that has been agreed, and therefore to concentrate on his work without additional distractions.

Negotiating the bill at the conclusion of the matter

It is possible to negotiate the bill once the matter has concluded. On the one hand, the matter has already been settled and therefore the client has already had the benefit of the transaction of interest to him, while on the other the lawyer believes, rightly or wrongly, that the matter has been settled and his bill is appropriate for it.

This in appearance leads to a situation of disequilibrium between the client and the lawyer when negotiating a reduction of the bill. As stated, this situation is more apparent than real, because in practice, even in cases where the client considers his bill to be unreasonable, he will discuss the matter with the lawyer. This discussion almost always ends either with the reduction of the bill by the amount agreed, or with the maintaining of the bill, according to which party convinces the other of the justice of the position he is defending. In most cases, situations of this kind, contrary to appearances, do not generate tensions between the client and the lawyer and do not prevent a flexible and fruitful relationship from continuing in the future.

Even where the client agrees with the amount of the bill, he may sometimes request the lawyer for certain facilities for its payment, either because of its amount or because the client's financial situation is not as satisfactory as he would wish. In practice, a reasonable request of this kind may be met without problems and does not cloud the relationship existing between the parties.

Breakdown of bills

A satisfactory client/lawyer relationship requires not only good quality work but also scrupulous attention to what is collected for it. Clients now request a breakdown of their bills more frequently. Rational policies for the billing system not only benefit the client but also lawyers themselves, as they facilitate collection of the bills.

A bill should consist of three basic parts:

(1) the professional fees themselves;
(2) all the expenses incurred by the lawyer on his client's behalf; and
(3) the tax withholdings that have to be made or the taxes levied on the services rendered.

Professional fees

A satisfactory bill should set out the services rendered quite clearly. The detailed breakdown of these services means that each matter dealt with should be duly separated from the others and the lawyer participating in it should be indicated. Next should be included the statement of the hours devoted to the matter, if the hourly tariff system has been selected. Here, the degree of detail varies according to the client's needs. The total number of hours must be stated and it is also possible, where required, to break down the hours devoted to each part of the work or item making up the bill and even to break it down according to the hour of each participating lawyer.

Then the list of lawyers should be given, their categories and the charge per hour for each.

Where the hourly policy is not followed, some of the items described above may be superfluous. However, a proper breakdown of the work performed should be included in any bill, whatever the billing method that has been agreed between the lawyer and his client.

If applicable, any advance payments received as provision of funds on account of the fees should be deducted from the total amount of the fees.

Expenses

Expenses of two kinds are usually generated in any transaction: those incurred with third parties and those arising from the client/lawyer relationship. In the system of billing by time, these expenses are not included in the hourly tariff. Neither is it customary for the expenses of a transaction to be covered in the system in which a fixed and closed bill is agreed, regardless of the time taken to conclude the transaction in question.

Expenses should be clearly and completely justified. The lawyer must provide his client with detailed information as to the expenses included in the bill, stating in the bill or as an appendix to it the various items making up the expenses such as telephone, fax, travel, translations, etc and justifying the use of the provision of funds, if any. At all times, the lawyer should be able to furnish the client, at his request, with the supporting documents, invoices, receipts, etc verifying the expenses incurred.

Taxes

It is a known fact that Value Added Tax is levied on professional fees in Spain at the general rate of 15 per cent. However, some bills bear VAT and others do not. If the bill is addressed to a resident on Spanish territory, then its amount is in fact increased by 15 per cent. This is not the case when the bill is addressed to a resident in another EU country. In this case, the invoice is issued without VAT and this tax would be levied in the country of destination, the recipient in an EU country being able to pass it on. For non-EU countries, the bill is also issued without VAT.

• TIMING OF BILLING •

There are no written rules or set policies on the timing of the issuing of bills. In practice, bills are usually issued quarterly in arrears where there is a relation of ongoing advice, so that the client receives the bill for one quarter within the first 20 or so days of the next quarter. In the case of a single or exceptional transaction, it is not unusual to wait for the transaction to be closed before sending the bill, unless the client prefers to be billed differently.

Nevertheless, other intervals may be taken, eg monthly, if the client so wishes. This system of monthly billing is more frequent where an annual retainer has been agreed on.

• FEE DISPUTES •

Unfortunately, on some occasions where a fee is in dispute, discussions break down and attitudes become radical. In these uncommon situations, neither party is able to convince the other and it proves impossible to close the gap between their positions. By adopting such a radical attitude, the loss is the lawyer's, who is left without a client, and there is loss to the client who fails to pay the bill where the transaction has not been closed. This is because existing Spanish legislation prohibits a lawyer from taking on the defence or advice of a client unless the client produces evidence to the bar association that he has paid the fees of the outgoing lawyer. Thus a situation could arise in which the client would be unable to use the services of another lawyer without paying the first one. It must be stressed, however, that in practice such situations are very rare.

• LEVEL OF EXPERIENCE NEEDED •

The decision as to which person should do the work involved is a problem which frequently arises. The greater the lawyer's experience, the more costly his services will be. However, the quality of the service must be guaranteed whatever the experience of the lawyer who renders it may be. If the client has confidence in the law firm he has selected, then he should let that firm decide which lawyer should work on the case. Law firms usually have controls to ensure that the lawyer chosen has the necessary qualifications for the work he performs. The quality of the product is always supervised and the quality/time ratio is combined so that, while ensuring the appropriate quality, only the time necessary is devoted to the matter.

TREATMENT OF FOREIGN NATIONALS UNDER LOCAL LAW

• RESTRICTIONS, REPORTS AND GOVERNMENTAL APPROVALS • OF FOREIGN INVESTMENT

The treatment of foreign nationals with regard to investments made in Spain is regulated broadly by Royal Decree 671 of 2 July 1992 on foreign investments in Spain and by various regulations of the Directorate General for Foreign Investments implementing it.

Foreign investments in Spain are classified into four categories:

- direct investments;
- portfolio investments;
- investments in real estate;
- other forms of investment.

The general principle is that all of these are liberalised, with no exception, save for non-EU foreign investments in sectors governed by special regulation, as mentioned below, and investments made by public bodies other than the European Union member states, in which cases the system of prior administrative authorisation is applicable. This system of prior administrative authorisation is also applicable to investments from non-EU countries which could have a detrimental effect on the Spanish economy.

Direct investments
Direct investments are those in which the investor acquires an interest that, considered alone or together with the interests already held by that investor, gives it a real influence on the management or control of the company in which the investment is made. Real influence is assumed to exist when the

investor's direct or indirect interest is 10 per cent or more of the company's capital, or when although that percentage is not reached, it permits the investor to form a part, directly or indirectly, of the company's body of administration.

The system applicable to these investments is that of prior administrative verification, whenever the foreign interest exceeds 50 per cent of the capital of the Spanish company receiving the investment either before it or as a consequence of it in addition any of the following conditions occur:

(a) where the amount of the investment exceeds 500,000,000 pesetas;
(b) where the foreign interest in the capital stock plus reserves exceeds 500,000,000 pesetas.

Prior verification is also necessary for loans of over 500,000,000 pesetas with a weighted average life of over five years.

Finally, where the foreign interest exceeds 50 per cent, if the investor is resident in a tax haven then prior verification is necessary even where the circumstances mentioned in paragraphs (a) and (b) above do not occur.

Portfolio investments

Portfolio investments are considered to be those made by the subscription for and acquisition of shares in Spanish companies, acquired both on or off the organised markets, investments made by the subscription for and acquisition of negotiable securities issued by public or private persons or entities and participation in Spanish group investment funds. These investments are free and no prior verification is needed.

Real estate investments

Investments in real estate consist of the acquisition by an individual or juridical person not resident in Spain of title to and other rights in rem on real property located in Spain. No prior verification is required for investments of this kind unless the investment in the real property acquired exceeds 500,000,000 pesetas or where, regardless of its amount, it originates from tax havens.

Other forms of investment

What are known as other forms of investment include those made in joint venture accounts, jointly-owned assets, foundations, economic interest groupings, co-operatives, etc. No prior verification is required for these investments unless their amount exceeds 500,000,000 pesetas or where, regardless of their amount, they originate from tax havens.

Finally, as stated above, specific sectors exist in which investments require express administrative authorisation. These sectors are gambling, television, air transport, radio and activities directly relating to national defence.

Nevertheless, the system of authorisation referred to is not applicable to residents in an EU member state unless the subject of the investment is the production of or trade in arms, ammunition, explosives and war materials, or the operation of final and bearer telecommunications services.

Administrative authorisation is also required for investments made by governments and entities of foreign sovereignty belonging to non-EU states.

• TAX TREATMENT •

Regarding the tax treatment of non-residents in Spain, a distinction must be drawn between income tax and Value Added Tax.

Income tax

Residents

Under the provisions of Acts 18/1991 and 61/1978, the following are considered residents in Spain for tax purposes:

(1) Individuals having their customary place of residence on Spanish territory. Customary place of residence on Spanish territory is deemed to include:
   (a) a stay on Spanish territory of 183 days in any one calendar year; or
   (b) location in Spain of the main nucleus or base of his business, or professional activities or economic interests.

(2) Corporations with legal status which are resident in Spain. Entities resident in Spain are:
   (a) where they are organised pursuant to Spanish law;
   (b) where they have their registered office on Spanish territory; or
   (c) where they have their actual seat of management on Spanish territory, ie the place where the administration and management of the business is effectively centralised.

Both individuals and corporations resident for tax purposes in Spain are liable to tax on their entire worldwide income, regardless of the place where it was obtained. In addition, individuals and corporations who are not considered residents for tax purposes in Spain are liable for taxation in Spain when they obtain income or capital gains produced on Spanish territory. Income considered to be obtained or produced on Spanish territory is that generated by:

- individual businessmen or professionals resident on Spanish territory;
- corporations or public or private entities resident on that territory;
- permanent establishments located in the territory.

The definition of a permanent establishment for tax purposes follows, along general lines, the definition contained in the OECD model convention to avoid double international taxation.

Non-residents

According to the 1993 Budget Act, the tax rates for income and capital gains obtained in Spain by non-resident individuals or corporations are as follows:

- 33 per cent where they are obtained through a permanent establishment located in Spain and, in the case of capital gains, obtained in Spain in the absence of a permanent establishment;
- 25 per cent in general in the case of income other than that set out in the preceding paragraph.

However, the following income obtained by non-residents in Spain is currently exempt from taxation in Spain:

(1) Interest and capital gains arising from movables, when obtained by persons or entities having their customary place of residence in other EU member states and which do not operate through a permanent establishment in Spain;

(2) Interest and capital gains arising from Spanish Public Debt where obtained by non-resident individuals or corporations that operate with a permanent establishment in Spain, the only exception being the interest and capital gains obtained from countries regarded by Spanish law as tax havens.

The tax obligations of non-residents in Spain are complied with by filing with the tax authorities the '210' tax return. At present, the filing of this form and payment of tax debts is not a prior requirement necessary to transfer the funds abroad.

The depository or manager of the property or rights of non-residents, or the payer of the income obtained by non-residents, is jointly and severally liable for the payment of tax debts in respect of the income obtained by or paid to non-residents.

Individuals and corporations non-resident on Spanish territory are similarly obliged to appoint an individual or corporation domiciled in Spain to represent them before the authorities regarding their income tax obligations.

Double tax treaties

The foregoing rules are applicable in the absence of a double tax treaty between Spain and the country of the non-resident obtaining income or capital gains on Spanish territory. However, Spain has signed double tax treaties with most of its neighbouring countries, including the following: Austria, Belgium, Brazil, Canada, Denmark, Finland, France, German

Federal Republic, Hungary, Italy, Japan, Luxembourg, the Netherlands, Norway, Portugal, the UK and Sweden.

The above treaties follow the standard form of the OECD convention with regard to definitions and the distribution of taxation authorities between the various countries. Consequently, income paid to non-residents in respect of interest dividends and royalties are liable to tax at rates below the generally established 25 per cent. Likewise, the double tax treaties entered into, with some exceptions, follow the policy of taxing capital gains obtained by non-residents in the country of residence of the transferor.

EC Directives

In addition to the double tax treaties, Spain recently passed Act 29/1991, giving effect to EC Directives 90/434 and 90/435. The first of these Directives refers to the common tax system applicable to mergers, spin-offs, contributions of assets and exchanges of shares. For the tax system of these transactions, Spanish law follows the Directive's policies relating to the non-taxation of capital gains on the above transactions, and to the evaluation for tax purposes of the elements received according to the amount allocated to them before the merger, spin-off, contribution and exchange transactions were carried out.

Act 29/1991 also gives effect to EC Directive 90/435 relating to the common tax system applicable to parent companies and subsidiaries of different member states of the European Union. The system established, applicable to entities having a direct interest of at least 25 per cent of the capital stock, has among other consequences the effect that profits distributed by a Spanish subsidiary to its parent company resident in another EU member state are not subject to taxation and/or withholding in Spain. The system of Act 29/1991 on parent companies and subsidiaries is not applicable where the majority of the voting rights of the parent company are held, directly or indirectly, by individuals or corporations which are not resident in EU member states, except where:

(a) the parent company actually conducts business directly related to the subsidiary's business;
(b) its purpose is the management and administration of the subsidiary through the appropriate organisation of material means and manpower; or
(c) it is proved that the parent was organised for valid economic reasons and not merely to obtain undue benefit from the tax system established in Act 29/1991.

Value Added Tax

The legal regime governing VAT is contained in Act 37/1992 of 28 December and in Royal Decree 1624/1992 of 29 December. Pursuant to the Act, goods delivered and services rendered between different persons or entities resident in different EU member states are subject to this tax (inter-Union acquisitions of goods) as are imports of goods.

Persons or entities carrying out transactions liable to Spanish VAT are obliged to file returns relating to the commencement, change and ceasing of activities determining liability for the tax, and to request a tax identity number from the authorities.

Persons carrying on a business or profession who are not established on Spanish territory may claim a refund of VAT paid by them or shifted on to them in that territory. Such persons who, although having a permanent establishment located in Spain, do not deliver goods or render services in that territory are equated to those who are not established within the territory for the purposes of the tax. The following conditions are laid down for the claiming of a refund by such persons who are not established in Spain:

(1) Those intending to exercise this right must be established in the European Union, or if not, they must prove reciprocity in favour of businessmen or professionals established in Spain.

(2) During the period to which the application for refund refers, the parties concerned should not, within the territory of application of the tax, have delivered goods or rendered services subject to VAT other than:

(a) services rendered in which the person liable for the tax as the recipient of the service is resident in Spain;

(b) carriage and ancillary carriage services, exempt from the tax under Arts 21, 23, 24 and 64 of the Act.

Those not established in the EU who propose to make use of the right to the VAT refund should have previously appointed a tax representative resident in Spain, from whom the tax authorities may demand a sufficient guarantee.

• ACCESS TO AND TREATMENT BY LOCAL COURTS •

The access of foreign nationals to Spanish courts is fully guaranteed by virtue of the basic right to the protection of the courts enshrined in Art 24 of the Spanish Constitution. This provision is applicable to foreign nationals pursuant to Art 13 of the Constitution and other related articles (eg Arts 27 and 28 of the Civil Code), all without prejudice to the provisions of bilateral and multilateral treaties.

Spanish and foreign nationals are also treated the same in that foreign persons are able to benefit from justice free of charge, provided that they meet the same requirements as those demanded from Spanish nationals for this benefit to be granted. On this matter, without prejudice to the provisions of bilateral treaties, the multilateral conventions should be borne in mind, among which should be noted Convention No 62 of the Council of Europe relating to the forwarding of applications for free legal assistance, dated 27 January 1977 (ratified by Spain on 29 November 1985).

Such access to justice is reserved to persons in full exercise of their civil rights. To determine this full exercise, the provisions of the respective personal law are applicable.

Juridical persons appear before the courts through the individuals who represent them legally.

Foreign nationals also benefit from all the procedural guarantees provided by the Spanish legal system. For example, the law makes special provision for evidence that has to be produced outside Spain, and further provides that foreign persons with insufficient knowledge of the Spanish language should be assisted by an interpreter when testifying, thereby guaranteeing adequate understanding of the sense and meaning of the procedural acts performed, and so forth.

• FOREIGN PARENT LIABILITY •

In principle, save where provided otherwise in bilateral or multilateral conventions, liability is confined to subsidiary entities or companies, since their legal status is independent of that of their parent companies.

However, it should not be forgotten that at present the theory of lifting the corporate veil is becoming widely accepted in Spanish case law. In such cases, an 'action for lifting and return' may take place, to reach the original or main party responsible (the parent entity).

• JURISDICTION OF LOCAL COURTS •

Spanish courts have cognisance of lawsuits arising on Spanish territory between Spanish nationals, between foreign nationals and between Spanish and foreign nationals, according to the provisions of Spanish legislation and the international treaties and conventions to which Spain is a signatory. Cases of immunity from jurisdiction and enforcement laid down by rules of public international law are excepted.

The Basic Act on the Judiciary describes the 'extension' of jurisdiction by defining its limits. In cases falling outside these limits, jurisdiction does not rest with the Spanish courts and consequently no body within the Spanish judiciary has competence.

The Spanish courts thus have jurisdiction in the following circumstances:

(1) *Exclusively*, on questions of:

(a) rights *in rem* and leases of real estate located in Spain;
(b) the organisation, validity, nullity or dissolution of companies or juridical persons domiciled on Spanish territory and with regard to the resolutions and decisions of their bodies;
(c) the validity or nullity of registrations made at a Spanish Registry;
(d) patent registrations or validity and other rights subject to deposit or registration where the deposit or registration was applied for or made in Spain;
(e) recognition and enforcement on Spanish territory of court orders and arbitration awards passed abroad.

(2) *In general terms*:
(a) where the parties have expressly or tacitly submitted to Spanish courts; and
(b) where the defendant has its domicile in Spain.
(c) in the case of the adoption of provisional measures or measures for security with regard to persons or property on Spanish territory that have to be complied with in Spain.

Tacit submission to the Spanish courts occurs, according to case law:
(a) With regard to the plaintiff:
  (i) when precautionary measures are requested prior to the complaint;
  (ii) when application is made for legal aid; or
  (iii) when the preliminary formalities of a lawsuit are commenced.
(b) With regard to the defendant:
  (i) when suspension of the proceedings is requested;
  (ii) when an appeal is lodged;
  (iii) when the respective term in which to lodge opposition to summary proceedings is requested; or
  (iv) when a counterclaim is brought against the plaintiff, even though a plea for change of venue is filed at the same time in the same brief of reply;

(3) *In the absence of the above criteria*, on questions of:
(a) declaration of absence or decease, where the disappeared party had his last domicile on Spanish territory;
(b) disqualification and measures for the protection of the person or property of minors or the incapable, where these have their customary place of residence in Spain;
(c) personal and economic relations between spouses, annulment of marriage, separation and divorce, where both spouses have their customary place of residence in Spain at the time of the complaint or where the plaintiff is Spanish and has his/her customary place of residence in Spain, and where both spouses have Spanish nationality, wherever they reside, provided that the application

is filed in mutual agreement or by one of them with the consent of the other;

(d) affiliation and parent/child relations, where the child has his/her customary place of residence in Spain at the time of the complaint or where the plaintiff is Spanish or resides customarily in Spain;

(e) constitution of adoption, where the adopter or adopted is Spanish or customarily resides in Spain;

(f) alimony, where the creditor thereof has his/her customary place of residence on Spanish territory;

(g) contractual obligations, where these were created or should be complied with in Spain;

(h) tort liabilities where the event giving rise to them occurred on Spanish territory or the author of the damage and the victim have their common customary place of residence in Spain;

(i) actions relating to movables, if these are located on Spanish territory at the time of the complaint;

(j) successions, where the deceased had his/her last domicile on Spanish territory or possesses real property in Spain;

(k) consumer's agreements, where the purchaser is domiciled in Spain in the case of sale by instalments of material movables or loans intended to finance their acquisition;

(l) service agreements or agreements relating to movables where the execution of the agreement was preceded by a personal offer or advertised offer made in Spain, or where the consumer carried out on Spanish territory the actions necessary to execute the agreement;

(m) insurance, where the insured and the insurer have their customary domicile in Spain;

(n) litigation relating to the operation of a branch, agency or commercial establishment, where this is located on Spanish territory;

(o) insolvency, the legislation regulating this shall be applicable.

• FOREIGN LANGUAGE DOCUMENTS AND DOCUMENTS • GOVERNED BY FOREIGN LAW

Documents executed in other countries have the same value in court as documents executed in Spain provided that they meet the following requirements:

(1) The subject matter or contents of the act or agreement is lawful by Spanish law.

(2) The parties have legal capacity to be bound pursuant to the laws of their country.

(3) The form and formalities required by the country where the acts or contracts were executed have been observed.

(4) The documents contain such verification and other requirements as is necessary for them to be accepted as authentic in Spain.

Any document worded in a language other than Spanish must be accompanied by its translation and copies of both. The translation may be prepared privately, in which case, if either of the parties objects to it within three days on the grounds that it is not faithful and accurate, it is remitted to the official Language Interpretation Department for its official translation.

• RECOGNITION AND ENFORCEMENT OF FOREIGN •
JUDGMENTS

There are several considerations to be borne in mind regarding the possibility of relying on the decision of a foreign judiciary as evidence before the Spanish courts. Judgments (particularly in the case of court decisions from common law countries) form a part of the general term 'foreign law' referred to in the last paragraph of Art 12.6 of the Spanish Civil Code, according to which:

> the person invoking foreign law should evidence its contents and validity by the means of evidence admitted in Spanish law. However, to apply it, the judge may also avail himself of the instruments of investigation he may consider necessary, issuing the appropriate orders for that purpose.

Supreme Court case law has construed this paragraph by understanding that application of foreign law is a question of fact and, as such, must be alleged and proved by the party invoking it. The precise nature of the existing law, its scope and its authorised interpretation must be proved in evidence, so that the courts are in no doubt as to its application. This is done through the appropriate duly-attested documents, and repeated practice is that when the Spanish courts are unable to accept grounds for the application of the foreign law with absolute certainty, they must judge and decide pursuant to Spanish law.

Consequently, prior approval or *exequatur* is not necessary if the intention is merely to use the foreign judgment as evidence in a lawsuit being pursued before the Spanish courts.

With reference to the recognition of foreign judgments, within the civil jurisdiction, Spanish courts are exclusively responsible for the recognition and enforcement on Spanish territory of court decisions and arbitration awards passed abroad. If the judgment for enforcement originates from a country where, according to case law, judgments passed by the Spanish courts are not enforced, then it will not be enforceable in Spain. Reciprocity is a fact and must therefore be alleged and proved by the party invoking it. It follows that failure to provide evidence of reciprocity is treated as though there is none.

The Supreme Court has stressed that the court may take cognisance of whether reciprocity does or does not exist, and that reciprocity may be evidenced by any of the means admitted in law; a certificate issued by a foreign court, by two court solicitors or by the consulate of the country of origin. When appraising the existence of reciprocity, case law plays a very important part (and has some value as a precedent).

If a judgment does not fall under any of the categories set out above, it will be enforceable in Spain if:

(a) it has been handed down at the conclusion of personal actions;
(b) it was not a judgment by default;
(c) the obligation, the performance of which was demanded, is lawful in Spain;
(d) the judgment meets the requirements for validity in the country where it was given, and also the requirements demanded by Spanish law for it to be duly attested in Spain.

Enforcement of judgments given in foreign countries is sought before the Supreme Court. The only exception is the case where enforcement rests with other courts pursuant to a treaty.

•

Alvaro Sainz Martin
J & A Garrigues
Antonio Maura 16
28014 Madrid
Spain

•

—— 13 ——

THE UNITED KINGDOM

——— • ———

CONTENTS

•

THE UNITED KINGDOM

•

THE UNITED KINGDOM

——— • ———

STRUCTURE OF THE LEGAL PROFESSION

The legal system of the UK is composed of three distinct jurisdictions: England and Wales, Scotland and Northern Ireland. In respect of each system, the legal profession falls into two mutually exclusive categories; that of solicitors and barristers who play different, though increasingly overlapping, roles.

Although there are differences in each of the three jurisdictions, they are very closely aligned. For example, laws passed by the UK Parliament apply to all three jurisdictions unless otherwise specified. Both for this reason and historically, the corresponding legal professions are for all practical purposes identical. For the purposes of this chapter, the position in England will be discussed. However, there is little difference in practice in the other jurisdictions, although different legislation regulates the details of the professions there.

There are three main structural differences between solicitors and barristers which impact on their respective roles:

(1) Barristers (other than barristers in a position of employment) have full rights of audience before all the courts of England and Wales (in the case of an English barrister). 'Rights of audience' refers to the right of an individual directly to address a judge or other judicial person in a court. The limitation on solicitors in this regard is that, although they have rights of audience before lower courts, and in certain interlocutory matters in higher courts, they presently have no right of audience in the High Court, the Court of Appeal or the House of Lords (the highest Court of Appeal). Solicitors' rights of audience currently are in the process of being extended.

(2) Barristers practise independently of each other, usually being grouped together in a chambers which may have a particular specialisation. In contrast, solicitors practise within partnerships (which are sometimes

quite large), individual solicitors within a firm usually not operating independently of others in the same partnership.

(3) Clients may not normally instruct barristers directly, but must do so through a solicitor (or, for example, through a chartered accountant).

As a result of their wider rights of audience, a barrister's practice typically focuses on his skills as an advocate. In addition, barristers frequently specialise in one or more speciality areas of the law and so also may serve as a consultant in that regard. As a result, a barrister normally will only be required in very specific circumstances and in addition to the services of a solicitor.

However, the practice of a firm of solicitors, particularly that of a larger firm, typically encompasses a very wide area of the law and so is able to act as a client's legal adviser for the full range of a client's business transactions. Firms are usually divided internally into specialised groups. Subject to their limited rights of audience, most firms also engage in advocacy.

Thus, commercial transactions are likely to be undertaken wholly by solicitors, although a barrister may be consulted on any unusually difficult point which may arise.

Depending on the nature of any litigation which is undertaken, one factor being which court will hear the case, solicitors may employ barristers in their capacity as advocates or as specialist consultants.

HOW TO FIND A SUITABLE LAWYER

The first step which a client must take in establishing a relationship with a lawyer is carefully to consider for what purposes the lawyer is sought. For example, instructing a lawyer in respect of a particular transaction will involve wholly different considerations from establishing a general services relationship with a firm of lawyers.

• RECOMMENDATIONS •

The most reliable method probably is to seek out recommendations from colleagues with relevant experience of the UK legal services market. 'Relevant experience' means that a recommendation from a colleague regarding experience in, for example, a shipping transaction, does not really carry much weight if the client is seeking anti-trust advice. In this regard, it should be noted that there is a size-related differential. While the very large firms of solicitors are likely to have considerable scope for possessing specialist knowledge and skills in a number of areas, the smaller or medium-sized firms are likely to be able to give specialised advice in only more limited areas. A corollary of this is that the very large firms are more likely to be able to provide a broad spectrum legal service to its clients if that is required, rather than more specialist advice. There are, of course, smaller firms with strong reputations in their specialist fields.

In seeking out recommendations, a useful source of information is likely to be lawyers in the client's own country who may have some greater or lesser knowledge of the UK legal services market. Seeking the recommendations of such lawyers will be particularly important where it is anticipated that the foreign lawyers and the UK lawyers will be working closely together.

• LEGAL DIRECTORIES •

A secondary source of information may be found in international legal directories such as *Martindale-Hubbell*, *Kime's International Law Directory* or *The Legal 500*, which is an assessment of solicitors' firms practising in the UK. A further source of information may be specialist trade journals which intermittently review market perceptions of firms specialising in that particular area. It is desirable that names extracted therefrom are tested against whatever market place perceptions can be obtained.

• ADVERTISING •

Solicitors (and barristers) are permitted to advertise, subject to strict rules governing the contents of such advertisements. In general, advertisements are neither a useful nor recommended way of identifying a firm of solicitors suitable to one's needs. Advertisements in the form of marketing brochures which highlight the firm's scope of practice and its areas of expertise are of some greater use. Such brochures may provide an opportunity to open a dialogue with the firm in question.

• BEAUTY PARADES AND PERSONAL INTERVIEWS •

For a larger, more complex or potentially high value transaction, a client may seek to identify a small number of potential firms of solicitors and subject them to a 'beauty parade'. The idea behind a beauty parade is that, after receiving a brief of the particular transaction, each firm provides a synopsis of its ability to deal with the transaction. The synopsis will include matters such as the firm's prior experience of transactions of that sort, the resources (possibly including the identity of significant people) that it anticipates it will devote to the matter and, perhaps, a preliminary summary of the general approach it sees as being appropriate to that particular matter. One advantage of such beauty parades is that the client is likely to benefit in terms of cost from the resulting competition.

Of course, all of the above approaches should, with appropriate modifications, be used in identifying a suitable lawyer. Thus, although the transaction may not be suitable to give rise to a beauty parade, it may be sensible, following the recommendation of a colleague, to interview a number of potential legal advisers to gain a perception of what is on offer. Interviews are useful not least because different firms of solicitors have different house styles and a client should, as far as possible, ensure that the house style of the firm matches his desires or needs.

FACTORS IN CHOOSING A SUITABLE LAWYER

• PROFESSIONAL QUALIFICATIONS •

Every solicitor and barrister will have completed higher academic studies together with professional training prior to being eligible to be admitted to the relevant arm of the legal profession.

Throughout their professional careers, solicitors are required to undertake a minimum level of professional education and training every year (in the form of seminars, courses, conferences, etc) to ensure that their legal knowledge and development remains well-informed and up to date.

As a result, in considering a prospective solicitor's professional qualifications, the focus very much should be on such a person's or firm's professional experience rather than on academic qualifications although the latter, of course, are not to be ignored.

• LANGUAGE ABILITY •

English is the common language of international business and this places UK lawyers in a most advantageous position in terms of the spoken and written word in relation to international transactions. Nevertheless, linguistic ability can be of paramount importance in enabling a client's legal needs to be met both professionally and commercially by his legal advisers.

Because of London's position as one of the world's leading financial and commercial centres many English law firms, particularly the larger ones, have access to a wide range of linguistic expertise from among their own personnel in London, their overseas offices, associates and connections. This facility also exists to a lesser extent in the principal provincial centres.

• TYPE OF TRANSACTION •

The type of transaction or project which a potential client is contemplating will have a great bearing on the choice of solicitor.

The first decision which will need to be made is whether English legal advice is required at all. It will be essential to seek the advice of an English lawyer wherever an English court might be considered to have jurisdiction. For example, if the proposed transaction involves entities established or resident in England or if it is proposed that the agreement should be governed by English law, an English court may have jurisdiction in any future litigation. English law often is used as the law governing international transactions not only because of London's position in the international market place, but also because English law is a highly regarded and well-developed legal system. This may be the case even where the transaction itself has no tangible connection with England.

Second, the type of transaction affects a potential client's choice in three ways:

- whether the transaction is of an international character;
- whether the transaction is of a highly specialised nature or involves a complex or difficult area of law;
- whether the transaction is large or complex, involving several different areas of law.

• FAMILIARITY WITH OVERSEAS CONTRACT TYPES •

Clearly, where a transaction has an international character, familiarity with different countries' legal systems and cultures will be an important factor in choosing an English legal adviser. Many London law firms, particularly the larger ones, have considerable experience of international transactions and an in-depth knowledge of contract types and foreign laws. Many will be able to draw on the experience accumulated by their overseas offices, associates and connections. This experience is unlikely to be found among provincial law firms, due to the strong focus of international legal business in London.

• SPECIALISATION IN TOPICS •

Where a transaction is highly specialised or complex, solicitors with appropriate expertise must be sought out and, where the transaction is large and involves several complex areas of law, the range of ability and expertise available within a firm of lawyers must be considered.

In both cases, because of the structure of the legal profession, it should be noted that one normally chooses a firm of solicitors with particular reference to individual solicitors therein. In this respect, size is an important differentiator in the English legal market. Only perhaps the largest firms in England have the ability to offer a high degree of specialisation and experience across a wide spectrum of legal activity. Other, smaller, firms will tend to specialise in particular fields, competing at the highest levels only in those particular areas of specialisation.

Many of the reference materials on English law firms differentiate between firms on the basis of specialisation. The following represents a non-exhaustive list of some of the international specialisations covered: asset finance and leasing, aviation, banking, capital markets, commodities, company/commercial, EC and competition law, construction, corporate finance, employment, energy, environmental law, financial services, insolvency, insurance, intellectual property, litigation, property, shipping and tax.

However, it becomes more complicated where the potential client is seeking a longer-term, or more general role for his English legal advisers.

Historically, recipients of legal services focused their strategy on a 'one-stop' approach, seeking to develop a relationship with one firm across several fields. This approach has the advantage of ensuring both that commercial and legal know-how relating to the client can be pooled firm-wide (leading to cost-savings and the development of client-specific expertise) and that a strong relationship can be built up between the client and its advisers. Recently, as the process of legal specialisation has continued, clients have sought to 'shop around', seeking specific services from the appropriate specialists within firms and to tender for specific services on a regular basis. This approach has the advantage of allowing the client to focus its resources on maximising the quality of advice in each relevant area and may also save costs in specific areas. The disadvantage is that close relationships will not so easily develop and the ability to obtain general advice is likely to be reduced.

• ASSOCIATE OFFICES IN BRUSSELS •

The potential client or the particular transaction may have a European Union dimension; for example, a cross-border transaction involving an EU member state will require a careful analysis of European legislation and may require lobbying within various EU institutions. In such cases it will be important to discover whether a particular law firm has a branch or associate office in Brussels or at least strong connections there.

• CLIENT CONFLICTS •

General guidelines concerning client conflicts are laid down by the Law Society of England and Wales, the body which regulates solicitors practising in these countries. The broad principle is that (subject to very limited exceptions) a solicitor must not accept instructions to act for two or more clients where there is a risk of conflict between the interests of those two clients. This guideline reflects a general fiduciary duty which exists in English law. Failure to comply with the guidelines is likely to result in disciplinary action being taken by the Law Society. Similar guidelines exist for solicitors practising in Northern Ireland and Scotland.

• RIGHTS OF AUDIENCE IN LOCAL COURTS •

As discussed above, solicitors and barristers do not have equal rights of audience. However, a potential client will normally instruct a firm of solicitors and where appropriate, the firm of solicitors will engage a barrister. If the case involves smaller or less complex matters, it may be desirable to consider the advocacy skills available within a firm of solicitors.

COMMERCIAL ARRANGEMENTS WHEN INSTRUCTING COUNSEL

• GENERAL •

The fundamental problem is how to obtain the best possible legal advice at the lowest possible cost. This does not mean simply obtaining a low cost legal service since this approach, if carried to its logical conclusion, would result in one taking no legal advice at all. What it means is attempting to obtain the right level of service and quality to fit the particular transaction or advice required. Accordingly, it is always a mix of cost against quality of service.

The level of legal skills required and the amount of legal expenses which should be incurred should correspond to the difficulty and importance of the matter in question. One would expect to incur much greater legal expense on a large and complicated acquisition across borders with commensurate tax problems than a small and technically simple acquisition of, for example, a single property.

The same thing applies when selecting the lawyers to advise on transactions. One should seek to use lawyers whose experience and practice most nearly matches the nature of advice required. Of course, the very large firms will tend to be able to advise on a very wide variety of matters and, particularly when the client is overseas, may by virtue of their experience with the client's jurisdiction be better able to assist.

However, the need to apply a 'horses-for-courses' approach remains. Using lawyers to handle transactions which are larger or different from those they commonly handle is likely to mean that the true value received will be low whatever the actual cost incurred. The same can be true if a firm is handling a transaction which is significantly smaller and simpler than those it normally handles since the firm's fee structure is likely to be geared to larger transactions.

Another major consideration is the speed at which a transaction is to be completed. This is particularly acute if a transaction is of some size and complexity since, in that case, the ability of the firm physically to provide the resources is a major consideration which will greatly affect the cost. It generally is the case that a well-ordered timetable, which is neither too tight nor too loose, results in the most efficient use of outside lawyers. Too tight a timetable will normally mean that excess resources have to be made available, whereas too slow a timetable can mean that too much time is spent.

Therefore, it is important, so far as possible, to identify the nature of the work required and the timetable before selecting the lawyers. Once these have been identified, it is not only easier to select the type of lawyer required, but also to agree the basis upon which the lawyers are to be remunerated.

Split profession

One must first bear in mind that the legal profession in England is split (see above). Thus, when dealing with lawyers in England a client is likely to be dealing with solicitors. In the event of litigation or in certain other circumstances a client may deal with barristers, either directly or through solicitors. The fees of barristers are negotiated with their clerks on a case by case basis. In these negotiations the clerks will take into account all factors considered by them relevant, including the size and complexity of the case, the experience of the barrister and the overall work load of the barrister. In litigation work the fees will be negotiated early on whereas in advisory work the fees will normally be settled after the advice has been given.

For the purposes of the rest of this section, the discussion assumes that the client is instructing solicitors.

Instructing the solicitor

A crucial aspect in how much a transaction will cost is how it is handled. Although it is often difficult to be certain as to the amount of work that will ultimately be required, particularly in larger transactions, one can seek to minimise unnecessary expense by careful instructions.

The handling of a very large matter like a government offer for sale of a privatised company's shares must be very different from that of a simple purchase of a small company or property or the giving of advice on a technical issue. The former is likely to need a large number of solicitors from different parts of a law firm whereas the latter should involve the absolute minimum of solicitors with experience of the particular issues involved.

The issue of proper matter management is one that needs careful attention. It is particularly important if the billing is on an hourly basis since if more solicitors are involved on the transaction then it is necessary for the fees go up proportionately.

When instructing solicitors the client should seek to specify:

- the nature of the work to be undertaken;
- if the client wishes to handle certain aspects of the transaction, or to get someone else to handle them, that the solicitor is not expected to involve himself in these aspects;
- the expected timetable for the transaction;
- the basis on which the client would wish to be billed;
- that the particular solicitors to work on the transaction are to be named and agreed;
- if there are any rules that the client wishes to impose on working methods, billing, etc.

This information will enable the solicitor to provide information called for and also to agree the billing arrangements.

What needs to be considered

It is sometimes considered that the only way to value a solicitor's work is to add up the time he or she spends on the work. In theory this has attractions but it fails to take into account the real value of the individual solicitor's speed of work, his specialist skills or the importance to the client of the transaction or the advice asked for. In order to be correct one would always have to select the best individual for each task and avoid any extraneous matters that could affect this. If one does not actually succeed in that selection it may well not be the most cost-effective method. Since the client, when selecting the solicitor, is not likely to have the level of information to be certain that these tests are met, one may prefer to use another method of settling fees.

There are numerous different approaches that can be adopted for remunerating solicitors. Different approaches may suit different types of clients or even different types of transactions for the same client. However, it should be borne in mind that, on any negotiation on fees, the solicitor will seek to achieve, over the whole of his business operations, an appropriate return for his work.

A further consideration is that, although there are clearly going to be circumstances where it is possible to obtain different rates from comparable firms for comparable levels of work, the reality is that, generally, one gets roughly what one pays for. It is necessary to identify the work that one will get for the price paid. Merely relying on the price is not sufficient.

A very low charge for a transaction may mean one of several different things, some of which are beneficial to the client and some of which are not. It could be because the solicitor has significantly greater experience of the particular type of work than his competitors and can do it more quickly and more easily than they can; equally, it could be that he intends to leave the work to the solicitors on the other side of the transaction. This approach could be a sensible use of resources or it could mean that his client is getting no legal advice at all, in which case the client will think that he is getting inexpensive legal advice but in reality he is paying for nothing.

There are numerous other examples which serve to emphasise that the client needs to know what service he wants. Thus, the selection of a solicitor appropriate for a type of transaction is at least as important as the actual fee negotiation. The latter is often more in the nature of a control.

• FEE STRUCTURE •

The law sets out the basis on which solicitors are required to bill clients. This is set out in the Solicitors' Remuneration Order ('the Order') which provides that a solicitor's remuneration for non-contentious business shall be such sum as may be fair and reasonable having regard to all the circumstances of the case and in particular to:

- the complexity of the matter or the difficulty or novelty of the question raised;
- the skill, labour, specialised knowledge and responsibility involved;
- the time spent on the business;
- the number and importance of the documents prepared or perused, without regard to length;
- the place where and the circumstances in which the business or any part thereof is transacted;
- the amount or value of any money or property involved;
- whether any land involved is registered land; and
- the importance of the matter to the client.

These provisions of the Order are akin to value billing, described below, in that the various aspects of value billing are covered in the Order.

The Order also provides that a client may require the solicitor to obtain from the Law Society (the body which regulates solicitors) a certificate stating whether in their opinion the sum charged by the solicitor is fair and reasonable or, as the case may be, what other sum would be fair and reasonable. If the Law Society specifies a lower sum, that will normally be the sum payable by the client.

Billing under the Order probably is the most commonly-adopted method of billing in England, even in the larger commercial transactions. It gives the client the ability to assess whether the solicitor's contribution was valuable and what he is prepared to pay for it. If he disputes the value of those services he has a mechanism to challenge it.

The main difficulty that clients may feel with reliance on the Order is that it maintains no control, as such, on the overall level of the fees. Thus, the fees in themselves may be wholly justifiable but the client may feel that at that stage it is too late to object if the overall level of legal costs has risen too high. Agreed billing arrangements may give a greater control over the overall level or at least give the client the ability to see what the costs are as the matter progresses.

It is open to the client whether or not to rely on the Solicitors' Remuneration Order. However, if both the client and the solicitor agree, they are free under the Order to agree specific billing arrangements.

• METHOD OF BILLING •

The most commonly agreed billing arrangements are set out below:

(1) **Hourly billing**: this involves billing at agreed hourly rates depending upon the seniority of the solicitors involved and the hours recorded.

(2) **Hourly billing with a success fee**: this normally involves billing at agreed hourly rates but (where the matter is non-contentious) with a special incentive or success rate depending upon agreed criteria, normally whether the transaction is successful or not.

(3) **Value billing**: this involves an assessment (and a negotiation) to reflect the value to the client of the work done and the charge may be at a premium or a discount to a given hourly rate, depending upon the nature of the transaction.

(4) **Fixed tariff billing**: this involves fixed-fee charging for specific types of work.

(5) *Ad valorem* **billing**: this involves billing by reference to the value of the transaction and may include an hourly rate as well.

Variants can easily be introduced, such as agreeing an overall cap on the total fees.

In order to decide which approach is the most appropriate it is necessary to appreciate what is meant by each term. The client can then seek to agree the billing basis to adopt.

Hourly billing and success fees

This, in theory, means that the client is getting the cheapest cost attainable in that it pays only for what it gets. The reality behind hourly rate billing is that it can disguise and perpetuate inefficient working practices without satisfying the client's desire for cost efficient billing. For example:

(1) Hourly billing means it is actually less profitable for the law firm to develop and use standard precedents or accumulated know-how which reduce the time involved to do a transaction. It may, of course, be argued that all firms will have precedents and that those that do not use them would rapidly become uncompetitive.

(2) Hourly billing can only encourage excessive time recording and overstaffing since the more time that is recorded the greater the income that can be received.

Hourly billing has its weaknesses. However, for many clients entering into transactions of an uncertain duration and in a different jurisdiction from his own, it may be the only basis upon which the client feels he can assess and, to some extent, monitor legal costs. In those cases, hourly billing may be appropriate.

The rates charged by firms in England on an hourly basis are often high by comparison with, for example, those in the US. In theory, this would mean that the legal costs in England should be higher than those in the US. In practice the reverse generally seems to be the case, probably because the actual method of recording time and perhaps the approach to handling transactions are different.

Where a matter has an uncertain prospect of success, hourly billing with success or incentive fees means that the client has split the risk of failure between it and the solicitor. It has the advantage in that the client has limited its downside while acknowledging that if the project goes through, the solicitor will be appropriately rewarded.

Value billing

Value billing is difficult to describe. It has been described as simply 'gut feeling' or 'what the market will bear'. That may be the result but it probably is not the correct approach. What it does mean is that the fee negotiations will take place at the end of the transaction.

The approach to preparing a value bill is not 'how much time did we spend doing the work?' but rather 'what did I do for the client?' and 'what was the value of the firm's service to the client?'. It also involves the solicitor trying to assess the client's perception of that value and the client being given the opportunity to challenge that assessment. In transactions where there is something akin to a 'going rate' it involves a judgment of whether the transaction in question is worth the 'going rate' or should be charged at a premium or discount to it.

It is sometimes the case that the solicitor simply multiplies the time spent by an hourly rate. This is not value billing but rather the application of a (normally hidden) hourly billing basis. Value billing has to involve judgment. One can calculate the time and by applying a charge to that time reach a bill. However, this will not show whether:

- the time has been properly recorded;
- the work was as efficiently handled as it could have been;
- the client obtained a benefit out of the firm's know-how or precedents;
- the client was particularly demanding (eg demanded 24-hour service seven days a week);
- the work was simple or complex and whether it involved original thinking;
- the transaction was large and valuable to the client (eg a very large issue or funding or a large acquisition).

Clearly, if the solicitor is asking himself these questions, then the client should reverse these questions and consider if he feels that the value is there. Although value billing does not involve time assessment, there is nothing to stop the client asking for information on the time worked in order to work out what excess there is over hourly rates.

The one thing to bear in mind if value billing is adopted is that it should go both ways – reduced rates for abortive or routine transactions as against increased rates for successful ones.

Fixed tariff billing
This is particularly appropriate in transactions where there is a large repeat business and one can expect that over a series of transactions, the cost can be predicted with some reliability. Generally, it is not appropriate as a billing method on transactions where there is any significant element of uncertainty since in order to factor in that uncertainty, it is likely that there will be a very large risk element resulting in an overly high quote if the matter is not successful.

Ad valorem *billing*

This generally is not used except in property transactions where the market has long recognised billing based upon the value of the transaction. In its pure form it is, in reality, not that dissimilar from value billing though the value ascribed is the value of the transaction rather than a mixture of the value of the work and the value of the transaction.

• TIMING OF BILLING •

This is a matter of client preference. Solicitors will normally submit bills when asked to do so. The timing may well depend on which billing method is adopted, though all methods can easily accommodate interim billing.

If the transaction has a fairly short timetable it is normally easiest to require the solicitor to submit his bill when the transaction is completed. If it is a long-running transaction then it is preferable to having regular interim billing. It is worth bearing in mind that because of the cash-flow benefits to the solicitor of regular billing he may well be willing to provide a discount on his fees to reflect the time value of the payment arrangements.

Whether or not interim billing is called for, it is normal for clients to expect to be kept regularly informed as to how much cost has been incurred on a matter.

When the basis of billing is agreed, then the information to be provided in, and if appropriate the format of, the bill can also be settled.

TREATMENT OF FOREIGN NATIONALS UNDER LOCAL LAW

The precise definition of 'foreign national' and similar terms under the law in force in the UK differs according to the area of law one is considering. For example, for the purposes of financial services regulation, the question is whether the person is carrying on investment business from a permanent place of business in the UK, but for taxation purposes it becomes a question of the place of central management and control (in the case of a company which is not incorporated in the UK). For the purposes of this section, except where noted otherwise, it is assumed that the foreign person is a corporate entity which fits squarely into the appropriate categories and has no other connection with the UK other than the investment, transaction, or litigation, etc contemplated.

• Restrictions, Reports and Governmental Approvals •
of Foreign Investment

Although there are no exchange controls in place in the UK, a foreign entity considering inward investment to the UK must consider a number of regulatory issues. Broadly, the main areas of investment activity which are regulated include investment business, banking, insurance, companies and building societies. Subject to specific exceptions, such regulation applies equally to UK and non-UK entities.

In the broadest of terms, such regulation usually lays down rules as to:

- who are fit and proper persons to engage in the regulated activity;
- how the activity should be carried out having regard to the interests of both regulated persons and consumers of the relevant services;
- how compliance with such rules is to be monitored; and
- what sanctions are to be imposed in the event of a breach of those rules.

By way of example, the regulation of investment business will be summarised, not because such rules necessarily reflect the rules of other areas of regulation, but because it is an area which often affects the activities of foreign investors in the UK.

Regulation of investment business
The Financial Services Act 1986 ('FSA') regulates the conduct of investment business in the UK by, *inter alia*, foreign persons. 'Investment business' is widely defined to include activities such as dealing in or arranging deals in or managing investments, giving investment advice, or establishing collective investment schemes. 'Investments' is similarly widely defined to cover, *inter alia*, shares, debentures, units in collective investment schemes, options, futures, etc.

The general rule is that the FSA prohibits the carrying on of investment business in the UK unless the person carrying on the investment business is an authorised or exempted person. Authorisation typically is obtained by becoming directly authorised by the Securities and Investments Board (SIB) or becoming a member of one of a number of self-regulating organisations.

Authorisation will not be required if the activity is an excluded activity. Examples of excluded activities are:

(a) where the transaction is to be entered into by a principal;
(b) if the transaction is between two parties who are corporate bodies within the same group or in connection with a joint enterprise;
(c) where the transaction is in connection with the sale of goods or supply of services; or

(d) where the transaction is in connection with the acquisition or disposal of shares in connection with the sale of a company (other than an open-ended investment company).

In each case there are detailed conditions to be satisfied.

Overseas persons also gain the benefit of additional exclusions from the need to be authorised. Thus, for example, authorisation will not be required in respect of dealings by an overseas person with or through an authorised person or an exempted person.

As noted above, a person will be an 'overseas person' if such person does not carry on investment business from a permanent place of business maintained by him in the UK. Whether a place of business is 'permanent' and 'maintained' by that person is a question of fact and would cover, for example, a person who establishes a UK office even if such office merely performs administrative functions in connection with investment business. However, the activities of an agent with a permanent place of business in the UK does not mean that the principal maintains a place of business in the UK. Also, a company with a branch in the UK may still be an overseas person for the purposes of the FSA providing that no investment business is conducted at that branch.

Generally, an unauthorised person may not issue investment advertisements in the UK unless approved by an authorised person. However, advertisements are exempt from that rule if they are only distributed to limited categories of investors (in general, authorised persons and substantial corporations or institutions) in accordance with the relevant investment advertisement exemption regulations. As noted above, investment advertisements may also be issued if their contents are approved by an authorised person. However, authorised persons are subject to rules governing when they can approve such advertisements.

Similarly, unsolicited calls may be made provided they are made in accordance with the relevant unsolicited calls' regulations of the SIB. In practice, these restrictions are most easily satisfied by restricting all communications to and dealings with persons in the UK to authorised persons and substantial corporations or institutions.

There are two serious consequences of a breach of the requirement for authorisation:

(1) The person concerned commits a criminal offence, although he has a defence if he can provide that he took all reasonable precautions and exercised all due diligence to avoid commission of the offence.

(2) Any agreement entered into by him which falls within the prohibition is, subject to to narrow exceptions, unenforceable by him (but the agreement will generally remain enforceable against him) and any money paid or property transferred can be recovered by the other

party together with compensation for loss unless the court orders otherwise.

• TAX TREATMENT •

The taxation of foreign persons may, for convenience, be treated in two discrete categories: that which arises from a foreign person trading within (as compared to trading with) the UK (ie operating its business through a subsidiary, branch or agency in the UK), and that which arises from a foreign person making inward investments into the UK.

Trading within the UK
A foreign entity might trade within the UK either by establishing a subsidiary (which will generally be UK incorporated and so resident in the UK for UK tax purposes), or by trading within the UK through a branch or agency. Depending upon which of these two categories the trade falls into, different taxation consequences follow.

Subsidiary
A subsidiary company incorporated in the UK will be resident in the UK for UK tax purposes. A subsidiary company incorporated elsewhere may be UK tax-resident if it is centrally managed and controlled in the UK.

In general, a company resident in the UK is subject to UK corporation tax (at the current standard rate of 33 per cent) on its worldwide income and gains, including profits of trade carried on in any part of the world. Relief may be given for any overseas taxes paid depending upon the provisions of any applicable double tax treaty. It should be noted that if a UK resident company is also a resident in another country, it might not be entitled to any such relief which might otherwise be available. However, dual residency generally will not arise if the subsidiary is effectively managed and controlled in the UK.

The foreign parent will not be subject to UK taxation merely by virtue of having a UK subsidiary, provided that the subsidiary acts independently of the parent and not as its agent.

If the subsidiary is funded by an equity investment, profits of the subsidiary's activities presumably will be repatriated to the foreign parent by way of dividend. When the subsidiary pays a dividend, it has to pay advance corporation tax (ACT) of ¼ on the net dividend. ACT paid on dividends is, within limits, able to be offset against the subsidiary's liability to corporation tax on its profits. The receipt of such a dividend by a foreign parent will not give rise to any further liability to UK tax thereon. However, the foreign parent may be entitled to claim a repayment from the UK Inland Revenue of all or part of the ACT, under any applicable double tax treaty.

To the extent that the subsidiary is funded by loan capital from the foreign parent, the parent will be able to extract revenue from the subsidiary by way of interest payments on the loans. While dividends are effectively payable only out of after-tax income, interest payments will generally be deductible by the subsidiary from its profits chargeable to corporation tax. Interest payments in long-term loans are generally subject to a withholding tax of 25 per cent, although this may be relieved in whole or in part by any applicable double tax treaty. If interest is paid as above not at an arm's-length rate, or there is too much loan capital as compared with equity in the subsidiary ('thin capitalisation'), the UK tax authorities could, under UK law and relevant treaties, deny a deduction for the payments and/or deny relief from withholding tax.

Losses sustained by the subsidiary may be set off against trading profits of the same trade in the future, or against other profits of the same accounting period and, in limited circumstances, of the immediately preceding accounting period. In general, no relief will be available to the foreign parent in respect of such losses.

Branch or agency

If a foreign entity does not establish a UK subsidiary, it will be taxable in the UK on its trading profits only if it trades in the UK (as opposed to trading with the UK), and does so through a branch or agency. A foreign entity will be considered to be trading within the UK where there is a specified or identifiable place in the UK at which the trade is being carried on. In deciding where a trade is being carried on, one of the most important factors will be the place where contracts for the supply of goods or services are made. Other factors include, in particular, the place where, in commercial terms, the profit of the transaction arises, as well as the place where the negotiations are conducted, the place of delivery, the place where the subject matter of a contract is to be found at the time of the sale and the country of receipt of the proceeds of sale.

Corporation tax

A foreign entity trading in the UK will be subject to corporation tax (at the current standard rate of 33 per cent) on:

(a) any trading income (wherever arising) insofar as it arises directly or indirectly from the trade carried on in the UK through a UK branch or agency and any income from property or rights used by, or held by or for the benefit of, the branch or agency; and

(b) gains realised or deemed to have been realised on the disposal of assets situated in the UK which are used in or for the purposes of or held for the benefit of the trade of the branch or agency.

There is also an 'exit charge' on realised gains on such assets when a non-UK resident company's branch or agency trade ceases or such assets are removed from the UK before disposal. As regards the transfer of the trade and assets of the branch to a UK resident company on the 'domestication' of the branch, any capital gains on the assets transferred may (by election) not be taxed immediately but will be deferred until disposal of the assets by the new company.

Income tax

Income tax (at the current rate of 25 per cent) is charged on other income which has a source within the UK, including passive UK source income such as interest and dividends on non-UK branch investments.

General

There is no UK tax on the repatriation of the profits of a UK branch to the foreign parent's home country. Branch losses may be able to be offset against the foreign parent's own profits.

Transfer-pricing

Attempts to reduce profits of a UK branch or subsidiary liable to UK taxation by 'transfer-pricing' arrangements under which the UK operation charges artificially low prices to or is charged artificially high prices by its foreign head office, parent or affiliate, are likely to fall foul of UK domestic transfer-pricing provisions, or the provisions of any applicable double tax treaty. Under the transfer-pricing provisions, the tax authorities have power to direct that for tax purposes the relevant transactions are to be treated as having been carried out on arm's-length terms.

Value Added Tax

Value Added Tax (VAT) is a concern for a UK branch or subsidiary. It is a general turnover tax which is charged on most supplies of goods and services made in the UK and on imports of goods and the receipt of certain services from overseas by a taxable person. Anyone carrying on business with a (or with an expected) taxable turnover exceeding the registration threshold (currently £37,600 per annum) is required to be registered as a taxable person for VAT purposes. Anyone failing to register is liable to significant penalties. VAT currently is charged on taxable supplies at a standard rate of 17.5 per cent or (in respect of certain supplies) at a zero rate. Certain types of supply are exempt from VAT.

Whenever a taxable person supplies goods or services to which VAT applies, its price should reflect the VAT for which the taxable person will be required to account to Customs and Excise. However, in accounting for VAT, the taxable person is able to take credit for VAT on goods and services supplied to it and imports made by it (except insofar as it uses them in making exempt supplies), so that, very broadly speaking, VAT is only borne by the end consumer of the goods or services.

Inward investment

The investments contemplated here are the acquisition of shares in a UK company and making loans to a UK company. Non-resident holders of securities are technically liable to UK tax on dividends and interest paid by a UK company (subject to provisions of any applicable double tax treaty). Such holders may be able to obtain relief under a treaty in respect of ACT paid on dividends or tax required to be withheld on interest (see above). By concession the UK tax authorities do not seek to recover tax (other than withholding tax) on interest and dividends paid to non-residents who have no other UK connection.

A non-resident company holding securities will not be subject to UK tax on disposal of those securities unless it is trading in those securities in the UK through a UK branch or it holds the securities for the purpose of a trading branch or agency in the UK. However, if a non-resident trades in securities through an agent in the UK, the non-resident may be assessed to income tax in the name of the agent unless, broadly, the agent is acting as such as part of its business of providing investment management services. Any tax charge pursuant to these rules may be relieved by an appropriate double tax treaty.

• ACCESS TO AND TREATMENT BY LOCAL COURTS •

As noted above, the English and Northern Irish legal systems have some differences between them, while the Scottish legal system is quite distinct, though all three jurisdictions share many common features. Because of the differences in the context of litigation, this section refers to English, rather than UK, courts or law, though in most cases the position in Northern Ireland and Scotland is not materially different.

The only restriction on a foreign plaintiff's access to English courts is that it may be required to give the defendant security for its costs. The court may, on the defendant's application, require a foreign plaintiff to deposit a sum of money in court or provide a bank guarantee in the amount of the defendant's costs. This is to secure the defendant against the danger that it might successfully rebut the plaintiff's claim but then be unable to recover its costs because the plaintiff has no assets in the country.

The defendant can only ask for security for its costs up to a given stage of the litigation and must then re-apply. It must justify the amount claimed.

Of course, a court will take into account a party's residence in deciding questions such as jurisdiction or the most convenient place for a case to be tried (see below), but in all other respects a foreign plaintiff or defendant is treated no differently from an English party.

• FOREIGN PARENT LIABILITY •

In general, English law adheres to the principle that a company is distinct from its shareholders and that they are not liable for its actions. This is so whether the shareholders are foreign or English. The main exceptions to this principle are where:

(a) the company acts as agent for its shareholders – that is, the shareholders authorise it to make contracts on their behalf, generally govern the company's business and receive the profits and bear the liabilities that result;

(b) a shareholder is a shadow director of the company – that is, the directors of the company are accustomed to act in accordance with the shareholder's directions or instructions. The shareholder may then be liable as a director of the company;

(c) a shareholder may be found to have conspired with a company in an unlawful act, or have assisted in the commission of a crime.

In these cases, the jurisdiction of the UK courts may be established over the shareholder.

• JURISDICTION OF LOCAL COURTS •

Since the UK (but not the Channel Islands or the Isle of Man) is a party to the Brussels and Lugano Conventions (see Appendix), English courts will take jurisdiction in proceedings against a defendant domiciled in another contracting state in accordance with those Conventions (see below). In proceedings against other foreign defendants, English courts will apply their own jurisdictional rules.

Jurisdiction under the Conventions is generally determined by domicile (see below). Under English law, an individual is domiciled in England if he is resident there and has a substantial connection with the country (which is presumed if he has been resident in England for the last three months). A corporation is domiciled in England if:

• it was incorporated there and has its registered office there; or

- its central management and control is exercised there.

Where the Conventions do not apply, an English court will take jurisdiction over a foreign defendant in two cases:

(1) If the defendant is served with a writ inside England. This can be done without leave of the court. The domicile or nationality of the defendant and the duration of the defendant's stay in this country are irrelevant. Service on an authorised process agent is sufficient to establish jurisdiction.

(2) If the plaintiff, with leave of the court, serves a writ on the defendant outside England. In order to obtain leave, the case must fall within at least one of certain specified categories, including:

(a) the action concerns a contract which was made in England, breached in England or governed by English law;

(b) in a tort action, the damage was suffered, or the tortious act committed, in England;

(c) the subject matter of the claim is land in England.

Additionally, the plaintiff must show a good arguable case on the merits, and the court must be satisfied that England is the forum in which the case can most suitably be tried.

Both of the above routes are subject to the defendant, once served, establishing that another court is more appropriate to hear the case and, accordingly, that the English court should decline jurisdiction. For example, a UK court may decline to exercise jurisdiction on the grounds that another court already has jurisdiction or on the grounds of *forum non conveniens*, ie that because of factors such as convenience, expense and the law governing the transaction, that the case can be more conveniently tried in another legal forum.

• FOREIGN LANGUAGE DOCUMENTS AND DOCUMENTS • GOVERNED BY FOREIGN LAW

Documents in a foreign language need to be translated if they are to be relied on at a hearing. The translation need not be notarised. If there is a dispute as to its accuracy, the court will hear evidence from expert witnesses called by the parties in order to decide the correct meaning of the document.

English courts frequently hear cases concerning contracts or torts governed by foreign law. They assume that the foreign law is the same as English law, except where the parties establish that it differs. Again, where the parties disagree as to the foreign law, the court will decide the issue on the basis of expert evidence.

• RECOGNITION AND ENFORCEMENT OF FOREIGN • JUDGMENTS

Enforcement of a foreign judgment in the UK depends upon whether the foreign judgment was obtained in a country which is a party to either the Brussels or Lugano Conventions (see Appendix), or to a reciprocal enforcement treaty.

The Brussels and Lugano Conventions
The English courts will enforce a judgment of a court in another contracting state in accordance with the rules explained in the Appendix. Once registered, such a judgment can be enforced like any English judgment.

Reciprocal enforcement treaties
Reciprocal enforcement treaties exist between the UK and Australia, Austria, Canada, many of the Caribbean islands, the Cayman Islands, Cyprus, Fiji, the Gambia, Ghana, Gibraltar, Guernsey, Guyana, Hong Kong, India, Isle of Man, Israel, Jersey, Kenya, Malaysia, Malta, New Zealand, Nigeria, Norway, Pakistan, Sierra Leone, Singapore, Sri Lanka, Swaziland, Tanzania, Uganda, Zambia, Zimbabwe and a number of other present and former dependencies. (The above list excludes those countries which have also ratified the Brussels or Lugano Conventions.)

As under the Brussels and Lugano Conventions, a judgment creditor must register the judgment with the High Court. Upon registration, the judgment shall, for the purposes of execution, be of the same force and effect as if the judgment had been a judgment originally given in the registering court and entered on the date of registration.

To be registered, a foreign judgment must be final and conclusive (notwithstanding that an appeal may be pending), and there must be payable under it a sum of money which is not a sum payable in respect of taxes, fines or penalties. It will not be enforced if it was obtained by fraud, if enforcement would be contrary to English public policy or if the original court acted without jurisdiction. Additionally, an English court will not enforce a judgment if enforcement would offend natural justice. A defence to enforcement proceedings based on natural justice is not restricted to the requirements of due notice and opportunity to put a case, but depends on whether the proceedings in the foreign court offended, in the English court's view, substantial justice.

If the applicant seeking to set aside the registration of the judgment can show that an appeal is pending or that the applicant is entitled to and intends to appeal the judgment seeking to be registered, the court may set aside the registration or stay the registration.

Except as noted above, an English court will not examine the merits of a foreign judgment. But an important difference from the Brussels Convention is that, under a reciprocal enforcement treaty, an English court will examine whether the foreign court had jurisdiction under the treaty rules. These are restrictive and a foreign court will be deemed to have had jurisdiction only if the judgment debtor:

(a) was plaintiff in, or voluntarily appeared in, the proceedings (other than to contest jurisdiction or the seizure of property); or

(b) agreed to submit to the jurisdiction of the court; or

(c) when the proceedings were instituted, was resident in or (if a company) had its principal place of business in the foreign country; or

(d) had a place of business in the foreign country (for most countries it is also necessary that the proceedings were in respect of a transaction effected through that place).

A foreign court is not regarded as having jurisdiction over land outside its own country.

Other cases
A judgment of a court in a country which is not a party to the Brussels or Lugano Conventions or a reciprocal enforcement treaty must be enforced by bringing fresh proceedings before an English court.

As long as the foreign judgment satisfies the conditions required under the reciprocal enforcement conventions (see above), the English court will treat it as creating a debt owed by the judgment debtor to the judgment creditor. It will not (save in fraud or public policy cases) examine the merits of the judgment. Therefore, summary judgment can usually be obtained within a few months.

•

David Cheyne
Linklaters & Paines
Barrington House
59–67 Gresham Street
London EC2V 7JA
United Kingdom
•

—— 14 ——

THE UNITED STATES

——— • ———

CONTENTS

•

THE UNITED STATES

•

STRUCTURE OF THE LEGAL PROFESSION

• LEGAL SYSTEM •

The United States' legal system consists of:

- federal laws and statutes, which generally apply throughout the US; and
- state and local laws and statutes, which are valid only in a particular state or locality.

This distinction is important because a combination of federal, state and local laws and statutes may be relevant depending on the particular issue on which the client seeks advice. Cases and transactions lacking any federal aspect are extremely rare given the lengthy tradition of enactment of laws and statutes at the federal level and the pre-emptive nature of the US constitution and many federal laws, which work to override conflicting state and local laws. If, however, a lawyer or law firm is not able to provide legal advice at the federal, state and local levels, a client may be required to hire a generalist leading law firm to handle the structuring or management of a particular transaction or matter and engage local counsel to deal with specific issues or matters relating to a particular state or municipality (eg local real estate laws).

• COURT SYSTEM •

The US court system may seem bewildering to those unfamiliar with its structure and federal systems of government. Most likely, a client involved in litigation in the United States would find itself before a court at the federal or state (or similar jurisdiction such as the District of Columbia) level. The federal level consists of federal district courts located in each state or similar jurisdiction. Appeals from those courts may be taken to a court of appeals, each of which hears cases from an area comprising several states or other similar jurisdictions. Final appeals may be taken to the US Supreme Court. Typically, appeals must be made by way of petition to the Supreme Court which will agree to adjudicate only those very few cases which it deems to involve sufficiently important or controversial legal questions.

Each state (or similar jurisdiction) has a similar court system. Cases are first heard by a state district court or by county courts spread throughout the state or by magistrates, with appeals allowed to a state court of appeals and then to a state supreme court. Matters involving questions of both state and federal law or where federal jurisdiction applies as a result of diversity between the domiciles of the parties, may be removed to the relevant federal court. Some states have courts dedicated to distinct areas of state law such as probate, property and criminal law.

Most local municipalities and counties have specific courts for dealing with domestic disputes, tax claims, property assessments and other issues involving local law which may not be of concern to most foreign clients. Other federal courts include:

- the US Claims Court, which adjudicates many tax and US government procurement cases;
- the US Court of International Trade; and
- the US Bankruptcy Courts.

These courts are responsible for adjudicating specialised areas of federal law, although appeal may be made from these courts to higher ranking federal courts.

• LAWYERS •

Jurisdiction

Lawyers in the United States must qualify to practise in a particular state or jurisdiction. Many lawyers are qualified in more than one state, with qualification in one jurisdiction often ensuring or facilitating the process of qualifying in another. To be qualified in a particular jurisdiction, the lawyer must pass an exam given by that state's governing legal organisation, often called a bar association. In addition, many states require lawyers to attend seminars or classes in order to retain their qualification to practise in that state.

Identifying the state or states in which a lawyer is qualified is especially important if a client seeks advice on litigation matters. Generally, a lawyer must be qualified in, or certified by, a particular state before appearing before that state's courts. In larger litigation matters, this distinction may be of less importance if the matter involves several states or both federal and state (or local) issues, although certain federal courts will require lawyers trying cases before them to hold a certificate for those courts.

In a business transaction, a lawyer's particular state qualification is often less important as a client will typically want to retain a lawyer or law firm with expertise on the type of transaction or the specific legal issues involved rather than experience in any given location. However, certain types of transactions, particularly those involving real estate and state and/or local regulatory issues, will have a more pronounced state and/or local law component. In such circumstances, a client will require a lawyer familiar with that state or a similar jurisdiction's laws. In a large transaction involving, for example, the acquisition of or taking security over real estate in several jurisdictions, one lawyer or law firm might be responsible for structuring the overall transaction and co-ordinating the work of lawyers qualified in particular states to handle title surveys, registrations and filings and the negotiation and delivery of real estate related opinions.

Generally, a US lawyer will only deliver an opinion as to the federal laws and statutes of the United States and the laws and statutes of the jurisdiction in which he or she is admitted, although many law firms or lawyers with an active transactional corporate practice will also deliver an opinion with respect to the general corporate law of Delaware, the jurisdiction of incorporation of many American companies (due to its progressive judiciary and developed body of statutory and case law for corporate matters). In transactions with a multi-state dimension, the limitation on the delivery of opinions described above may not be crippling since the common law and many state statutory schemes are similar or based on uniform models. Accordingly, lawyers will be willing to deliver opinions concerning another state's law based upon their own state's laws, subject, of course, to the necessary exceptions and assumptions. In transactions with a more evident local component, the client may insist on opinions rendered by lawyers qualified to practise in each relevant jurisdiction.

Organisation
Most lawyers in the US have formed partnerships or law firms. Many of the larger firms in the major commercial markets have offices in several states, the District of Columbia and/or in other countries. With the exception of a few highly specialised areas, which are often provided by either very large or very small firms, most of the larger firms in the major cities offer the same general range of legal services, especially in the fields of litigation and the standard areas of 'business' practice: finance, general corporate, anti-trust, taxation, environmental, regulatory, pension, intellectual property, leasing, aircraft and ship financing and labour work.

A law firm with as broad a jurisdictional and practice area base as possible can be advantageous to a client, since one law firm may be able to advise on most or all aspects of a complicated transaction or litigation and render the necessary legal opinions. The larger law firms should also be aware of the sensitivities involved in handling matters for non-US clients and may have attorneys with language expertise or experience of the law in different countries. Firms in the smaller cities and towns will most likely be better able to advise on those matters with an exclusive local element.

HOW TO FIND A SUITABLE LAWYER

Before instructing a lawyer in the United States, a client should carefully consider the scope and extent of the legal advice needed.

• RECOMMENDATIONS •

One of the best methods for identifying a suitable lawyer is through 'word of mouth' – relying on the recommendations of colleagues, friends, lawyers in the client's home jurisdiction and others who have worked with a lawyer or law firm in the United States. A direct recommendation may be more efficient for finding counsel than any of the other methods described below.

Any of the foregoing persons who have hired a US lawyer should be in a position to evaluate the quality of work performed, the knowledge and experience of particular lawyers, the cost and time efficiency of the service provided and the style and methods of the particular attorney in question. Any client relying on a recommendation in choosing a lawyer should ask how that lawyer was found and what criteria were used in his or her selection. Specific attention should be paid to the recommending party's impression of the quality of that lawyer's colleagues and the depth of personnel and logistical support able to be dedicated to any particular matter.

It is important to establish the nature and complexity of legal services actually supplied to the recommending party. The quality of legal services offered by the same firm may vary considerably among individuals and practice areas, and further investigation may be warranted if the required legal advice is in a different area or of a greater complexity than that forming the basis of the recommendation.

A client should also ask its local legal counsel for recommendations, particularly if such counsel is in a position to evaluate the nominated attorney's qualifications and will be working closely with the proposed US lawyers.

• LOCAL LAW SOCIETY OR BAR ASSOCIATION •

There are many legal associations in the United States which can recommend appropriate legal counsel. Most of them are state and municipal organisations, with responsibility for discipline of attorneys, continuing legal education, and the organisation of legal services for non-profit entities and lower income individuals (known as legal aid or *pro bono* work). Nationwide bar associations may be useful in selecting a practitioner in a highly specialised or technical area, such as intellectual property or maritime work.

• LEGAL DIRECTORIES •

Legal directories are also a source for finding US legal counsel. The *Martindale-Hubbell Law Directory* is the best known of these. This multi-volume compendium lists lawyers practising in firms, professional associations and corporate law departments and as solo practitioners by locality in all US jurisdictions as well as most jurisdictions outside the United States. The listing for one firm with an office in one city will include information on that firm's branch or associated offices, thus facilitating the search for attorneys with a multi-jurisdictional practice.

The primary advantage of *Martindale-Hubbell* is its exhaustive listing of biographical information on individual attorneys, including details of each lawyer's academic background, areas of specialisation, publications, membership in academic and professional associations and language ability. In some cases, *Martindale-Hubbell* lists a firm's or association's representative clients and practice areas by category, although this latter listing is not descriptive and does not include information on any firm's relative strengths and weaknesses or its areas of relative experience or inexperience. Another valuable feature of *Martindale-Hubbell* is its inclusion of summary legal digests for the various US jurisdictions with a brief description of the most important laws and statutes in effect in each such jurisdiction. Two volumes of *Martindale-Hubbell* are devoted to the listing of attorneys by practice area, although this may be of little practical use to a client evaluating the merits of potential legal counsel.

Clients looking for legal representation on an initial basis may find the complete *Martindale-Hubbell* more useful as a tool for evaluating the competence and background of specific attorneys. The more compact *Martindale-Hubbell Bar Register of Prominent Attorneys* provides the basic information contained in the larger edition and is more likely to be of use to non-US companies seeking legal representation for most of their legal needs. It may be appropriate to consult *Martindale-Hubbell* after receiving a preliminary evaluation of a given lawyer or law firm, especially to investigate the background, qualifications and specialities of the particular firm or lawyer.

In addition to *Martindale-Hubbell*, each major US city also publishes a listing of lawyers in that jurisdiction, although this often amounts to little more than an alphabetical roster of those admitted to practise law and their contact details.

Basic information about the more prominent US legal firms can also be found in *The Lawyers' List* and *The American Bar Reference Handbook*. Three UK publications, *Kime's International Law Directory*, *The International Law List* and *The International Financial Law Review's Guide to the World's 1000 International Business Law Firms*, may also be useful to those clients with large-scale business transactions with a US aspect or involved in litigation before a US court.

• ADVERTISING •

Advertising by lawyers in the United States is both permitted and widespread. Mass media advertising is typically directed at individuals who may need legal services as a result of personal injury, family problems or financial difficulties. Most non-US clients requiring representation will find this form of advertising unsuitable for their requirements. Interestingly, this freedom to advertise only dates from US Supreme Court decisions in the 1970s, and mass-media advertising remains subject to standards of truth in advertising and full disclosure contained in the Model Rules of Professional Conduct (the 'Model Rules') promulgated by the most important body governing the American legal profession, the American Bar Association (the 'ABA').

Law firms, especially larger firms, regularly distribute brochures in their attempt to attract new business. These brochures may be helpful as a preliminary means of evaluating a particular firm's suitability, competence and relevant experience. Firms may also distribute articles, memoranda on salient legal issues, newsletters and other publications written by their attorneys as a promotional method. The larger firms may also sponsor seminars for potential clients or participate in conferences on legal or business issues of particular interest where potential clients might be in attendance.

• CHAMBERS OF COMMERCE AND EMPLOYERS' • CONFEDERATIONS

Another possible source for finding an appropriate provider of legal services is any particular city's or area's chamber of commerce or business promotion office. These offices are probably more useful in providing recommendations for advice on those matters with a substantial local component rather than assisting clients in finding general legal representation.

The US embassy or consulate in the client's home jurisdiction may be able to provide a list of lawyers and law firms with offices in that jurisdiction.

Businesses involving the manufacture of goods or provision of services may consider referring to a local, national or international organisation to which similar US businesses belong. These organisations and their members may furnish recommendations for US legal counsel with particular expertise in the required fields.

• LOCAL VISITS AND PERSONAL INTERVIEWS •

Upon narrowing the choice of potential law firms, it may be appropriate to conduct face to face interviews with the candidates. In a particularly large transaction or where longer-term representation is sought, it may be sensible to conduct a 'beauty parade' which involves interviewing and visiting potential candidates to handle a specified matter, ascertaining their suitability, competence and compatibility with the client, the client's customer or any opposing party, and asking for descriptions of the work to be performed and the potential cost. In a competitive legal market, any responsive fee estimate or cap, as the case may be, from such a beauty parade should be based on realistic assumptions as to the timetable, complexity of work and manpower required for a given transaction or case and should be made subject to the non-occurrence of delays and contingencies over which lawyers and their clients have no control. The process of selecting counsel, however, need not be so formal and may consist of a few visits to or interviews with possible candidates.

FACTORS IN CHOOSING A SUITABLE LAWYER

• PROFESSIONAL QUALIFICATIONS •

A US lawyer's professional qualifications typically begin with the lawyer's academic training. Generally, a person must have successfully completed an undergraduate degree at a recognised university to be accepted into a US law school. Following graduation from law school, lawyers qualify to practise law in a particular state by taking the state's bar exam, which will test both general case law and the legal rules particular to the relevant state, as well as the application of the Model Rules. One notable exception is California where admission to the bar does not require any specific degree of formal education.

Upon successful completion of the required examinations and subject to personal recommendations and character and background checks, a lawyer will be admitted to the state bar. As discussed below, lawyers in certain practice areas (eg tax litigation) must have special qualifications or certification to appear before certain courts. Also, a lawyer's professional experience is an important qualifying factor. As mentioned earlier, directories such as *Martindale-Hubbell* provide summaries of a lawyer's qualifications and academic background.

• LANGUAGE ABILITY •

Generally, language ability should not be an issue in selecting a US lawyer or law firm unless, of course, the client is seeking to retain a legal adviser who is conversant in the language of the client's home jurisdiction or if special language skills are required due to the nature of the particular transaction or matter involved. If special language skills are required, most large US firms employ lawyers fluent in at least a few of the major international commercial languages. In fact, many US firms will have branch or associate offices in foreign countries that are staffed with lawyers possessing appropriate language capacity.

• TYPE OF TRANSACTION •

The type of transaction is one of the more important criteria in identifying which lawyers should be dedicated to the matter at hand. First, the type of transaction will dictate whether or not a US law firm is required or appropriate and, if so, may dictate the state or other jurisdiction in which the lawyer must be qualified.

If the transaction is relatively routine and involves the law of only one particular state, a lawyer or law firm with a general practice covering such transactions should be adequate. If, however, the transaction transcends many legal jurisdictions (either in the United States or internationally) and involves an understanding of, or an ability to work with, the laws of those jurisdictions, a client should consider selecting a firm that has some exposure to and experience in completing and co-ordinating such complex, multi-jurisdictional transactions. For example, an international acquisition might include a target company whose business is conducted in several countries, while a cross-border securitisation might involve the purchase of receivables in different countries with very different legal and regulatory regimes. A global public offering of securities will require understanding of US securities laws and their interaction with the securities law of other jurisdictions. In such transactions, the lawyer or law firm selection should have the substantive legal skills as well as the ability to co-ordinate and manage the required legal teams to complete the deal effectively and efficiently.

If a US lawyer is needed in connection with an international transaction involving a number of countries and legal systems, the choice of a lawyer or law firm will depend, in part, on the law that is selected to govern a particular transaction and the complexity and importance of the issues which are the subject of the transaction. Many international financing and other business transactions, for example, are governed by New York law as a result of New York's established reputation in the global business market and its respected and commercially-oriented laws and court system. The long standing of New

York law and New York courts has also resulted in the relative scarcity of some of the more idiosyncratic laws and cases adopted in other US jurisdictions. Finally, under New York law the parties to a contract or transaction involving amounts in excess of a certain dollar level (currently, US$250,000) can select New York law to govern any contract or document whether or not such contract or document has any relation to New York and expect to have such choice of law upheld in a New York court.

• FAMILIARITY WITH OVERSEAS CONTRACT TYPES •

If a particular transaction is US based but involves a substantial non-US element or if a US lawyer is required for domestic US advice in connection with a transaction based outside the US, the client should consider a lawyer or law firm familiar with non-US transactions and international contract types. Most large US firms or firms with a foreign office will have this capacity. In such situations, time and cost savings may result from an existing familiarity with foreign regulatory systems, the interpretation and application of the relevant non-US contracts and the structuring and negotiation of non-US transactions. Of course, if the transaction or matter for which the client requires US advice is entirely or primarily a US matter or very specialised, a firm with local qualification or the appropriate expertise would provide the best service, notwithstanding its comparative lack of familiarity with contracts originating outside the US.

• SPECIALISATION IN TOPICS •

Many of the larger US firms have teams or departments of lawyers who concentrate in the standard areas of legal practice, such as litigation, tax, pensions, anti-trust, environmental, corporate and securities, banking and finance. If a client's needs, however, relate only to one particular area (for example, specialised tax advice, estate planning or intellectual property), smaller, more specialised firms may be better equipped to render the necessary advice in a more timely and cost-efficient manner. If, however, the client needs access to more than one of these specialist areas on the same transaction (for example, to complete an international acquisition) a larger firm may be more appropriate.

If a client is looking for a long-term relationship with a particular lawyer or law firm, the client may prefer a 'one-stop' shop for general legal advice but source its requirements for specialised or expert advice on a transaction or matter specific basis from individual lawyers, lawyers from various firms or 'boutique' firms.

Finally, the client may choose to use a more cost-efficient firm for routine transactions while relying on more expensive practitioners for more complex, higher profile matters. Obviously, how a client sources its US legal advice may change from time to time as relationships change and requirements develop.

• ASSOCIATE OFFICES IN BRUSSELS •

With a number of non-US firms and lawyers operating in Brussels and most purporting to provide similar services, many foreign clients requiring representation in Brussels are likely to have engaged counsel with a presence in Brussels. A number of US firms do maintain offices in Brussels and this may be a criterion for selecting a US firm if the client is interested in developing a multi-jurisdictional relationship with one law firm or has a particular need for legal representation in Brussels but has not yet established a relationship with a firm with a Brussels presence. Obviously, the client's needs for a lawyer or law firm in Brussels will depend upon the degree to which the client requires advice on matters involving European or Belgian law.

• CLIENT CONFLICTS •

New clients seeking to employ a law firm will be subject to a 'conflict of interest' check which may result in the firm's inability or unwillingness to take on certain potential new clients. Moreover, 'conflict of interest' checks will also be used on new matters involving existing clients in order to prevent an adverse effect on the firm's or lawyer's representation of other existing clients. Most firms have developed conflict policies based on the principles contained in the Model Rules which are intended to ensure that lawyers will represent their clients zealously and effectively without consideration of competing interests.

Specifically, Model Rule 1.7(a) provides that an attorney may not represent a client

> if the representation of that client will be directly adverse to another client, unless (1) the lawyer reasonably believes the representation will not adversely affect the relationship with the other client and (2) each client consents after consultation.

Model Rule 1.7(b) provides that representation of a client may not be undertaken if it would be

> materially limited by the lawyer's responsibilities to another client or to a third person, or by the lawyer's own interests, unless (1) the lawyer reasonably believes the representation will not be adversely affected, and (2) the client consents after consultation.

Model Rule 1.7, which attempts to reconcile the principle of loyalty to a client with the needs of lawyers to attract business from different sources and not be dependent on any one client, relegates to individual lawyers and firms the responsibility of ensuring that different clients with potentially divergent interests are effectively represented. Moreover, because many large-scale corporate clients use different American law firms to satisfy their various legal needs on a regular basis, it is not surprising that many firms have institution-alised 'Chinese wall' policies and procedures between certain individuals and practice areas in the firm who are acting on behalf of one client, the representation of which may be potentially adverse to a second client.

In order to work on behalf of both such clients, the responsible parties within the firm will solicit both parties' consent to their respective represen-tation. The firm should ensure that the practitioners working for each such client have no professional contact with, or discussions between, each other and that all documents and other sensitive information are isolated from the other group. While Chinese walls are common and taken seriously by the firms involved, any prospective client which wishes to avoid even the slightest potential for conflict of interest should not feel pressured into accepting a Chinese wall from the firm proposing the dual representation.

• RIGHTS OF AUDIENCE IN LOCAL COURTS •

As discussed above, lawyers qualified in a particular jurisdiction will generally be permitted to appear before the courts of that jurisdiction but may need independent or additional qualifications to appear in front of certain courts sitting in that jurisdiction. For example, special certification is required before a lawyer is qualified to appear before most federal courts and the tax courts in most states. Appearance before courts other than those of a lawyer's home jurisdiction may be made by oral or written motion often at the behest of the litigants or the guest lawyer's local counsel.

COMMERCIAL ARRANGEMENTS WHEN INSTRUCTING COUNSEL

Once a client has identified a suitable lawyer or firm of lawyers for a particular matter, it is important that both lawyer and client have a clear understanding of the commercial arrangement between them. While many of the elements of such an arrangement (eg time constraints, number and seniority of lawyers involved, billing considerations) may be discussed during the process of identifying the lawyer or law firm, certain specific details should be understood by both sides prior to commencing substantive work. Many of these details will likely have an impact on the ultimate cost of the services to be provided.

Before agreeing on a specific commercial arrangement, the responsible or contact lawyer must appreciate the amount and nature of the work expected from the lawyer or law firm and the role the client expects the lawyer to assume in the particular transaction or matter being considered. A careful description of the task at hand and a clear communication of the client's expectations will help ensure that the service ultimately provided by the lawyer meets the client's needs and minimises the opportunity for disappointment at the end of the engagement. Moreover, this approach will help form the basis of a working relationship for the project and for potential future matters.

Accordingly, a client should keep the following considerations in mind when instructing a US lawyer or law firm:

(a) whether there will be any division of labour between the US lawyer or law firm and the client's in-house lawyers and, if so, the allocation of responsibilities;

(b) the number of lawyers and level of seniority that the client expects to work on the matter;

(c) the names of any specific lawyer or lawyers the client prefers to work on the matter;

(d) any special timetable or other timing constraints (eg fiscal year-end or other reporting requirements, related transactions);

(e) any special billing constraints (eg timing, form, content); and

(f) any other working rules or methodology that the client would like to establish at the outset (eg cost updates, progress reports).

Obviously, these are only general considerations and may not be relevant for every engagement. For example, the number and seniority of the lawyers involved will depend, in part, on the complexity, the documentary require-ments and the urgency of the transaction or matter.

Clients should generally expect partners in US firms to take a more pro-active, visible role in transactions or cases on a day to day matter than do their counterparts in firms outside the US. Any client working with a US lawyer for the first time should be cognisant that the final fee for legal services ultimately rendered will reflect the hourly rates of partners and other senior professionals dedicated to the matter.

• FEE STRUCTURE •

ABA Guidelines: the Formal Opinion

The ABA and local bar associations require that all legal bills be 'fair' and 'reasonable' in light of all the circumstances surrounding a matter. Recent controversies over legal fees have prompted the ABA to issue a formal opinion (Formal Opinion 93-379, Billing for Professional Fees, Disbursements and Other Expense of 6 December 1993, the 'Formal Opinion') which aims to refine and promote the application of the ethical standards contained in the Model Rules to the fairness and reasonableness of legal fees and disbursements.

The Formal Opinion attempts to clarify the actual effect of Model Rule of Professional Conduct 1.5 (and an analogous provision, Model Code of Professional Responsibility DR 2-106, which is in effect in a minority of US states) on billing. Aside from reiterating the fundamental principle that legal fees should be reasonable, Model Rule 1.5 also requires that all methods of determining fees, including those discussed below are acceptable as long as they are used reasonably and in the appropriate circumstances. In determining reasonableness, the factors to be considered are:

(a) the time and labour required, the novelty and difficulty of the questions involved, and the skill requisite to perform the legal services properly;

(b) the likelihood, if apparent to the client, that the acceptance of the particular employment will preclude other employment by the lawyer;

(c) the fee customarily charged in the locality for similar legal services;

(d) the amount involved and the results obtained;

(e) the time limitations imposed by the client or by the circumstances;

(f) the nature and length of the professional relationship with the client;

(g) the experience, reputation and ability of the lawyer or the lawyers performing the services; and

(h) whether the fee is fixed or contingent.

Model Rule 1.5 also states that lawyers representing clients on a first-time basis should communicate to the client, preferably in writing, the basis or rate of the fees and disbursements intended to be charged either before or shortly after commencing performance. This obligation also requires that invoices eventually rendered be as lucid and informative as possible. False or misleading communication about the lawyer or the lawyer's services (ie communications containing material misrepresentation of fact or law, or omitting a fact necessary to make the statement considered as a whole not materially misleading) are prohibited under Model Rule 7.1. For example, bills computed on a straight time basis should contain a breakdown of disbursements into the actual type of charges incurred.

The Formal Opinion reiterates the policy grounds underlying the ABA's standards on the reasonableness of legal fees. On the one hand, the client should be able to rely on the integrity of a professional yet, on the other hand, the lawyer should be able to expect fair compensation under the circumstances so as to preserve his other incentive to represent the client effectively and zealously and to protect his or her financial and professional independence. One of a lawyer's chief responsibilities is to advance the legal process efficiently without unnecessary continuous toil or overstaffing a project.

The ethical standards of billing by the American legal profession is specifically addressed in the Model Rules and the Formal Opinion. If a lawyer is capable of accomplishing a task more efficiently than originally anticipated, the lawyer is free to suggest to the client a premium or success fee as compensation for his work. Such lawyer may not, however, according to the Formal Opinion, use the fortuity of his efficiency to bill the client for hours not actually spent to the client. As a corollary, if a lawyer's work is more time-consuming or difficult than originally intended, the lawyer should bill those hours actually spent or even consider renegotiating the original fee estimate or cap agreed to by the client providing reasons for the higher than anticipated fees or disbursements.

A client should pay only for those out-of-pocket disbursements reasonably incurred in connection with his representation. A client should not be expected to shoulder any share of general overhead expenses (such as rent, utilities, malpractice insurance or general secretarial expenses); these costs should be considered part of a lawyer's professional fees. An exception to the foregoing arises for certain disbursements reasonably allocated to the cost of other disbursements properly charged to a client. For example, a pro rata share of a service contract for photocopying or facsimile machines may be billed as a fixed portion of the per page cost of the photocopying or facsimile charges otherwise paid by the client. Similarly, costs incurred for the services of third party professionals, such as court reporters, technical consultants or local counsel, if billed through the main lawyer, should only reflect the hourly charges and disbursements directly charged by the third party professional (including at a discounted rate, if applicable), and may not reflect any of the main lawyer's fees unless directly incurred in connection with the employment of the third party.

• METHOD OF BILLING •

As with most of their counterparts outside the US, US lawyers generally bill their clients for time and actual disbursements incurred on a particular matter. Most US law firms and legal practitioners have traditionally billed for their professional services on a strict hourly basis. However, the actual procedures and methods for calculating a legal bill will depend to a large extent on the lawyers involved and the nature of the matter.

Legal time is normally recorded by increments of time (usually consisting of ten or 15-minute intervals) spent per lawyer, paralegal, outside consultant or other professional. Hourly rates for US lawyers range widely between and even within markets and often depend on the type or complexity of a given transaction or case. The high end of the scale (lawyers in the major firms in the bigger markets) might be in the vicinity of US$250-450 per hour for a partner and US$100-250 per hour for an associate. Most surveys traditionally put this figure as somewhat lower than that for their English and central European counterparts although a comparison of the basis of an attorney's hourly rates may have little relevance in terms of analysing the final price paid for the legal services provided for completion of a case or a transaction. Most firms also charge time on an incremental basis for the services or paralegals, researchers, docket clerks and similar professionals.

Generally, more routine matters which could be handled by virtually any firm in a certain market will be billed on a straight time basis, while more complex, time-consuming transactions will often be charged at a premium. Premiums are often characterised as 'success fees', as a means of creating incentives to lawyers to take a more commercial, pro-active role in a transaction and thus add greater value than would be the case for a more routine transaction where attorneys are merely reacting to the legal aspects of a routine transaction, the terms of which have already been decided by the principals. A premium can be agreed as a fixed 'add-on' to the actual time and disbursements incurred or it can be included as part of an overall fee, thus encouraging attorneys to work as efficiently as possible so that their fee for actual time does not eclipse their potential profit earned. If the transaction or matter is one for which a premium above normal rates may be applicable, the potential premium should be negotiated in advance.

Disbursements are normally delineated by category. Common out of pocket costs for which law firms expect reimbursement are secretarial overtime, facsimile, telephone, courier, photocopying, automated legal research, filing and registration fees and the fees and expenses of local counsel employed to advise on matters as to which the main law firm is not experienced or licensed to practise.

Other alternatives to straight hourly billing with or without a premium (or means of obtaining legal services on a basis other than hourly billing) include the following.

Blended rates

With this billing method, the firm will set an hourly rate for its services reflecting the probable configuration of attorneys dedicated to a matter. This creates an incentive to lawyers to use more expensive practitioners only as and when necessary, although less highly leveraged firms (those with a comparatively low associate-partner ratio) may be able to accomplish the work with more efficient senior attorneys.

Sliding scales

A client and its lawyer may come to an agreement that routine matters are charged at a rate lower than those for which a particular firm's expertise would be crucial to the success of a matter.

Flat fees

A law firm or lawyer may agree an absolute cap on legal fees and, sometimes, disbursements for the matters of either a routine, standardised nature or considered as a 'loss leader' necessary to retain or attract other business.

Transaction percentage

A client may agree to pay the lawyer a fee based on a fixed percentage of the total transaction value. This method is most common in real estate transactions.

Volume discounts

A law firm may enter into an agreement with a client, usually a long-term institutional client, for all or a well-defined portion of that client's work to be done by the firm at reduced hourly rates or for a flat fee for a specific period. For example, a common arrangement might involve a law firm taking a certain portion of a client's work, such as documentation of risk management products, small dollar amount loans or routine pleadings, for a reduced percentage of the firm's normal fees. This volume discount arrangement is often a means of establishing a long-term relationship between a law firm and its institutional clients and is intended to facilitate engagements on other more remunerative transactions.

Secondments

This is a corollary to the volume discount and sliding scale schemes described above. Financial institutions or companies which have a very limited or no legal department will often use their leverage with their preferred or potential lawyers to employ a legal professional to work on an in-house basis for a flat fee, often computed on an bi-annual or annual basis. The secondee will provide legal services to the client on a much lower hourly basis than if the client had referred the work actually done to the law firm on a case by case basis. Clients may find this arrangement advantageous in that they will be able to rely on the expertise and experience of the secondee's entire firm. A secondment arrangement has the added benefit that the client is able to terminate the secondment in case of a downturn in the quantity of work without any of the costs and difficulties involved in dismissing a staff attorney.

Contingency fees

One unusual feature of US lawyers' billing methods is the contingency fee arrangement, where certain lawyers, mostly in the personal injury and defamation fields (but not, according to Model Rule 1.5(d), in the majority of domestic relations matters or criminal cases), will not charge clients fees for legal time but will take a certain percentage of any damages or monetary judgment awarded to their clients and be reimbursed for costs and expenses. The contingency fee system is viewed by some practitioners as controversial. Its proponents claim that it gives genuinely aggrieved plaintiffs the ability to seek adjudication of their injuries which they might otherwise not use because of the high costs of lawyering and litigation, while its critics argue that it leads to litigiousness.

It must be noted that the ABA does not prohibit or encourage any of the foregoing methods of billing; it merely attempts to instil ethical standards into the billing methods which lawyers and their clients are free to negotiate.

• TIMING OF BILLING •

As mentioned above, the method and timing of billing should be discussed between the lawyer and client in the early stages of the engagement. While the actual timing of issuing an invoice will depend on the nature of the transaction or matter, both client and lawyer can benefit from interim billing. By issuing interim bills, the lawyer helps the client to spread its legal expenses more evenly throughout a particular accounting period and provides the client with a regular check on the cost of its legal services. This may be especially important on major transactions or litigation matters that involve a large team of lawyers over an extended period of time. For the lawyer, interim billing helps manage the cashflow needs of the lawyer or law firm, something which more lawyers and law firms have begun to focus on as they begin to manage their practices in a more businesslike manner.

Whatever billing arrangements are finally agreed, a client should expect to be kept informed with respect to progress on the legal matter, including cost updates. This is especially important where a cap or similar arrangement has been agreed at the outset or where there is an agreement to revisit arrangements when a legal fee approaches a previously determined limit.

• FEE DISPUTES •

The Model Rules defer the matter of disputes between clients and their attorneys over fees to the procedures outlined by local bars. Many of these procedures were developed in the 1970s as bar associations became aware of the prevalence of fee disputes and the unsuitability of the judicial process to adjust fees on the one hand and the perceived weakness in the bargaining power of most clients on the other. Arbitration procedures in some states are open to those who wish to make use of them, while others are binding upon the lawyer, if the dispute is submitted to arbitration by a client, although, generally, a lawyer may not impose arbitration upon an unwilling client. In some jurisdictions, such as California, disputes between a lawyer and client as to fees which have been subject to an arbitral award may still be tried before a court of law in the absence of an agreement between the parties to be bound by the arbitral award. The statutes in effect in some states, such as California, provide that recovery of costs and expenses may be awarded to the prevailing party and that sanctions may be effected against attorneys who refuse to comply with arbitral awards (including placing errant attorneys on involuntary inactive status).

The question of resolution of fee disputes is left to the relevant jurisdiction in which the lawyer practises. The comment to Model Rule 1.5 merely implores that a lawyer should conscientiously consider submitting to any arbitration, mediation or other fee dispute resolution procedure established by his local bar and should follow any existing statutory scheme as to the fixing of fees, for example, in probate matters. Clients should, however, take comfort in the bargaining power they have in settling possible fee disputes. A client can use the threat of withdrawal of other business or the redirection of future legal work to another lawyer or firm as leverage in resolving any dispute, assuming of course it is sufficiently satisfied with the quality of the lawyer's services to attempt an amicable resolution of the disputed amount of the invoice. Lawyers tend to be mindful of any potential damage to their reputation in a closed society of learned professionals. Finally, there is adequate case law precedent in most states for overturning egregious fees for legal services.

TREATMENT OF FOREIGN NATIONALS UNDER LOCAL LAW

The United States has traditionally maintained an open policy toward foreign direct investment with a comparatively non-interventionist approach to business in general. This *laissez-faire* policy, combined with the attractiveness of the world's largest single market and continuing economic and political stability, has no doubt contributed to the ongoing importance of the US as a destination for capital from sources outside the US.

This description of regulations affecting foreign investment in the US is a summary only and any investment in the United States, regardless of the type or location, should be made only after consultation with legal, accounting and tax professionals with special attention paid to regulation at the federal, state and local levels.

• BUSINESS ENTITIES •

Generally, most businesses in the United States are organised as corporations or partnerships, although there are various types of each such form. All business entities are formed under the statutory framework in effect in a certain state and subject to that state's own regulations as to business entities, as well as the laws and statutes in effect in each location where that organisation does business. One basic distinction between the various alternatives for organising a business in the US is the concept of limited liability.

Unlimited liability

Sole proprietorship

The sole proprietorship is the simplest form of business enterprise. All capital is supplied, and all risks are assumed, by the proprietor. The owner usually serves as manager of the business and has day to day involvement in its affairs. Despite the comparative simplicity of this form of ownership, sole proprietorships are subject to the same taxpaying and filing requirements as larger entities. A sole proprietorship may survive its proprietor or may terminate at his or her will or upon his or her death, incapacity or insolvency.

General partnership

A partnership is generally defined as an association of two or more persons to carry on as co-owners a business for profit. Each partner assumes unlimited liability for partnership obligations. No special formalities are required to operate as a partnership, and a partnership may be deemed to exist even if not intended, if the parties' actions are consistent with that of a partnership. The Uniform Partnership Act, adopted in most states, specifies the rights and obligations of the parties in the absence of a partnership agreement. Law firms, accounting firms, movie production companies, merchant banks and other professional organisations tend to be organised as general partnerships.

A partnership may buy, sell and own property and may sue or be sued in its own name. The partnership is treated as a pass-through conduit under federal and state tax laws, with individual partners rather than the partnership recognising income and losses. Transfer of a partnership interest and any of the partnership's assets usually requires the approval of all or the majority of partners. A partnership dissolves upon the death, legal incapacity, bankruptcy or, if no term for the partnership has been agreed, the demand of any partner.

Unincorporated joint ventures

An unincorporated joint venture is similar to a partnership but it does not maintain the status of a distinct legal entity and is typically limited in duration and purpose to a single commercial undertaking or a series of related undertakings. Joint ventures have been used by many non-US and US companies in the manufacturing and natural resources industries, where economic and political factors dictate a circumscribed alliance of convenience rather than the establishment of a long-term institution.

The liabilities assumed by the joint venturers are similar to those assumed by partners in a partnership. However, each joint venturer generally has less power to bind the other with respect to third parties than partners in a general partnership. Much like a partnership, a joint venture is treated as pass-through conduit for tax purposes. Interests in the joint venture may be transferred in accordance with the joint venture agreement. The legal regime governing joint ventures is derived from the common law of contracts and sometimes from partnership law in effect in the relevant state.

Limited liability

Limited partnerships

Limited partnerships share the attributes of general partnerships but have one or more limited partners whose liability for partnership obligations is limited. A limited partnership must have at least one general partner who assumes unlimited liability for partnership obligations. However, the general partner itself may be an entity of limited liability, such as a corporation. The special tax attributes of limited partnerships ensures their usefulness in oil, gas and other natural resource ventures.

The attraction of a limited partnership for its limited partners is that the limited partner remains liable only to the extent of its investment in the partnership. The Uniform Limited Partnership Act and the Revised Uniform Limited Partnership Act, adopted in most states, regulate the formation and governance of, admission of partners to and withdrawal of partners from, assignment of partnership interests in, and dissolution of, such partnerships. The relative uniformity of state regulation of partnerships has meant that, unlike corporations, limited partnerships tend to be organised in the states where most partners reside or where they do most of their business. Delaware, however, is often the state of choice because of its well-developed law relating to business organisations.

A limited partner may participate in major decisions of the partnership but is prohibited from participating in the day to day management and control of the business. There is ample case law for the proposition that a limited partner's involvement in such day to day management of the business will result in the limited partner's interest being treated as that of a general partner, thereby assuming unlimited liability for the partnership's obligations. A limited partner may freely assign its interests in the limited partnership, subject to any restrictions in the partnership agreements. Also, a limited partnership is dissolved not upon a limited partner's death, legal incapacity or bankruptcy but, rather, in accordance with the partnership agreement or otherwise with the consent of all partners. Like corporations, limited partnerships are required to make routine filings in their state of formation.

Corporations

A corporation is legally and logistically the most complex form of business entity to organise and manage, but such complexity has not prohibited even modest sized entities from using the corporate form. The vast majority of larger US corporations are organised under the laws of Delaware which, as noted above, has maintained a corporate law and judiciary favourable to business for most of the 20th century.

Initially, the promoters of a corporation must select a corporate name for approval by the Secretary of State in the proposed state of incorporation. Next, one or more incorporators must file with the Secretary of State a charter document, usually called the Articles of Incorporation (or the Certificate of Incorporation for a Delaware corporation), which establishes the corporation as a separate legal entity. Among other provisions, the Articles of Incorporation specify the classes and number of shares of authorised stock and the designated agent for service of process. The authorised number of shares is usually greater than that which is actually issued. Capital is contributed by shareholders, either through subscription arrangements or public offerings. A corporation is chartered only in one state. Following incorporation, however, a corporation may choose to conduct business in other states and must qualify to do business in each such state – such qualification is a relatively straightforward procedure. In some states, 'doing business' includes owning real property or borrowing money, although special care should be taken in certain states which afford very liberal constructions to the question of what constitutes 'doing business' and which may void or make voidable contracts entered into by corporations which inadvertently fail to gain official approval to do business in those states. Corporate income and assets will be taxed pursuant to the rules of each state in which it does business.

At the first meeting of the corporation, by-laws (the internal rules governing the corporation) are adopted and the initial board of directors is elected. Upon the election of directors, the incorporators resign. The directors elect officers to conduct the day to day management and operations of the business. Directors and officers should observe all formalities of the corporation's existence, including the maintenance of adequate books and records. Case law in each state establishes the fiduciary duties of care and loyalty owed by a corporation to its shareholders. Once incorporated, a corporation may buy, sell and own property, enter into and enforce contracts, and sue and be sued. A corporation has unlimited duration but may be dissolved by merger with another corporation, by voluntary dissolution upon the vote of a majority of its shareholders, or by involuntary dissolution by court order due to deadlock among shareholder or shareholder actions proving fraud or unfairness or waste of corporate assets.

Because the corporation is a separate legal entity, the liability of each shareholder is limited to the amount of its investment in the enterprise although, in certain cases such as those described below, shareholders may be forced to assume liability for corporate obligations. The extent of transferability of shares in a corporation depends on whether the entity is closely held or publicly traded. Corporations maintain a continuity of existence which survives the death or disability of any shareholder. Corporations are subject to 'double taxation', first to the corporation on income earned, and second to the individual shareholders on dividends received.

S corporations

Certain companies with fewer than 35 shareholders (who must be individuals, estates or certain trusts and if non-US persons must be resident in the state of incorporation) may elect to form a corporation which qualifies for special tax treatment under the US Internal Revenue Code of 1986, as amended (the 'Tax Code'). S corporations are taxed much like partnerships, with income not required to be recognised by the corporation but only at the shareholder level.

Limited liability companies

A growing number of states have introduced legislation creating a new type of business entity: the limited liability company. As the name suggests, the company generally insulates its members (a limited liability company does not have shareholders) from liability like a corporation, but it may be described as a hybrid with both corporate and partnership characteristics. A limited liability company, however, must be structured so that it does not have more corporate than non-corporate characteristics and, generally, must possess at least two of the following three non-corporate characteristics: limitation on duration, limitation on transferability of members' interests and decentralised management.

A limited liability company is not subject to the 'double taxation' dilemma faced by shareholders of a corporation. Members pay federal income tax on the earnings of the corporation in accordance with their respective investments, much like a general partnership. The affairs and conduct of the business of a limited liability company are generally governed by its articles of organisation, an operating agreement and the statutory scheme of the state of organisation.

• BRANCH VERSUS SUBSIDIARY •

A non-US corporation seeking to establish operations in the US should consider, among other things, the following factors in determining whether a branch or a domestically incorporated subsidiary is the most appropriate vehicle:

- effective market penetration;
- limited liability;
- capital requirements and accessibility;
- the ability to obtain local financing; and
- tax treatment.

Some of the fundamental differences between branches and subsidiaries are discussed below.

Branches of non-US corporations

In most cases, a branch office of a non-US corporation wishing to do business in the US need only procure a licence from the state in which it chooses to do business. A branch does not require a permanent physical presence in the US but instead may be established through the periodic presence of employees or agents of the foreign corporation in the US. Capital is provided by the parent, and the parent assumes liability for the branch's operations. The branch, however, must maintain adequate books and records showing the branch's attributable taxable income for US income tax purposes.

Subsidiaries of non-US corporations

Any non-US corporation wishing to establish a domestic subsidiary will be required to incorporate that subsidiary in an appropriate state. Assuming that the subsidiary is adequately capitalised and corporate procedures and all relevant laws are observed, the foreign parent should be insulated from the liabilities of the subsidiary. Some exceptions to this general principle are discussed below. Financing from the US capital and debt markets may also be more readily available to a subsidiary than to a branch. Additionally, as long as the foreign investor does not engage in other activities in the United States, only the subsidiary will be taxed by the federal government on its business income.

• RESTRICTIONS, REPORTS AND GOVERNMENTAL APPROVALS •
OF FOREIGN INVESTMENT

The US regulatory climate is very favourable to foreign investments, with investments from non-US sources generally afforded the same treatment as those from US investors. For example, there are no exchange controls and foreign investors may bring funds freely into the United States, borrow funds in the United States and repatriate both capital and profits abroad. There are no federal requirements to register foreign capital. However, certain foreign investments may need to be reported or subject to government approvals, as described below.

Despite this general freedom on investment, the US federal government has imposed investment restrictions in several commercial areas, usually as a result of perceived national security concerns. The areas covered include defence production, aviation, atomic and nuclear energy, coastal and freshwater shipping, communications and media, mining on federal lands and utilities.

At the state level, certain sectors such as banking, public utility and insurance are regulated so as to prevent or restrict investment by non-state residents, although those regulations are not specifically directed at non-US residents. Accordingly, it is always prudent to review the relevant state law and regulations to understand if any investment restrictions apply.

Import controls and trade agreements

The United States has effected 'antidumping' statutes intended to counteract price discrimination and other anti-competitive practices by a foreign company. Price discrimination occurs when a foreign manufacturer sells goods for a price in the United States lower than in its home or a third country or lower than its manufacturing costs in an attempt to gain a dominant or monopolistic market position in the United States.

Certain industries in the United States may be protected from foreign competition under s 301 of the US Trade Act of 1974, as revised by the Omnibus Trade and Competitiveness Act of 1988. While the application of s 301 is extremely rare, it provides a mechanism for a US company or industry to request the United States Trade Representative to retaliate against foreign businesses if the country of those businesses has denied US persons their rights under trade agreements or has otherwise discriminated against US businesses. If invoked, s 301 is used as a political tool to threaten countries accused of discriminatory trade practices with the preferred statutory method of retaliation being the imposition of duties rather than an outright ban on or restriction of the importation of a given product.

The United States prohibits or restricts the import of some products and requires licences or permits on others. Prohibited imports include controlled substances, obscene materials and products manufactured by convicted criminals or forced labour. Licences or permits are required for the importation of weapons and ammunition and products from certain countries deemed hostile to the United States or with which commerce would not be considered in the United States' national interest. Such proscribed countries include, at the time of writing, Cuba, Haiti, Iraq, North Korea and Serbia. Import restrictions apply to such commodities as alcohol, animals, certain drugs, meat, poultry, milk, dairy, fruit and nuts and products of the foregoing, petroleum and petroleum products, and trademarked items. Absolute annual quotas are imposed on certain imports, including some dairy products, animal feeds containing milk, cotton and cotton waste, clothing and textiles, peanuts, sugars, syrups, molasses, cheese, chocolate, ice cream and wheat. Also, country of origin marking requirements exist for imported products.

In most cases, tariffs are levied on an *ad valorem* basis, but may also be assessed on an item specific basis. Tariffs on some products are assessed on a sliding sale after initial quotas for those products have been met. The average tariff on industrial products ranges from 4 to 5 per cent. In addition to tariffs, the United States charges a user fee on all imports and a harbour maintenance fee on imports arriving by water. Also, excise taxes are assessed on certain imports including luxury items, intoxicating substances and petroleum products.

The United States has entered into free trade agreements with Israel (1985) and, pursuant to the North American Free Trade Agreement, with Mexico and Canada (1994). Many commentators expect the scope of the North

American Free Trade Agreement to be expanded to other countries in Latin America. These agreements eliminate or reduce tariff and non-tariff trade barriers and are designed to increase economic growth and development in each country. Under the Caribbean Basin Initiative, duty-free entry of many products is granted to Caribbean countries. The United States is a member of the General Agreement on Tariffs and Trade, and has also entered into most favoured nation agreements with many of its trading partners, providing for reduced duty on the vast majority of products.

Reporting requirements
Any foreign entity must comply with certain reporting requirements, of which the most obvious is taxation, discussed below. With a few limited exceptions, all types of business will be regulated by laws and statutes enacted by federal, state and/or local agencies. Some of the more prominent agencies responsible for regulating the more common areas of commercial and financial activity include the Department of Agriculture, the Interstate Commerce Commission, the Federal Aviation Authority, the Federal Communications Commission, the Food and Drug Administration, the Environmental Protection Agency, the Federal Reserve System, the Comptroller of the Currency, the Federal Deposit Insurance Corporation and the Patent and Trademark Office and the Copyright Office. Any entity operating in the US should work with counsel to establish a compliance and reporting system suitable for that entity's business.

Most foreign investment is required to be reported to the Bureau of Economic Analysis of the Department of Commerce. This reporting requirement arises when a foreign entity or person owns or controls 10 per cent or more of a US business enterprise and must be updated periodically. The filing entity must submit details on transactions between the foreign and US entity and certain agreements governing their relationship (eg loan, lease, licence and royalty agreements). Exemptions from reporting are available for small investments (generally less than US$1,000,000) while the reporting requirements are reduced for investments under US$20,000,000, subject to several conditions. Other exemptions apply to limited partnership interests. In most cases exemptions from this reporting requirement are not self-executing and require a specific filing. Reports filed are generally kept confidential, even from taxing authorities. Failure to report can result in penalties and, if wilful, imprisonment. A few states impose similar reporting requirements.

Exon-Florio
The Exon-Florio Amendment to the Defense Production Act of 1950 ('Exon-Florio') is a broadly drafted statute which empowers the President of the United States to block or unwind an acquisition by a foreign individual, company or government control of a business engaged in interstate commerce in the United States if there is credible evidence that such acquisition could

impair the US national security. While 'national security' is not defined, transactions involving a US company that has contracts with the US Department of Defense or the US Department of Energy may be *prima facie* suspect of threatening the US 'national security'. Relatively few acquisitions have been challenged under Exon-Florio and while there is no legal duty to file a notice under Exon-Florio, a proposed transaction can be reviewed and advance clearance can be obtained if a voluntary notice is filed with the Committee on Foreign Investment in the United States (CFIUS), the US governmental agency delegated authority to review and investigate transactions potentially covered by Exon-Florio. A non-US person contemplating an acquisition of a US business involving products, services or technologies relevant to US national defence should seek appropriate legal advice and consider notifying the CFIUS to obtain advance clearance of its proposed acquisition.

Anti-trust reviews

Restrictions are also placed on certain acquisitions of US businesses that may have an anti-competitive effect. As a general rule, the US anti-trust laws attempt to foster competition and to eliminate monopolies and unreasonable restraints of trade. The anti-trust laws are complex and the level of enthusiasm with which such laws are enforced tends to vary over time with the changing policies of different US administrations. Private parties may also sue competitors and potential acquirers in connection with anti-trust violations and claim injunctive relief and/or treble damages. Proscribed activities include price fixing, horizontal market division, refusals to deal, resale price maintenance, territorial resale restrictions, tying arrangements, price discrimination and other activities which have the effect of substantially lessening competition. Except as described in the next paragraph, no prior approval or filing under the US anti-trust laws is required for an acquisition of a US business.

Hart-Scott-Rodino notification

The US government screens transactions that may have an anti-competitive effect by requiring filings and advance clearance for acquisitions of US businesses under the Hart-Scott-Rodino Antitrust Improvements Act of 1976 (the 'HSR Act'). The HSR Act does not focus on foreign transactions alone but affects many foreign acquisitions. Generally, the HSR Act requires both parties to an acquisition to notify the Federal Trade Commission and the Anti-trust Division of the Department of Justice if:

(a) the acquisition in question involves one person (under the HSR Act, a person includes the ultimate parent entity or ultimate controlling individual of a person and all entities that it controls) with US$100 million in annual net sales or total assets and another person with US$10 million in annual net sales or total assets; and

(b) as a result of the acquisition:

(i) the acquiring person holds either 15 per cent or more of the acquired assets or voting securities; or

(ii) the value of the assets and voting securities acquired equals or exceeds US$15,000,000.

Certain exemptions exist and may be available to the parties in certain situations.

Each party to an acquisition must file a Hart-Scott-Rodino notification, which must be accompanied by a US$25,000 filing fee. A waiting period (beginning on the date a complete notification form is submitted) must expire before the acquisition may be consummated. In most cases, the waiting period is 30 days (20 days for cash tender offers) unless extended by either the Federal Trade Commission or the Department of Justice by a request for additional information. The notification must include information about the parties involved, the transaction at issue and market information about the products manufactured or services provided by the parties involved in the acquisition. If full information is submitted promptly, anti-trust clearance should not impede the acquisition unless there is a genuine issue of anti-trust law. A request can be made for the early termination of the statutory waiting period and, unless a real anti-trust issue exists, early termination is typically granted. If the parties fail to notify an acquisition which is subject to the HSR Act or consummate the transaction prior to the expiration of the waiting period, they will be subject to civil penalties of up to US$10,000 per day.

• EXCHANGE CONTROLS AND OTHER REGULATORY ISSUES •

There are no exchange controls imposed by the United States and no restrictions on the flow of currency into or out of the country. However, if US$10,000 or more is physically taken into or out of the country, an information return (Form 4790) must be filed with a customs officer.

As mentioned above, the United States has effected laws and regulations covering virtually all areas of commerce. While this may require considerable planning time by the potential investor, it also provides stability and certainty of treatment once an investment decision has been taken. Two of the more distinctive aspects of the US regulatory landscape, environmental regulation and securities laws, are discussed below.

Environmental regulation
Environmental regulation is considerably more extensive in the United States than in other countries and foreign investors should pay special attention to the environmental aspects of their business. Under US environmental laws, a current owner of property, under certain circumstances, can be forced to incur monetary costs for the acts of prior owners and/or occupiers of the property or

even latent environmental conditions in the land itself. Accordingly, it is very important to consider whether an investment involves contaminated property or an entity that uses or produces hazardous substances. Under extreme circumstances, secured lenders financing a contaminated property may be forced to shoulder clean-up and/or compliance costs. Enforcement of violations of environmental laws can often be aggressive and the resulting sanctions may involve fines exceeding the purchase price of the property or imprisonment.

Securities regulation

Any person acquiring or selling securities in the United States or in a transaction involving US persons must consider the application of US securities laws. At the federal level, US securities laws are administered by the US Securities and Exchange Commission (the SEC). Generally, under the Securities Act of 1933 (the 'Securities Act'), offers and sales of securities in the United States must be registered pursuant to a registration statement filed with the SEC, unless the offer in question qualifies for an exemption from such registration. One such exemption is the so-called private placement exemption which, for example, typically would apply to the sale of shares in a privately-held company to a small group of sophisticated investors. The preparation of a registration can be an expensive and time-consuming process, and the registration statement must be reviewed, approved, and declared 'effective' by the SEC prior to the consummation of any sale of securities to which it relates.

The Securities Exchange Act of 1934 (the 'Exchange Act') regulates the trading of securities and requires that issuers of securities and certain insiders (see below) file certain periodic reports. For US domestic corporations, reports must be filed annually on Form 10-K and quarterly on Form 10-Q. For non-US corporations, reports must be filed annually on Form 20-F and, under limited circumstances in which such information is required to be made public in the home country or is disclosed to non-US securities authorities or is otherwise distributed to shareholders, quarterly or semi-annually on Form 6-K. Where the SEC's disclosure requirements for foreign companies is substantially equivalent to the disclosure required of domestic companies, limited accommodation for certain foreign companies may exist. For example, the SEC may allow a non-US company to include financial statements which have not been prepared in accordance with US Generally Accepted Accounting Principles (GAAP) as long as the effects of any significant differences between GAAP and the non-US accounting principles are disclosed.

In recent years, the SEC has made and continues to make considerable efforts to adapt US securities regulations to the increasing internationalisation of capital markets. The adoption in 1990 of Rule 144A, which facilitates the placement and trading of debt and non-listed equity securities with and among qualified institutional investors in the United States without registration under US securities laws, and Regulation S, which excepts certain offshore offerings from registration, are two noteworthy examples.

In addition to registration and reporting requirements, the federal securities laws prohibit short-swing profits (ie profits generated from the purchase and sale of publicly-traded securities when such purchase and sale are made less than six months apart) by insiders (ie officers, directors and shareholders owning 10 per cent or more of the shares of an outstanding class of stock). Short-swing profits made by insiders may be disgorged and paid over to the issuer. Beneficial owners of 5 per cent or more of the outstanding securities of a publicly-listed company must file reports disclosing such ownership, the relationship with the issuer and certain other related information. Fraud in the purchase and sale of securities (including insider trading) is highly regulated under federal securities laws and prohibited under Rule 10b-5 of the Exchange Act. Penalties for failure to comply with the provisions of the Securities Act and the Exchange Act involve both civil and criminal sanctions.

Finally, in addition to the SEC's requirements, each state has its own securities laws (known as 'blue sky' laws) which specify that state's registration and reporting requirements.

The primary public trading markets in the United States, which also impose regulations on purchases and sales of listed securities, are the New York Stock Exchange and the American Stock Exchange, both located in New York. Smaller stock exchanges are located in Boston, Chicago, Philadelphia and San Francisco. In addition, over-the-counter markets include NASDAQ (National Association of Securities Dealers Automated Quotations) and the NASDAQ National Market System. A separate application must be made for listing on an exchange or over-the-counter; registration with the SEC will not effect such a listing.

• TAX TREATMENT •

The US taxation rules are complex and subject to frequent revision, often as a result of changes in the political orientation of various US institutions. The following is a summary overview of US tax regulations and all but the simplest tax planning should be done only after consultation with a qualified tax attorney and/or accountant.

Taxation in the United States may be imposed at the federal, state and local levels. The principal taxing authority is the US federal government, which imposes income, excise and estate and gift taxes. Most state and some local taxing authorities also impose income, sales, franchise and capital-based taxes as well as property, gift and estate taxes. Often these authorities use an entity's federal tax reporting as the basis for determination of such entity's local tax liability.

One significant feature of US tax law is that resident aliens (non-US citizens) and domestic US entities (those formed under US law) are subject to US tax on their worldwide income. Foreign corporations and non-resident aliens typically are taxed only on income arising in the United States, often referred to as US source income. Once US source income arises, such income is generally taxed on a net basis if the foreign corporation or non-resident alien is carrying out a trade or business in the United States and such income is 'effectively connected' with such trade or business. If not engaged in a trade or business in the United States, such persons are generally subject to a flat 30 per cent tax on the gross amount of their income from United States' sources. Tax treaties between the US and foreign countries can substantially affect taxation.

Certain states (including California) tax US businesses on their worldwide income, even if not connected with the US. California has recently enacted an election to foreign companies to permit taxation only on US based income. Accordingly, the location of a proposed investment and the locations in which a foreign company plans to do business in the United States should be carefully discussed with competent US tax advisers.

The US Internal Revenue Service (the IRS) oversees the application of US federal tax laws. The IRS has established extensive requirements for filing returns and other information. Typically, filings must be made at least annually, although most entities are required to make payments of estimated tax on a quarterly basis. In addition, many businesses are required to pay quarterly payroll taxes for wages paid to employees.

One important tax planning consideration is the use of debt in a corporation's capital structure. As discussed above, the application of the US tax laws can result in the double taxation of corporate income. Interest payments on debt, while treated as income to the recipient, are generally deductible against net income by the corporation paying the dividend.

US tax laws may also require withholding of a certain percentage of interest and income paid to foreign entities and non-resident individuals.

Generally, US tax laws focus on substance over form. If a primary motivation for a particular transaction or investment structure is the avoidance of tax, the taxing authorities may challenge the tax characterisation of a given transaction nominated by the taxpayer. In cases of ambiguity, a business should seek an advance ruling as to the IRS' treatment of its tax position.

• EMPLOYMENT •

Labour laws
The relation between employers and their employees is regulated primarily by federal law, although state statutes and common law may be applicable in

certain situations. The National Labor Relations Act protects employees' rights to organise and bargain collectively with an employer, and the Occupational Safety and Health Act of 1970 sets health and safety standards for the workplace. The national minimum wage is currently set at US$4.25 per hour (the actual rate, however, may vary depending on the state or other jurisdiction and the type of employee), with at least one and one-half times the hourly rate required to be paid for overtime work (generally work performed over 40 hours per week). Employees in the United States are accustomed to payment at least twice per month. If a pension plan is offered, the employer must comply with provisions of the Employee Retirement Income Security Act of 1974 as amended by the Multi-employer Pension Plan Amendments Act of 1980, non-compliance with which can result in the imposition of liens and fines against the employer. Also, unless a bona fide work-related requirement exists, employment discrimination on the basis of race, national origin, religion, sex, age or disability is prohibited. Wrongful discharge claims by former employees can be minimised by instituting proper procedures for review and documentation of employee performance.

Work permits
Foreign nationals are required to have both a passport and an immigration visa to be eligible to work in the United States, and harsh penalties apply to employers who hire illegal aliens. Application for a visa may be made at US embassies and consulates. Non-immigrant foreign nationals who enter the United States on a temporary basis for business purposes generally seek B, E, H or L visa classifications. The B visa classification admits individuals for business stays less than six months, but US income cannot be earned during the stay. The E visa classification admits persons from countries with which the US maintains a treaty of commerce and navigation seeking to engage in substantial business or make substantial investments in the US. E visas are usually issued by US diplomatic officials pursuant to special requests. The H visa classification admits foreign nationals who possess special abilities or will receive special training. The L visa classification admits executives and managers with specialised knowledge necessary to the operation of US business enterprises. Spouses and minor children may be admitted under the E, H or L visa classifications.

• ACCESS TO AND TREATMENT BY LOCAL COURTS •

As a general rule, any US court at the federal, state or local level must have both 'subject matter' jurisdiction and 'personal' jurisdiction over the particular matter before the court. Unless both of these jurisdictional conditions are met, the court will have no power to adjudicate a particular matter. Subject matter jurisdiction is generally concerned with the appropriateness of the matter to be heard by the court, while personal jurisdiction addresses the propriety of bringing a specific person before the court in question. Often the basis of personal jurisdiction is the degree of fairness involved in having a defendant appear before a court. The analysis focuses on whether the defendant has sufficient contact with a jurisdiction from its presence, property or business activities there. A related legal concept (*forum non conveniens*) generally seeks to have cases heard in the most convenient court, considering, for example, the location of the litigants or the majority of witnesses.

Generally, state courts are courts of general jurisdiction and will almost always have subject matter jurisdiction over cases turning on an interpretation of that state's laws. US federal courts, in contrast, only are permitted to hear certain types of cases. For example, federal courts will hear cases involving an interpretation of federal law where an amount in controversy (currently US$50,000) is specified or where the parties involved reside or maintain businesses in different jurisdictions. For most non-US clients, federal courts should be available because federal courts are specifically given subject matter jurisdiction for suits brought by a 'foreign citizen'.

As certain recent highly-publicised trials in the US make apparent, the system and style of litigation before US courts is very different from that in other countries, and non-US persons seeking to use the court system to resolve disputes should be aware of the costs, delays and logistical burdens inherent in litigation in the US.

• FOREIGN PARENT LIABILITY •

As a general rule, setting up a US subsidiary should not result in exposure to the foreign parent. This is in contrast to setting up a branch office, for which the foreign entity has full liability.

In the case of a US subsidiary, there are certain limited situations in which a US court will 'lift the corporate veil' and hold a foreign parent liable for the debts and other liabilities of the US subsidiary. This emphasis on substance over corporate formalities will only occur in extreme circumstances when the court feels redress is necessary. Typically, this requires a substantive disregard for corporate formalities and an insufficiently distinct separation of the US subsidiary from its parent. These rules, however, apply equally to US parent companies and their domestic subsidiaries. Generally, assuming corporate formalities are observed, a foreign parent should not be liable for its US subsidiary's liabilities except in extreme circumstances involving fraudulent or tortious behaviour.

• JURISDICTION OF LOCAL COURTS •

As a general rule, any assets located in the United States can become the subject of US legal proceedings and a judgment obtained against a defendant in another country can generally be enforced against that defendant's assets located in the United States, as described below. Judicial conceptions of fairness play an important role in deciding whether a non-resident entity can be brought before a US court. A foreign entity doing business in the United States is liable to be sued in the United States courts if problems arise. For example, if a foreign company sold a product in the United States which injured a US person, the injured US person could probably sue the foreign company in the state in which the injury occurred. It is possible that a foreign parent company may be made party to an action in the US even if it has specifically organised a US subsidiary for the purpose of handling its US operations and that US subsidiary has already been named in the suit. See the discussion of foreign parent liability above.

• FOREIGN LANGUAGE DOCUMENTS AND DOCUMENTS • GOVERNED BY FOREIGN LAW

Before being presented as evidence, foreign records must be certified or otherwise fit within certain categories of exceptions to certification applicable under US law. All foreign language documents submitted to US courts must be submitted in English or with an English translation.

US courts will generally attempt to apply the law of the foreign jurisdiction to documents governed by foreign law. It is very important to draw the court's attention to the appropriate governing law at the beginning of the judicial process. In US federal courts a failure to notify the court about the proper governing law may result in the irrevocable application of the relevant US law despite the intent of the parties. Evidence of how foreign law affects the facts before the court, either through translations of foreign statutes, regulations and cases or by expert testimony must also be produced or the application of foreign law to the issue may be disregarded. US federal courts are also allowed to investigate independently foreign law and its effect on a particular case.

While US courts will typically apply the law of the foreign jurisdiction to documents governed by foreign law, there are limited exceptions to this rule. For example, an issue may arise if the chosen foreign law has no connection with either party or the transaction. Other exceptions may arise because the foreign country's laws are deemed to violate US public policy or the public policy of the state in which the US court is located. The analysis by a court of the validity of a choice of foreign law often varies from state to state and the application of foreign law to a particular case should be carefully discussed with counsel before commencing litigation.

• RECOGNITION AND ENFORCEMENT OF FOREIGN • JUDGMENTS

Typically a final judgment issued by a court outside the United States will be recognised in the United States without any additional procedures other than a motion for summary judgment and enforcement in the state where execution against the defendant is sought. There is, however, no US federal law on enforcement of foreign judgments and the US is not party to any recognition treaty such as the Brussels or the Lugano Conventions (see Appendix). Accordingly, the states may take different approaches in their enforcement of foreign judgments.

Many states, including California, New York and Illinois, have adopted the Uniform Money-Judgment Recognition Act which provides that recognition of foreign country judgments may be refused on two fundamental grounds. A court will not be permitted to enforce the judgment if a foreign court was not impartial or did not adjudicate the defendant pursuant to principles of due process of law or did not have jurisdiction over the defendant either under the foreign country's own laws or basic principles of international law.

A US court also has discretion to refuse to enforce the judgment of a foreign court for reasons such as lack of subject matter jurisdiction over the defendant, inadequate notice to the defendant, fraud in obtaining the judgment and the incompatibility of the judgment with the public policy of the state in which enforcement is sought. While these are all discretionary grounds for denying enforcement of a judgment and may not ultimately prevent enforcement, a vigorous defence to enforcement based on any of the foregoing should be sufficient to avoid summary judgment and force re-examination by a US court of at least those aspects of the case still in controversy. As the grounds on which a judgment may not be recognised are based on case law as in effect from state to state, advice from counsel should be obtained before seeking to enforce a judgment rendered by a non-US court.

•

Mark R Uhrynuk, Thomas C Wexler and Stefan H Sarles
Mayer, Brown & Platt
162 Queen Victoria Street
London EC4V 4DB
United Kingdom

•

— • —
APPENDIX
— • —

This appendix deals with litigation under the Brussels and Lugano Conventions and is applicable to all EU and EFTA countries.

BRUSSELS AND LUGANO CONVENTIONS

The Brussels Convention on Jurisdiction and the Enforcement of Judgments in Civil and Commercial Matters was signed at Brussels on 27 September 1968. It has since been amended. The Lugano Convention on Jurisdiction and the Enforcement of Judgments in Civil and Commercial Matters was signed at Lugano on 16 September 1988.

The Brussels and Lugano Conventions ('the Conventions') establish a regime with regard to jurisdiction and the enforcement of judgments as between those states that are parties to the Conventions ('contracting states'). Both Conventions apply to all civil and commercial matters, whatever the nature, except to matters pertaining to, among others, revenue, administrative matters, insolvency or arbitration.

The Brussels Convention has been adopted by all EU member states. The Lugano Convention extends a very similar regime to the European Free Trade Association (EFTA) countries (Austria, Finland, Iceland, Norway, Sweden and Switzerland). As at March 1993, only France, Luxembourg, the Netherlands, Portugal, Sweden, Switzerland and the UK have ratified the Lugano Convention. The other EU and EFTA countries are expected to do so in the near future.

• JURISDICTION •

Jurisdiction under the Conventions is generally determined by the domicile of the defendant – that of the plaintiff is irrelevant. Domicile must be determined according to the national law of the state determining domicile.

Although the starting point is that a defendant domiciled in a contracting state must be sued in that state, in some cases a defendant domiciled in one contracting state may also be sued in the courts of other contracting states. The main such cases are as follows:

(1) In matters relating to a contract, a defendant may be sued where the obligation giving rise to the claim was to be performed;

(2) In matters relating to tort, a defendant may be sued where the harmful event occurred (either the tortious act or the damage caused);

(3) Where a dispute has arisen out of the activities of a branch or agency, a defendant can be sued where the branch or agency is located;

(4) Under insurance or consumer contracts, the insured or consumer may sue where he is domiciled;

(5) In a case involving several defendants, all the defendants may be sued in the country where any one defendant is domiciled.

However, in some cases the courts of only one country will have exclusive jurisdiction, regardless of the country in which the defendant is domiciled and regardless of the above cases. Examples are proceedings relating to land, a company's constitution or the registration of intellectual property rights.

Where more than one of the Convention countries may have jurisdiction, jurisdiction will belong to the court first seised of the action.

Jurisdiction clauses

If at least one party is domiciled in a contracting stage, the court named in a jurisdiction clause must accept jurisdiction. If no party is so domiciled, the named court may, but does not have to, take jurisdiction.

• ENFORCEMENT OF JUDGMENTS •

Subject to the restricted scope of operation of the Brussels Convention (see above), judgment given in a contracting state to the Brussels Convention shall be recognised in all other contracting states without any special procedure being required. The same principle applies, *mutatis mutandis*, to the Lugano Convention except that the Lugano Convention will only apply where either the country in which the original judgment was given, or the country in which the judgment is to be enforced, is not a member of the European Union.

Under the Conventions, a court that is asked to enforce a judgment of another contracting state court may not examine the merits of the decision or (with a few exceptions) question whether the court giving judgment had jurisdiction under the Conventions. Therefore, a defendant must challenge jurisdiction before the original court, not wait until the judgment is to be enforced in his own country.

A court may only refuse enforcement on certain specified grounds. These include:

(a) the court giving judgment did not have jurisdiction and it was an insurance or consumer case or an exclusive jurisdiction case (see above);

(b) it would be contrary to public policy;

(c) the judgment was given in default of appearance, and the defendant was not duly served with the document instituting the proceedings in the foreign court in sufficient time to enable him to arrange for his defence.

Under the Lugano Convention the exceptions are slightly wider.

It should take about one month (two months where the judgment debtor is domiciled in another contracting state) for a judgment to be registered or declared enforceable.